The Wizard of Mecosta
Russell Kirk, Gothic Fiction, and the Moral Imagination

Camilo Peralta
Joliet Junior College

Series in Literary Studies

Copyright © 2025 Vernon Press, an imprint of Vernon Art and Science Inc, on behalf of the author.

All rights reserved. No part of this publication may be reproduced, stored in a retrieval system, or transmitted in any form or by any means, electronic, mechanical, photocopying, recording, or otherwise, without the prior permission of Vernon Art and Science Inc.

www.vernonpress.com

In the Americas:
Vernon Press
1000 N West Street, Suite 1200
Wilmington, Delaware, 19801
United States

In the rest of the world:
Vernon Press
C/Sancti Espiritu 17,
Malaga, 29006
Spain

Series in Literary Studies

Library of Congress Control Number: 2024930739

ISBN: 979-8-8819-0170-7

Also available: 978-1-64889-853-2 [Hardback]; 979-8-8819-0000-7 [PDF, E-Book]

Product and company names mentioned in this work are the trademarks of their respective owners. While every care has been taken in preparing this work, neither the authors nor Vernon Art and Science Inc. may be held responsible for any loss or damage caused or alleged to be caused directly or indirectly by the information contained in it.

Every effort has been made to trace all copyright holders, but if any have been inadvertently overlooked the publisher will be pleased to include any necessary credits in any subsequent reprint or edition.

Cover design by Vernon Press. Image by Russell Kirk Center for Cultural Renewal, CC BY 2.5 https://creativecommons.org/licenses/by/2.5, via Wikimedia Commons.

For Li and Annette,
the Chinese and conservative beauties, respectively.

Acknowledgments

First, I wish to thank my wife, Li, for her patience and support during the past few years. I also want to thank my parents, Esteban and Margarita; my sister, Lucia, her children, Allison and Silas; Julia and Cho; and all of my family, friends, colleagues, students, and classmates.

I am especially grateful to Annette Kirk, E. Wesley Reynolds, and Kris Beers at the Russell Kirk Center for Cultural Renewal. In the Spring of 2021, I was granted a Wilbur Fellowship, through which I was able to spend several months in Mecosta writing, researching, and talking with those who knew Dr. Kirk well, including several of his children. Special thanks to Felicia Kirk Flores for her constant encouragement and to her husband, Marcos, for the coconut lattes!

I owe a debt of gratitude to Jovan Tripkovic and Sean Hadley for (at various times) keeping me company in Mecosta and providing valuable feedback on this work-in-progress.

Finally, thanks to Morgan Chalfant for being such a good office neighbor all those years in Kansas, during which I was occupied with the writing of this manuscript.

ad majorem Dei gloriam

Table of Contents

	Acknowledgments	v
	List of Tables	ix
	Introduction	xi
Chapter 1	Kirk's Life and Work	1
Chapter 2	Kirk's Inimitable Style	23
Chapter 3	The Gothic Tradition in England and America	43
Chapter 4	Order in the Soul and Commonwealth	65
Chapter 5	Timeless Moments	85
Chapter 6	Kirk, Johnson, and the Conservative Gothic Tradition	101
Chapter 7	Kirk, Evelyn Waugh, and the Art of Political Satire	123
Chapter 8	T. S. Eliot and *Lord of the Hollow Dark*	141
Chapter 9	Manfred Arcane	161
	Bibliography	179
	Index	193

List of Tables

Table 2. 1. Allusions to the Bible in Kirk's novels   30
Table 2. 2. Allusions to Greeks and Roman Authors   31
Table 2. 3. Allusions to Shakespeare and Eliot   32
Table 2. 4. Allusions to British authors   33
Table 2. 5. Allusions to Shakespeare   39

Introduction

The Wizard of Mecosta: Russell Kirk, Gothic Fiction, and the Moral Imagination offers an extended analysis of the fiction of Russell Amos Kirk, a central figure in modern American conservatism who is, indeed, sometimes referred to as "the father" of the same.[1] He is best remembered today for 1953's *The Conservative Mind*, a study of social and political thought from the time of Edmund Burke to the early twentieth century, which served as a "catalyst" for American conservatives of all persuasions and helped "to precipitate a new political identity in America."[2] Kirk's thesis in that work is that "conservatives have adhered to [certain] principles or sentiments with some consistency, for two centuries," dating back to Burke's *Reflections on the Revolution in France*; that, in other words, and whatever their disagreements on specific policies or beliefs, all modern conservatives are the spiritual descendants of Burke.[3] Along with William F. Buckley, Jr., founder of *National Review*, Kirk played a pivotal role in the nascent rise of the conservative movement during the 1950s and 60s: Buckley himself insisted that neither the magazine nor the movement would have existed without Kirk.[4] In thousands of newspaper columns, scholarly articles, and well-researched books, Kirk promoted conservative principles while attempting to preserve what T. S. Eliot referred to as the "permanent things": the core values and beliefs of Western civilization.

But why another book about Kirk, and why now? The decades since his death have seen the release of several excellent studies of Kirk's life and thoughts. In 1999, just five years after Kirk's passing, James E. Person published *Russell Kirk: A Critical Biography of a Conservative Mind*. His intentions in this slim volume were, he admits, relatively modest: "I have tried to craft a critical primer, an introduction to Kirk's thought that will serve the intelligent, interested reader … and at the same time provide a starting point or springboard for scholars who will in time depart from this study to write more in-depth works on

---

[1] Matthew Continetti, "The Forgotten Father of American Conservatism," *The Atlantic*, 19 October 2020, https://www.theatlantic.com/ideas/archive/2018/10/russell-kirk-father-american-conservatism/573433/.
[2] Mark C. Henrie, "Conservative Minds Revisited," *Modern Age* 45, no. 4 (2003): 291, OmniFile Full Text Mega (H. W. Wilson).
[3] Russell Kirk, *The Conservative Mind: From Burke to Eliot* (1953; repr., New York: Regnery, 2016), 9.
[4] Gerald Russello, *The Postmodern Imagination of Russell Kirk* (Columbia, MO: University of Missouri Press, 2007), 2.

[Kirk]."⁵ The first of these more "in-depth works" appeared about a decade later: Gerald Russello's *The Postmodern Imagination of Russell Kirk*. Kirk's "affinity" for "postmodern themes," Russello argues, anticipates the rise of a strain of "conservative postmodernism" in the present, which may offer a possible solution to the fractured state into which American conservatism began to dissolve even in its early days.⁶ More recently, Bradley J. Birzer's *Russell Kirk: American Conservative* considers the "life, mind, and, at least by my hope and desire, Platonic soul of Russell Kirk as a lens through which to view the world of the mid-twentieth century."⁷ Birzer benefitted from having unprecedented access to Kirk's unpublished manuscripts, including letters and diary entries.

A variety of non-academic sources has also promoted Kirk's legacy. The most important of these is the Russell Kirk Center for Cultural Renewal, which is based at his ancestral home in Mecosta, MI, and recently celebrated its twenty-fifth anniversary. Headed by Kirk's wise and vigorous widow, Annette, the center pursues Kirk's life work of "linking together generations past and present in an educational journey to discover and nourish the roots of America's political, economic, and religious order."⁸ In 2018, a collection of Kirk's letters, edited by Person, was published with favorable reviews. As Luigi Bradizzi writes, the collection "fills a gap in our knowledge of Kirk … There are no surprises in these letters that would contradict the very strong impression communicated in his other works that he was a man of civility, decency, great intellectual seriousness, and deep cultural conservatism."⁹ In honor of the centenary of Kirk's birth in 2019, the State of Michigan installed a commemorative plaque outside his house in Mecosta. As proof of Kirk's enduring appeal in the twenty-first century, *The Imaginative Conservative* has been active for the past decade. "We address culture, liberal learning, politics, political economy, literature, the arts, and the American Republic in the tradition of Russell Kirk, T.S. Eliot, Edmund Burke, Irving Babbitt … and other leaders of Imaginative Conservatism."¹⁰ The website, co-founded by Birzer and named after a favorite phrase of Kirk's, promotes his thinking to an online readership that spans the globe.

---

⁵ James E. Person, "Preface" to *Russell Kirk: A Critical Biography of a Conservative Mind* (1999; repr., Lanham, MA: Rowman & Littlefield, 2016), x.
⁶ Russello, *Postmodern Imagination*, 12-26.
⁷ Bradley J. Birzer, *Russell Kirk: American Conservative* (Lexington, KY: University Press of Kentucky, 2015), 10-11.
⁸ "About Us," *The Russell Kirk Center*, accessed 5 May 2023, https://kirkcenter.org/about-us/.
⁹ Luigi Bradizza, Review of *Imaginative Conservative: The Letters of Russell Kirk*, *Independent Review* 23, no. 4 (2019): 637, *Academic Search Premier*.
¹⁰ "About Us," The Imaginative Conservative, accessed 23 May 2023, https://theimaginativeconservative.org/about-us.

But Kirk was more than a social and political thinker. He was also a prolific author of fiction, whose short stories and novels encompass several different genres, ranging from Gothic romance to political satire. He had a special knack for horror, which mirrored his lifelong fascination with the supernatural. "Kirk's ghostly achievements form their own creative legacy," James Panero writes appreciatively, "one not necessarily advantaged by Kirk's more prominent political association as a founding father of the American conservative movement. Yet they were all of a piece."[11] Person, Russello, and Birzer all devote sizable sections or even multiple chapters to explications of Kirk's stories and novels. *The Imaginative Conservative*, likewise, regularly publishes perceptive articles exploring the nuances of Kirk's fiction. To my knowledge, however, no one has yet undertaken a full-length study of the *entirety* of Kirk's fiction, which spans twenty-two short stories and three full-length novels written over nearly thirty years. This is surprising because Kirk was no more of a historian and social critic who happened to dabble in fiction than T. S. Eliot was an essayist who also wrote poetry. Whatever modesty he feigns in his memoirs,[12] it is apparent that Kirk regarded literature as a potent force for conveying conservative ideas and attempted to effectuate his views through the stories and novels he wrote. As Vigen Guroian observes: "It is in his fiction that Kirk puts to the test his principles."[13]

By focusing exclusively on his fiction, this monograph is intended to fill a prominent gap in the field of Russell Kirk's studies. That this gap exists is evident from recent protests, such as one in the *Catholic Herald*, that "Kirk's talent as a writer of fiction is effectively unknown in the literary world and treated as mere addenda to his philosophizing within the circle of Kirk enthusiasts."[14] As the title of James Barasel's article holds, Kirk's fiction has been "unjustly ignored" by critics—a belief shared even by many of those who have written extensively about the subject.[15] In the same manner that Kirk attempted to bring attention to neglected thinkers such as Albert Jay Nock or Peter Viereck, I hope that, by promoting a greater appreciation for Kirk's fiction,

---

[11] James Panero, "Introduction" to Russell Kirk, *Old House of Fear* (New York: Criterion Books, 2019), ix.
[12] Russell Kirk, *The Sword of Imagination: Memoirs of a Half-Century of Literary Conflict* (1995; repr., Grand Rapids, MI: Eerdmans, 2002), 250-51. Kirk explains that he wrote his first novel "mostly for his own entertainment" or "amusement."
[13] Vigen Guroian, introduction to *Ancestral Shadows: An Anthology of Ghostly Tales*, by Russell Kirk (Grand Rapids, MI: Eerdmans, 2004), vii.
[14] James Barasel, "Russell Kirk's fiction is unjustly ignored," *The Catholic Herald*, 8 August 2019, https://catholicherald.co.uk/russell-kirks-fiction-is-unjustly-ignored/.
[15] E.g., Person, *Critical Biography*, 150: Kirk's Manfred Arcane is "one of the most memorable, though critically neglected, heroes in modern literature."

this book can help return him to public prominence. Kirk used the phrase "moral imagination" to describe what he regarded as the most distinguishing feature of great literature, that it be ethical or even didactic. The moral imagination seeks to promote an understanding of the ancient and inherited principles held by those living within a certain community and direct the reader towards an appreciation of the permanent things that are shared by all men and women, past, present, and future. "The aim of great books is ethical," he explains, "to teach what it means to be a man."[16] In a general sense, this monograph will explore traces of the moral imagination in the stories and novels that Kirk himself wrote. Each chapter, however, will focus on a different aspect of his fiction, as discussed below.

Since this is primarily an extended work of literary criticism, it may be helpful to describe the hermeneutics I will employ in my analysis of Kirk's fiction. As Gregory Castle asserts, there has been much hand-wringing in recent decades about the alleged "death" of literary criticism or theory (for the sake of simplicity, I use these terms interchangeably); scholars today seem less interested in theory than in "meta-theory," or the "institutions and sociopolitical conditions that produce theoretical ideas and discourse."[17] Vincent B. Leitch, conversely, believes the young twenty-first century to be a time of "literary renaissance," albeit one that assumes a "characteristically postmodern form" marked by extensive "disorganization" and "disaggregation," with dozens of viable approaches to interpreting fiction.[18] Neither of these approaches seems particularly suited to an analysis of Kirk's writing since he was vocal in disclaiming any adherence to specific worldviews or ideologies,[19] and his stories and novels are obscure enough to warrant the use of more traditional methods. In fact, and perhaps unsurprisingly given the subject, I shall employ in this book a variation of one of the more traditional forms of literary theory known as "New Humanism," which was developed in the early twentieth century by two individuals who strongly influenced Kirk's approach to criticism: Irving Babbitt and Paul Elmer More.[20]

---

[16] Russell Kirk, *Enemies of the Permanent Things: Observations of Abnormity in Literature and Politics* (1984; repr., Peru, IL: Sherwood Sugden & Company, 1988), 16.
[17] Gregory Castle, *The Literary Theory Handbook* (Hoboken, New Jersey: Wiley-Blackwell, 2013), 47.
[18] Vincent B. Leitch, *Literary Criticism in the 21st Century: Theory Renaissance* (London: Bloomsbury Academic, 2014), vi.
[19] Kirk, *The Conservative Mind*, xv. "The book distinctly does not supply its readers with a 'conservative ideology,'" he writes, "for the conservative abhors all forms of ideology." See also "The Drug of Ideology," reprinted in Kirk, *The Essential Russell Kirk*, 348-64.
[20] Person, *Critical Biography*, 152.

Like Philip Sidney, Samuel Johnson, and Matthew Arnold before them, Babbitt and More sought a means by which to reconcile the latest developments in art with the history of English letters and its place in the whole Western tradition dating back to the ancient Greeks. Arnold, the late Victorian poet and critic, had feared that "the decline of religion would leave an increasingly divided society with no common system of beliefs, values, and images, with potentially disastrous consequences."[21] This danger was also acutely felt by Babbitt and More, who attempted to develop "a universally applicable code for humanity based on traditional philosophical teachings of the East and the West."[22] Although their concern for religion, ethics, and traditional values would be viewed with scorn by many academics today, the kind of moral criticism they pioneered had numerous adherents throughout the twentieth century and beyond, including M. H. Abrams, T. S. Eliot, Wayne Booth, and Kirk himself. Indeed, Kirk may have borrowed the term from Burke, but his emphasis on the moral imagination probably owes more to Babbitt and More in the long run. In this book, an expanded form of my dissertation, I am purposefully eschewing the political, destabilizing hermeneutics utilized in many contemporary schools of criticism (i.e., those inspired by structuralism, deconstruction, and their various derivations) in favor of a more unitive and moral approach, based upon the ideals of the New Humanists.

Outline

Chapter 1 is divided into two parts: the first offers a biography of Kirk, and the second a bibliography of his fiction. Both are, by necessity, cursory; my intention in describing key events from the author's life is to provide the reader with sufficient detail for being able to place the ensuing discussion of his work in the proper context. This is especially important, I believe, because so many of Kirk's stories have a basis in reality: "Though inconsistently," as Birzer explains, "Kirk uses his own experiences or those of those close to him for backgrounds and characters."[23] A basic understanding of the author's life is necessary for making sense of a story like "There's a Long, Long Trail A-Winding," which features thinly-veiled characterizations of members of the Kirk household and family. Likewise, in my overview of Kirk's fiction, I do not intend to describe the plots of all of his stories and novels but focus on those that are representative of his development as a writer or that reflect important

---

[21] Peter Barry, *Beginning Theory: An Introduction to Literary and Cultural Theory* (Manchester, England: Manchester University Press, 2009), 25.
[22] Li Tonglu, "New Humanism," *Modern Language Quarterly 69*, no. 1 (March 2008): 62, doi: 10.1215/00267929-2007-025.
[23] Birzer, *American Conservative*, 295.

themes, such as his concern with an order or his unique view of time. The major sources for information about Kirk's life and work are the biographies written by Person and Birzer, Kirk's memoirs, and his letters.

In Chapter 2, I provide an analysis of Kirk's inimitable writing style. Almost any page from *The Conservative Mind* will furnish an example of his distinctive prose, which can be distinguished by its elaborate sentence structures, deliberately archaic or obscure vocabulary, and frequent allusions or references to other sources. Take, for instance, this sentence from Chapter IX, which is part of a longer discussion of James Fitzgerald Stephen's opposition to utilitarianism: "The realm of politics and the realm of morals do not exist in separate spheres, Comte notwithstanding; the state exists to enforce a moral system, to redeem men from the impulses of the flesh and their ignorance."[24] Incredibly, Kirk's writing style becomes even more exaggerated in his fiction, especially in stories involving his most popular and enduring character, the dashing, erudite adventurer, Manfred Arcane. My focus in this chapter is mainly on Kirk's use of allusion: whether implied or explicit, these references enable Kirk to instigate a multifaceted conversation between himself, the reader, and the author being alluded to. His approach stands in marked contrast to how many of his contemporaries employed allusions chiefly in an undermining or ironic manner and how they are viewed today by many academics. Thus, although it is tempting to dismiss Kirk's allusions as ostentatious, I believe that he viewed them as one of the most fundamentally conservative acts in which he, as a writer of fiction, might engage.

"Mine was not an Enlightened mind," Kirk famously admitted. "It was a Gothic mind, medieval in its temper and structure."[25] Hence, it should prove no surprise that, as a writer of fiction, he excelled in the type of story that is set in a haunted castle and features the occasional ghost or two. In 1962, he even wrote an *apologia* for the supernatural, or Gothic, fiction written by M. R. James, Charles Williams, and Kirk himself. He referred to it as "A Cautionary Note on the Ghostly Tale," and it exists in two slightly different forms, which I compare at the start of Chapter 3. My interest here, however, is in the authors who most inspired his approach to this venerable genre. Kirk identified Anne Radcliffe and Sir Walter Scott as being particularly influential on the composition of his first novel, *Old House of Fear*.[26] Scott, the author of several epic poems and the popular Waverley series of historical novels, undoubtedly had the greater impact, especially on Kirk's use of music, poetry, and dialect to promote patriotic ideals. Of writers hailing from the other side of the Atlantic,

---

[24] Kirk, *The Conservative Mind*, 308.
[25] Kirk, *The Sword of Imagination*, 68.
[26] Ibid., 250.

he probably owes the most to Nathaniel Hawthorne, who explored New England's Puritan legacy in his classic books and stories, including *The Scarlet Letter*, *The House of the Seven Gables*, "Young Goodman Brown," and "Rappaccini's Daughter." As much as Kirk may have learned from each of these figures, he ultimately proved himself to be his own writer, especially through his willingness to acknowledge the existence of the supernatural.

In Chapter 4, I examine Kirk's concern over the decline of order "in the soul and in the commonwealth," as depicted in his fiction. In *The Roots of American Order*, he insists upon the importance of order in maintaining a just and free society: "The good society is marked by a high degree of order, justice, and freedom. Among these, order has primacy, for justice cannot be enforced until a tolerable civil social order is attained, nor can freedom be anything better than violence until order gives us laws."[27] Order in the state, he adds, is closely connected with order in the individual, and vice-versa; rising disorder in the one inevitably precipitates a loss of order in the other. Many of his stories feature individuals struggling to contend with various disorders of the soul, including greed and the kind of fanatical devotion to duty exhibited by the villains in "Behind the Stumps," "Ex Tenebris," or *Old House of Fear*. In other stories, such as "Lex Talionis," essentially good characters struggle to survive in their dangerously disordered societies. Above all, Kirk warns, we must resist the temptation to look to the government to solve the problem of declining order in the soul and commonwealth alike; it was such thinking, he believed, that led to the election of Lyndon B. Johnson as President of the United States in 1964, precipitating both the Vietnam War and the rise of the welfare state.[28]

Chapter 5 is devoted to an exploration of Kirk's unique views on time, eternity, and the afterlife. His main influences are Eliot and the Jesuit priest Martin D'Arcy, who assured Annette one evening that she and her husband would always be united in marriage, even after their deaths. Furthermore, D'Arcy promised all of the things they had ever enjoyed during their lifetimes would be available to them in Heaven, not as memories only, but as experiences to be lived again and again whenever they so desired.[29] Kirk was clearly taken with the idea, for he repeated the story in several letters and made it a core part of his beliefs about the afterlife, which also draws heavily from Eliot's discussion

---

[27] Russell Kirk, *The Roots of American Order* (1974; repr., Wilmington, DE: ISI Books, 2014), 6.
[28] Kirk, *The Sword of Imagination*, 319-23.
[29] Ibid., 340-42.

of time and "timeless moments" in *Four Quartets*.[30] Several of his stories are basically allegorical depictions of how one's fate after death is determined by and irrevocably linked to certain timeless moments experienced while alive. As Person explains,

> The damned, the sainted, and those in the process of purgation exist in the eternal present, the damned stuck like flies in amber within the sins that separated them from God and man, the pilgrims doing penance for sins that still prevent access to Heaven, and those who have been purged rejoicing forever within the stations in Heaven appropriate to their respective degrees of saintliness.[31]

Kirk's final novel, *Lord of the Hollow Dark*, presents the most comprehensive view of these matters, with characters undergoing redemption, damnation, and purgation all in a single week.

Compared to his stories, Kirk's long fiction has been especially neglected by critics. Perhaps this is due to their relative lack of success compared to his stories: of his three novels, only the first ever experienced any critical or popular success. It has been republished several times, most recently in 2019. The other two, by contrast, have long been out of print. In any case, they are the focus, consecutively, of Chapters 6 - 8, in which each of Kirk's novels is compared with the work of a conservative author who likely influenced its composition in some way. Chapter 6, for instance, will explore Gothic themes in Kirk's *Old House of Fear* and *A Journey to the Western Islands of Scotland*, the 1775 travelog by Samuel Johnson. I have already noted Kirk's penchant for Gothic romance and horror, which has been analyzed recently by James Panero, Scott Beauchamp, and Birzer, inter alia.[32] Contrasting *Old House of Fear* with Johnson's travelog is one way that I hope to bring a fresh perspective to my analysis of Kirk's first novel. Both are set at least partly in the Hebrides, a chain of islands off the western coast of Scotland that has long enjoyed a reputation for supernatural occurrences. Despite writing in very different genres, Kirk and Johnson depict the Hebrides in a similar manner, combining elements of traditional conservatism and Gothicism. For Kirk and Johnson, the volatile

---

[30] T. S. Eliot, The Complete Poems & Plays (London: Faber & Faber, 1969), 192 ("Little Gidding" I). Eliot writes, "Here, the intersection of the timeless moment / Is England and nowhere."

[31] Person, *Critical Biography*, 118.

[32] Bradley J. Birzer, "When Russell Kirk Was Really Scary," *The American Conservative*, 19 October 2018, https://www.theamericanconservative.com/articles/when-russell-kirk-was-really-scary/. Birzer here claims, however, that Kirk's fiction is too disturbing to qualify as "mere" Gothic fiction.

waters and rugged peaks that surround the Hebrides are more than just indelible features of the landscape: they serve as genuine barriers protecting the inhabitants from the destructive forces of modernity.

Chapter 7 will focus on one of Kirk's least-understood and appreciated books, *A Creature of the Twilight: His Memorials*. He refers to it as a "romance" or "black comedy,"[33] but it is really a political satire in the vein of Joseph Conrad or Evelyn Waugh. The novel is set in a fictional African kingdom, Hamnegri, which is being wracked by civil war. It introduces Kirk's best-known literary creation, the wily and erudite Minister without Portfolio, Manfred Arcane. The influence of Conrad, through novels such as *The Secret Agent*, *Under Western Eyes*, and, especially, *Nostromo*, is apparent enough, especially since Kirk discusses his admiration for the Polish-British writer in several essays and letters, even naming him one of his most "exemplary" conservatives in 1993's *The Politics of Prudence*.[34] Aside from Mark C. Henrie,[35] few critics have shown much interest in exploring Kirk's debt in this work to the brilliant satires of Waugh, namely *Scoop* and *Black Mischief*—both of which, I believe, played a larger role in shaping the plot and tone of *A Creature of the Twilight* than any of Conrad's works. It is curious that Kirk, who was always so willing to acknowledge his sources, does not have much to say about Waugh when discussing this book. I end by proposing possible explanations for that reluctance.

Kirk's third and final novel, *Lord of the Hollow Dark*, is the subject of Chapter 8. It is his most ambitious and thematically complex, which he describes as "in form a Gothick romance, by intent a symbolic representation of the corrupting cults that had come up from underground in the latter half of the twentieth century."[36] In the week leading up to Easter Sunday, a group of pilgrims gathers at the behest of an evil cult leader at an abandoned castle in Scotland. Perhaps the most unusual aspect of this admittedly odd book is that every character is forced to adopt a pseudonym taken from a poem or play by T. S. Eliot: e.g., Arcane calls himself "Gerontion," and there is also a "Marina," a "Sweeney," and so on. This chapter will combine a close reading of *Lord of the Hollow Dark* and selected works by Eliot in order to determine what Kirk's choice of pseudonyms reveals about either the motivations of his characters or how he interprets them in Eliot's. The use of pseudonyms in this book (each of which can be construed as an allusion to Eliot) illustrates the dialogic aspect of his literary style, as explained in Chapter 2. In order to fully understand *Lord of*

---

[33] Kirk, *The Sword of Imagination*, 375.
[34] Russell Kirk, *The Politics of Prudence* (Bryn Mar, PA: Intercollegiate Studies Institute, 1994), 73-74.
[35] Henrie, "Conservative Minds Revisited."
[36] Kirk, *The Sword of Imagination*, 433.

the Hollow Dark, its readers must first (or eventually) familiarize themselves with the characters' namesakes in Eliot's poems. This formidable challenge may help to explain, in part, the novel's relative lack of success.

I will conclude this book with a chapter devoted to one of Kirk's most intriguing and original characters, Manfred Arcane. From Arcane's first appearance in *A Creature of the Twilight*, it is clear that Kirk hit upon something very special in this brilliant but enigmatic figure, who "haunted" the author's imagination until he decided to bring him back for more adventures.[37] Altogether, Arcane appears in four stories and novels: in chronological order, these are *A Creature of the Twilight*, "The Last God's Dream," *Lord of the Hollow Dark*, and "The Peculiar Demesne of Archvicar Gerontion." The slow gestation of this character is evident, however, in stories Kirk wrote long before his second novel, including "Lex Talionis," "Uncle Isaiah," and *Old House of Fear*. Suppose it is true, as Birzer suggests, that Kirk regarded Arcane as his alter ego. In that case, I believe that tracing his development through the author's fiction can give us a sense of Kirk's evolving conception of himself as he grew from middle to old age. What can be learned about the "Wizard of Mecosta," one wonders, from his greatest literary creation, the "Father of Shadows?"

What soon becomes evident from the careful study of Kirk's fiction is how well it synthesizes the political and social views he tried to express through countless essays, lectures, and books. Through his stories and novels, he illustrates for the reader some of the precise dangers that threaten the disordered soul or state, whether they be the rapacious greed of an old miser, as portrayed in "Fate's Purse," or the failed ambitions of colonizers and colonized alike, such as those satirized in *A Creature of the Twilight*. Kirk was sometimes accused of being an "impractical dreamer" and of not offering solutions to the problems he had written about over the years. But, as he frequently attested, the problems of order in the soul and the commonwealth or the fates of our immortal souls are hardly matters that can be addressed through policy recommendations or catchy slogans. By dramatizing these issues and relying on the moral imagination to convey his thoughts about them instead, he makes it possible for "conscience to speak to a conscience,"[38] for readers of different times and places to join in the great conversation of which Kirk's voice was but one of many, though an especially eloquent and convincing one. Even after the recent celebration of the centenary of his birth in 2019 and the renewed interest it

---

[37] Kirk to Caroline Lecuru, 22 April 1988, in *Imaginative Conservative: The Letters of Russell Kirk*, ed. James E. Person (Lexington, KY: University of Kentucky Press, 2018), 279. A similar sentiment is expressed by Kirk in the Prologue to his 1979 story collection, *The Princess of All Lands*, vii.

[38] Kirk, *Essential Russell Kirk*, 206.

sparked in his life and works, it is clear that there is still much to be said about the Gothic, mystical, and frequently magical fiction of Russell Amos Kirk.

Chapter 1

Kirk's Life and Work

The centenary of Russell Kirk's birth was celebrated in 2019. When he died in 1994, his eulogists seemed unsure of what to make of him. To William H. Honan, writing for *The New York Times*, Kirk was a "seminal conservative author" and "founder of the modern conservative movement."[1] The *Independent*'s Richard Dalby hailed him as "an American social philosopher."[2] William F. Buckley, Jr., founding editor of *National Review*—to which Kirk contributed thousands of columns over the years—attempted to capture something of the multifaceted talent of his friend in the first issue published after Kirk's death: "He was omnipresent, coming at us from every direction. He wrote a seminal book and, for many years, a syndicated column. He lectured, gave speeches, wrote ghost stories and histories, and edited anthologies."[3] When one writes of Kirk today or introduces him to one's students, it is hard to know just how to refer to him exactly. Author? Historian? Social critic? He was all of those things and more. In temperament, belief, and action, Kirk was more a man of the twentieth than the twenty-first century. (One could go back even further than that without straining credibility.) Already out of time and place when he was alive, in death, Kirk is in danger of being totally forgotten, not just by his fickle fellow citizens but by his successors in the conservative movement, which he helped found and gave a name to decades ago.

Whatever else one can say about Kirk, he was, in many respects, a paradoxical figure. As comfortable as he was in the presence of the high and mighty, he preferred the company of his humble neighbors in rural Mecosta, MI. A productive scholar and engaging lecturer, he nevertheless scorned permanent academic appointments. Kirk was a staunch defender of the need for a natural aristocracy, even and especially in these demagogically democratic United States.[4] And yet, he was also a true "man of the people," who for years agreed to host in his own home and without the slightest expectation of financial compensation any number of refugees, unmarried mothers, and other victims

---

[1] William H. Honan, "Russell Kirk is Dead at 75, Seminal Conservative Author," *The New York Times*, 30 April 1994, Section 1, 13.
[2] Richard Dalby, "Obituary: Russell Kirk," *The Independent*, 30 June 1994.
[3] William F. Buckley, "Russell Kirk, R. I. P.," *National Review* 46, no. 10 (30 May 1994): 19.
[4] See the section on Tocqueville in Chapter 6 of *The Conservative Mind*, especially 220-21.

of remorseless fate. A self-styled "Bohemian Tory," Kirk fancied himself one of the last of the Romantics. Something of his variable nature can be gleaned from the enormous list of nicknames he has collected over the years, which include "America's Conservative Patriarch," "the Washington Irving of Michigan," and "the Wizard of Mecosta."[5] This last, somehow, seems especially suited for Kirk, who identified strongly with the flat, treeless land of his forebears and performed daring feats with his pen that could only be described as magical. Perhaps, then, that is how he ought to be remembered: not as author or critic, but as wizard!

But Kirk was a prophet, too, as Gleaves Whitney reminds us; his middle name, Amos, was taken from one of the great augurs of the Old Testament, who dared to criticize the Israelites "for being obsessed with luxury, trampling on the rights of the poor, and abandoning the true faith."[6] These are all charges Kirk himself would level against his contemporaries, who were no more receptive to the message than were the ancient Jews. Now, almost thirty years after his death, is it any wonder that this country is in such dire straits—caught between the Scylla of ascendent progressivism and the Charybdis of fractured, impotent conservatism? "I believe we must either recapture the soul of American conservatism," warns Mickey Edwards, "or we will ultimately destroy the country that the founders created, that the Constitution guaranteed, and that the rights of a free people demand."[7] Where is the modern-day Kirk (or Burke or Cicero), who will rouse us from our decadent, suicidal slumber? Until one emerges, we could do worse than try to make up for the hard-headedness of previous generations, who ignored the wizards and prophets sent to vex them. Kirk was one such man, whose efforts to redeem the times and defend the permanent things through the moral imagination are recounted in these pages. Before beginning my analysis of his fiction, I will offer a brief overview of the author's life and creative works.

Kirk's Life

Russell Kirk was born in Plymouth, MI, now a far-flung suburb of sprawling and decayed Detroit. One hundred years ago, though, it was a quiet enough town of some three thousand inhabitants—a veritable paradise for a young boy filled with curiosity and imagination, such as Kirk turned out to be. He certainly remembered it fondly in his memoirs:

---

[5] Birzer, *American Conservative*, 358.
[6] Gleaves Whitney, "The Swords of Imagination: Russell Kirk's Battle with Modernity," *Modern Age* 43, no. 4 (2001): 318.
[7] Mickey Edwards, *Reclaiming Conservatism: How a Great American Political Movement Got Lost—and How It Can Find Its Way Back* (Oxford: Oxford University Press, 2008), 160.

A good town to be born into, Plymouth was old as civilization goes in Michigan, founded by New Englanders in the 1820s. Although only twenty miles by rail to the west of Fort Street station in Detroit, Plymouth in 1918—and indeed until the Second World War—remained a tranquil place with handsome old houses (nearly all of them vanished today), tree-shaded streets, and a square on the New England model.[8]

Though most Americans today know little about their ancestry, except what they are told from a website, and though many of us now hold only a few generations of native blood in our veins, Kirk had traced the deep roots that held both branches of his family to North America. On his mother's side, he was descended from the Plymouth Colony of southern Massachusetts, founded in the early seventeenth century. The religious zeal that had prompted the Pierces and Johnsons to leave England in search of the freedom to worship as they pleased had subsided, over the centuries, into a "vague stubborn apprehension of a world beyond the world," a kind of non-denominational spiritualism, which blossomed, eventually, into Kirk's Roman Catholicism.[9] The paternal branch of the family was made up of Kirks and Simmonses, long-time residents of southern Michigan who descended from hardy stock in Edinburgh and Galloway. Even as a young man, Kirk would feel the pull of his ancestral roots in Scotland calling him back across the ocean.

This lifelong critic of higher education knew well the target of his barbs, for he earned his degrees from schools of vastly different sizes, missions, and locations. He attended Michigan State College of Agriculture and Applied Sciences (now Michigan State University) from 1936 - 1940, departing with both a BA in History and an enduring dislike of pragmatic, utilitarian educational policies, such as those employed by then-president John A. Hannah. Kirk's frequent jabs at the school and at Hannah seem to typify his quixotic efforts in the larger cultural wars in which he took such an active part, for, despite his complaints, no one can deny that MSU has only gotten larger and more obsessed with sports in the years since he last attended and taught there. From his home state, Kirk departed for the Deep South and Duke University, where he wrote a Master's thesis that was eventually published in 1964, *Randolph of Roanoke: A Study in Conservative Thought*. Though he didn't spend much time in the region after leaving Duke, the South continued to have a strong appeal for Kirk; he thought it the bastion of one of two native strains of American conservatism (along with New England), which was represented best by staunch

---

[8] Kirk, *The Sword of Imagination*, 3.
[9] Ibid., 5.

traditionalists such as Randolph and John C. Calhoun, and utterly destroyed as a consequence of the Civil War and Reconstruction.[10]

In 1942, he was drafted into the US Army and sent to Dugway Proving Ground in Utah: "one of the most desolate and most salubrious spots in all the world," as he recalled much later.[11] Kirk spent the war writing erudite letters to friends and family back in Michigan, which bear the unmistakable influence of the Stoic philosophy he had begun studying in earnest. Though only in his twenties, Kirk was already cultivating the habits of mind and body that would later come to serve him so well. Somehow, he found the time to balance his formal duties with long walking tours of the surrounding areas, his voluminous reading, and a punishing rate of correspondence. As a soldier, he also had numerous opportunities to witness the inefficiency and indifference of government bureaucracy first-hand. While in Florida for training, he saw chemical weapons being tested on live subjects, including animals and human beings.[12] Kirk disagreed strongly with Truman's decision to drop atomic bombs on Japan and was still fretting over it in letters written decades later.[13] His opposition to the wars in Vietnam and Iraq must be understood in light of these experiences in the Army. After being discharged, he returned to Michigan and took up a teaching position at his alma mater.

Kirk only lasted a few semesters there before departing to pursue his doctorate at the University of St. Andrews. The appeal of Scotland's oldest university for Kirk should be obvious. As a young man with a strong inclination towards history and tradition, he must have been eager to reconnect with family roots that had not been watered since the arrival of the Kirks in the New World centuries prior. He took to St. Andrews and Scotland immediately: "I believe there could be no pleasanter place for a man to loll away his days," he confided in a letter written in his first term.[14] Kirk soon became acquainted with many of the great families belonging to the local nobility, taking a special interest in their houses; for the rest of his life, he retained an interest in architecture and a love of all neglected, mysterious things.

Meanwhile, he had begun to explore the history of conservative thought in the West, gradually coming to believe that it could be traced to the mind and pen of the Anglo-Irish statesman Edmund Burke. In Burke's opposition to the French Revolution and his steadfast defense of prescription, tradition, and the "great primeval contract of eternal society," which connected the living with the

---

[10] See the chapter on these two figures in Kirk, *The Conservative Mind*, 150-84.
[11] Kirk, *The Sword of Imagination*, 58.
[12] Ibid., 70.
[13] Kirk to Christopher Derrick, 9 July 1984, in *Letters*, 254.
[14] Kirk to William C. McCann, 18 October 1948, in *Letters*, 42.

dead and the yet-unborn,[15] Kirk saw the guiding principles of all subsequent branches of modern conservatism. Kirk submitted his dissertation for the degree of *litterarum doctorem*, or doctor of letters, in 1952; it was published the next year as his most enduring and important work, *The Conservative Mind*. And with that, a career in humane letters was launched that would change the world in ways obvious, subtle, and as-yet unrecognized.

Many excellent analyses of *The Conservative Mind* have been offered in the seven decades since it first appeared; it has been republished numerous times in several languages, attesting to its enduring ability to attract the attention of serious readers the world over. Writing in *Modern Age*—a journal founded by Kirk in 1957—upon the fiftieth anniversary of this book, Mark C. Henrie summarizes its influence on American culture. "In 1953, Kirk's book acted as a catalyst, helping to precipitate a new political identity in America. It inspired intellectual élan in a nascent *movement* that would become, perhaps, the most significant feature of the public life of the United States in the twentieth century. Indeed, Kirk's book provided that movement with its very name."[16] Though that influence is, regrettably, somewhat diminished in the years since Kirk's death, his arguments remain as potent and lucid as ever. Boldly, he denounces the eagerness of his fellow Americans to abandon traditional values for the sake of mere abstraction, especially in the name of progress and equality. "Liberalism, collectivism, utilitarianism, positivism, atomistic individualism, leveling humanitarianism, pragmatism, socialism, ideology ('the science of idiocy,' said John Adams) — these were some of Kirk's targets."[17] Contemporary readers may be struck by how much of the book seems to anticipate subsequent developments in American culture, such as affirmative action and the growth of the welfare state. Kirk never played the role of prophet better.

The Conservative Mind made him something of a household name in the US, though its financial rewards would ever pale in comparison to its outsized influence. Still, he felt secure enough in his intended career as a professional writer to quit his teaching position at MSU and purchase a home in Mecosta, which had been in his family for generations. "Piety Hill" was to become his base of operations for the rest of his days: "the Last Homely House," in the

---

[15] Edmund Burke, *Reflections on the Revolution in France*, ed. L. G. Mitchell (1790; repr., Oxford: Oxford University, Press, 2009), 97.
[16] Mark C. Henrie, "Conservative Minds Revisited," *Modern Age* 45, no. 4 (2003): 291.
[17] George H. Nash, *The Conservative Intellectual Movement in America Since 1945* (Wilmington, DE: Intercollegiate Studies Institute, 1998), 110.

words of an old friend,[18] where Kirk could rest whenever he grew weary of his frequent travels or seek refuge from the hardscrabble ideological battles that filled the years ahead. Eventually, it became a *home* to him in the truer sense of that word, as well: a place in which to raise a family and entertain guests and friends. But for some time, Kirk lived happily enough as a bachelor, writing and amassing a library that would eventually number in the several thousands of volumes. Also, in the 1950s, he met two individuals who would come to have a profound impact on his life: William F. Buckley, Jr., and T. S. Eliot. The former, the brash young founder of *National Review*, traveled to Mecosta to personally recruit Kirk to his fledgling magazine. After a night of heavy drinking, Kirk agreed and would go on to write thousands of articles for Buckley over the next twenty-five years.[19] With Kirk on staff, though not on its letterhead, *National Review* soon established itself as the "spokes-journal of American conservatism,"[20] a position it would hold for much of the latter half of the twentieth century.

Eliot's friendship with Kirk was never as warm as the one he enjoyed with Buckley. However, the elderly poet undoubtedly had a much greater influence on him, especially as a literary critic and writer of fiction. Early in life, Kirk realized that the two were working towards similar ends. As he writes in his memoirs:

> From the beginning, it had been Eliot's purpose to defend "lost" causes, because he knew that no cause worth upholding is lost altogether. He had sworn fealty to the permanent things, understanding that these permanent things are not the creations of men merely. As the inheritor of the purpose of Vergil and Dante, Eliot endeavored to "redeem the time, redeem the dream."[21]

Kirk managed to impress Eliot with a review of his 1953 play, *The Confidential Clerk*. By the time of their first meeting, he was already planning a major study of Eliot, though he would not get around to writing and publishing it until after Eliot's death in 1971. It was from Eliot that Kirk borrowed many of his favorite

---

[18] Kirk, *The Sword of Imagination*, 344. The "old friend" is Jas Scott-Moncrieff, son of George Scott-Moncrieff, whom Kirk had met and befriended during his studies in Scotland. The reference is to Rivendell, the house of the elf-lord Elrond in J. R. R. Tolkien's *The Lord of the Rings*.

[19] Birzer, *American Conservative*, 163.

[20] Peter Steinfels, *The Neoconservatives: The Men Who Are Changing America's Politics* (New York: Simon and Schuster, 1979), 48. Kirk declined to be named on the letterhead of *National Review*, though he was among its most prominent and frequent contributors.

[21] Kirk, *The Sword of Imagination*, 214.

phrases, including "permanent things," which refers to the core values and beliefs of Western civilization, as passed down to modern Americans from ancient Greece and Rome by way of Jerusalem and London. Through his mature cycle of meditative poems, *Four Quartets*, Eliot also influenced Kirk's understanding of how time functions in a Christian framework. Kirk's stories and novels show the marked influence of these poems on their author, as I discuss in Chapter 4.

In 1960, Kirk met Annette Yvonne Courtemanche, a college student and Roman Catholic. The story of their courtship would make for a very fine, if old-fashioned, romance novel, with the two exchanging affectionate but chaste letters for several years before finally deciding to marry in September of 1964. Her piety helped push Kirk towards a formal embrace of Catholicism, though he could never in his life be accused of being "a pillar of the Church," i.e., someone who attended Mass regularly, observed all of the feast days, and so on. Still, he served "tolerably well as one of its flying buttresses."[22] The two settled down in Mecosta, where they had four children together, and accepted all of the unwed mothers, political refugees, or whatever other "flotsam and jetsam of the twentieth century's disorders" happened to show up at their doors, desperate for help or a place to stay.[23] Annette took care of the household duties so that Kirk could focus on his writing. He was blessed to be outlived by her and their children together; since his death, she and they have sought to carry on his legacy in several ways. Most notably, the Russell Kirk Center for Cultural Renewal, founded by Annette in 1995, has hosted more than 5600 students and 400 scholars over the years;[24] they have, in turn, spread enthusiasm for Kirk's writings throughout their respective communities. It is possible that, through the activities of the Center, Annette may end up winning as many or more admirers of her husband's work as he was able to earn during his lifetime.

As early as the 1950s, Kirk had been criticized for offering specific proposals about what conservatism should look like in practice, for being too concerned, in other words, with theoretical rather than practical considerations. Even his

---

[22] Kirk, *The Sword of Imagination*, 239. In a letter sent to Buckley, Kirk claims that his conversion to Catholicism was mostly due to "what Newman calls *illation*," but, surely, it is no coincidence that his formal entrance into the Church took place shortly before his marriage to Annette in September 1964. See Kirk to William J. Buckley, 2 March 1992, in *Letters*, 337-49.
[23] Kirk, *The Sword of Imagination*, 348.
[24] Lee Edwards, "The Marriage That Shaped American Conservatism," *Intercollegiate Studies Institute*, 20 August 2019, https://isi.org/intercollegiate-review/marriage-shaped-american-conservatism/.

defenders readily acknowledge that "Preoccupied as he was with the revival of the Permanent Things, the Moral Imagination, and the Roots of American Order, when Kirk's baroque mind turned to matters of state, he did not write much about power politics and foreign adventures, at least not much by his standards ... When [Kirk] did write about the affairs of nations he preferred to state principles rather than to offer policy proposals or information."[25] And yet, in 1964, Kirk agreed to play an active role in the presidential campaign of Barry Goldwater, serving as an advisor, writing speeches, and promoting his policies in articles and newspaper columns.[26] By the time of Goldwater's crushing defeat at the hands of Lyndon B. Johnson, Kirk was no longer part of the candidate's inner circle but continued to support Goldwater publicly and in private. The experience may have soured him on the prospect of taking an active role in politics again, though Kirk proudly notes his involvement in the campaign in a 1990 letter written to John Engler.[27] On the other hand, perhaps the defeat of 1964 merely confirms the wisdom of Kirk's hesitation to commit himself to formal policies. Had Kirk's political ambitions ever been realized, he may not have had the time or inclination to write any of the great books he published during the 1970s.

The first of those is the already-mentioned treatise on the poet whom Kirk regarded as the greatest of his lifetime: *Eliot and His Age: T. S. Eliot's Moral Imagination in the Twentieth Century*. Drawing from many years of reflection on Eliot's prose, poetry, and plays, as well as their close, though not overly intimate, personal relationship, Kirk is able to offer what is still regarded as one of the definitive studies of Eliot's life and work. The Anglo-American poet, he declares, was "the principal champion of the moral imagination in the twentieth century,"[28] the latest and perhaps most eloquent disciple of Burke. He traces the development of Eliot's thought across his whole career as a poet and playwright, showing how, even before his conversion to High Anglicism in 1927, Eliot was still "searching for sources of knowledge and love" beneath the skeptical, relativistic *façade* of modern society.[29] If professors of English still valued their traditional mission to promote the serious discussion of literature, Kirk's book on Eliot would be a widely-assigned text in courses on

---

[25] John Willson, "A Foreign Policy for (Probably Not Very Many) Americans," The Russell Kirk Center, 3 March 2009, https://kirkcenter.org/essays/a-foreign-policy/.
[26] Birzer discusses Kirk's role in Goldwater's campaign in Chapter 7 of *American Conservative*, 245-282. Kirk treats the same subject in Chapters 10 and 11 of his memoirs, 249-98.
[27] Kirk to John Engler, 26 November 1990, in *Letters*, 329. Engler served as governor of Michigan from 1991 to 2003.
[28] Russell Kirk, *Eliot and His Age: T. S. Eliot's Moral Imagination in the Twentieth Century* (1971; repr., Wilmington, DE: ISI Books, 2008), 4.
[29] Ibid., 60.

Modernist and twentieth-century literature, for a livelier and more knowledgeable account of Eliot's work has never been published. But it is clear that no one is reading *Eliot and His Age*, let alone assigning it in their courses, since the same, tired charges of Eliot being a misogynist or an anti-Semite are still being repeated well into the twenty-first century, despite Kirk's convincing rebuttal of both claims in 1971.[30]

His other great work of the decade is a historical overview of the major influences on American society and culture, *The Roots of American Order*. Kirk identifies those roots as belonging to four cities.[31] Jerusalem, the home of Christendom, represents the influence of the Old Testament, especially the Hebrew prophets, who were ever in the minds of the founders of the American republic. Athens symbolizes the art, philosophy, and democratic ideals of Hellenic Greece. Rome, of course, stands for the piety and the manly virtues of the ancient Romans. From London, finally, Americans have inherited their great patrimony of English law and letters, which, regrettably, they have never been at greater peril of forgetting than in the present. "Into the writing of the Declaration of Independence and of the Constitution of the United States," Kirk concludes, "went much of the legacy of institutions and thought" of these four ancient civilizations.[32] Response to this work was largely favorable, and Kirk had high hopes for it, himself. He spent several years trying to secure narrators for a proposed film of the book, which was to be produced by Pepperdine University.[33] Alas, the project never came to fruition, and Kirk's sober account of this country's founding remains as neglected by professors of history as his thoughtful study of Eliot is by their colleagues in English.

Kirk's influence, which had peaked in the 1960s, remained strong throughout much of the following decade. He published often in both serious and popular journals and reached untold thousands through a weekly newspaper column and regular appearances on national television. He was invited to lecture at college campuses around the country, traveled widely at home and abroad, and bent the ears of popes and presidents. In 1975, on Ash Wednesday, a fire erupted at Piety Hill. There were no deaths, and the destroyed portions of the house were quickly rebuilt, but the event clearly carried great symbolic weight

---

[30] For Kirk's response to criticism of Eliot's treatment of his wife and relationships with other women, see *Eliot and His Age*, 30-33, 44-45, and 348-49. Kirk defends his friend against charges of anti-Semitism in *Eliot and His Age*, 175-76.

[31] Kirk, *The Roots of American Order*, 6. Chapters 2 - 4 cover the varying influences of these respective cities, and are summarized below.

[32] Ibid., 393.

[33] See Person's introductory note to the letter from Kirk to Charlton Heston, 28 December 1985, in *Letters*, 258-59.

for Kirk. "The Kirks' restoration," he later recalled, "was more successful than those of the Stuarts or the Bourbons had been. Burke had written that an enduring society must be a blending of the old with the new. The Kirks had accomplished just that with [the rebuilding of] their house."[34] That process lasted many years, and by the end of it, Kirk seemed to have lost some of his inner fire and surrendered to the same flames that had devoured so many priceless family keepsakes. By 1980, he was in his early sixties and beginning to slow down, at least physically, if not mentally. He still produced an inordinate number of articles and letters each week, but it is telling that, in his memoirs, he devotes only fifty out of four hundred pages to the last twenty years of his life.[35] Similarly, Birzer, in his otherwise meticulous study, covers the decades since the fire of Ash Wednesday to Kirk's death in 1994 in an astonishing three pages![36]

Had he really accomplished so little of lasting value during the 1980s and 90s? By no means, but his triumphs during those years, belonging more to home and hearth, are not so easily chronicled. Due to the destructive influence of the telephone, he argued, one is often "unable to find documents that might make fairly clear what actually happened in some struggle or controversy of a generation or a decade gone."[37] And though Kirk himself steadfastly avoided using telephones except when necessary,[38] a similar lack of documentation—of best-selling books and quantifiable awards and honors—makes it difficult to assess his accomplishments during the latter decades of his life. Surely, his greatest achievement, and one that he would have regarded as far more valuable than anything he wrote or said, is having successfully raised the four children he had with Annette. Many of his heroes, including Burke and Eliot, had miserable home lives. Still, Kirk's marriage was as happy and affectionate as any that can be enjoyed between man and woman on this earth. Nor is there any indication that Kirk had a strained relationship with any of his children. When Felicia, the third oldest, was in college, or about the age at which daughters tend to clash most with their fathers, she decided to write a paper

---

[34] Kirk, *The Sword of Imagination*, 359. Kirk refers to himself in the third person throughout his memoirs.
[35] Ibid., 395-469. Kirk doesn't stick to a strict chronological order in *The Sword of Imagination*. But the final section of Chapter 14, "Musings in Taiwan," begins in 1974; the last parts of the book were composed shortly before his death. Person provides an overview of Kirk's final years in *A Critical Biography*, 17-19.
[36] Birzer, *American Conservative*, 391-93.
[37] Kirk, *The Sword of Imagination*, 254.
[38] Birzer, *American Conservative*, 381. Birzer simply notes that Kirk "despised the device."

about him for class.³⁹ The next-eldest, Cecilia Kirk Nelson, serves today as Publication Manager of the Kirk Center. They are all grown now, mothers with families of their own, but still involve themselves in their mother's efforts to preserve Kirk's legacy. Here is no family filled with black sheep or scandal.

If it is true, as the ancient Athenian lawgiver Solon argues, that one cannot know the happiness of a man until he has died,⁴⁰ then the manner of Kirk's passing surely proves how fortunate he was. He greeted death with his old Stoic resolve and with the more recent optimism inspired by his conversion to Christianity. In his last days, he read Shakespeare, talked with friends and family, and put his affairs in order. His daughters returned to Piety Hill so that they could all be with him during his final days; together with Annette, they watched him take his last breath.⁴¹ However much he'd struggled, in life, against the turning tide of the twentieth century, Russell Kirk had accomplished much in managing to stem that tide, at least for a little while. Often, in his memoirs and other works, he refers approvingly to a doctrine espoused by Fr. Martin D'Arcy regarding the timelessness of human existence. "Heaven is a state," Kirk quotes him as saying, "in which all the good things of your life are present to you whenever you desire them ..."⁴² The Wizard of Mecosta had lived for seventy-six years and spread much magic during his time on earth. Who knows? Perhaps Fr. D'Arcy is right, and he continues to do so in Heaven.

Kirk's Fiction

Though Kirk is remembered today mostly as a social critic and historian, he was also an accomplished writer of fiction—a fact that often takes his admirers by surprise. Many of the scholarly articles and reviews written about his fiction tend to include a disclaimer to that effect. In his examination of the transcendent "Presence" that suffuses Kirk's ghostly tales, for instance, Scott Beauchamp notes the difficulty in simply acquiring them; many of Kirk's stories and novels have long been out of print.⁴³ Even in 2003, a critic for *National Review* saw fit to applaud the timeliness of a new, two-volume collection of Kirk's stories, seeing that the originals were so "hard to find."⁴⁴ Kirk enjoyed

---

³⁹ Kirk, *The Sword of Imagination*, 415. See, also, the missives Kirk wrote to Andrea and Cecelia, respectively, in his *Letters*, 353-54 and 308-10.
⁴⁰ Herodotus, *The Histories*, trans. Robin Waterfield (Oxford: Oxford University Press, 2008), I.32.
⁴¹ Person, *Critical Biography*, 17-19.
⁴² Ibid., 341. This is one of the major themes in Kirk's fiction, which I examine more fully in Chapter 3.
⁴³ Scott Beauchamp, "Horror and Eternity," *Modern Age* 60, no. 3 (2018): 52.
⁴⁴ Ray Andrew Newman, "Spirit world," *National Review* 55, no. 25 (2003): 39.

varying degrees of success as a writer of fiction. Some of his short stories, which typically involve horror or supernatural themes, were always popular, with "There's a Long, Long Trail A-Winding" winning an award for best short fiction from the Third World Fantasy Convention in 1976.[45] One of his books, at least, was a national best-seller.[46] But most of his fiction has been overlooked by scholars, especially in the years since his death. Even his short stories have yet to receive the sort of extended analysis typically accorded to authors of Kirk's stature. However successful his stories or novels may have been in the past, none ever approached the enduring influence and acclaim of his great historical and political tracts, especially *The Conservative Mind*. Furthermore, the liberal professoriate that has come to dominate many English departments in recent decades has shown little interest in rehabilitating the reputation of conservative authors such as Kirk, thus ensuring his continued obscurity in the fields of literature and literary criticism.

Birzer, one of Kirk's biographers, divides his fiction into three periods: the early (written between 1949-1953), the middle (1961-1967), and the late (1976-1984). He refers to these as Kirk's "hell-purgatory," "purgatory," and "purgatory-heaven" phases, respectively.[47] Though useful, it is worth noting that Kirk's novels, at least, defy such simple attempts at categorization. Another biographer, Person, distinguishes between "two basic sorts" of stories written by Kirk: those that emphasize "the reality of evil" and those that explore "the nature of justice through violent retribution."[48] Government intrusion, revenge, and redemption are all major themes to which Kirk turns repeatedly in his short fiction. Most of his stories, moreover, take for granted the existence of the supernatural, whether in the form of ghosts, miraculous occurrences, or the afterlife. As both Birzer and Person note, and as Kirk himself readily acknowledged, he took metaphysical matters rather seriously and had done so for most of his life. "As easily as it had come to the young William Butler Yeats," he writes in his memoirs, "acceptance of the uncanny came to Russell Kirk: it was a matter of course in his family."[49] Even as a baptized Christian, Kirk continued to believe in ghosts and was always fond of Halloween.

During his lifetime, Kirk oversaw the publication of three collections of his short fiction: *The Surly Sullen Bell* in 1964; *The Princess of All Lands* in 1979; and

---

[45] Kirk, *The Sword of Imagination*, 375.
[46] Ibid., 250. According to Kirk, *Old House of Fear*, published in 1961, sold more copies than "all [his] other books combined."
[47] Birzer, *American Conservative*, 294.
[48] Person, *Critical Biography*, 112.
[49] Kirk, *The Sword of Imagination*, 16.

Watchers at the Strait Gate in 1984.[50] Just as many have been released in the years since his death, but for the sake of convenience, I shall stick here with the arrangement Kirk selected. The first includes some of his earliest published fiction, which appeared in *London Mystery Magazine* in the early 1950s. It received favorable reviews, like one published in the *Beaumont Enterprise* on 6 January 1963: "Writing with apparent ease, obvious smoothness, and skilled attainment of sustained interest and suspense, Dr. Kirk has produced a volume which is unique in this era and will no doubt be hailed by the many who like this kind of escape literature."[51] "Behind the Stumps" is representative of the offerings found in Kirk's first collection. It concerns a determined government official, Cribben, who travels to fictional Pottawatomie County in rural Michigan to conduct a census of its stubborn and impoverished residents. He learns, the hard way, the truth of Kirk's assertion that there must be a "healthy tension between order and freedom" in any genuine democracy, that even representations of the most powerful nation on earth must respect the ancient customs and beliefs of its lowliest citizens.[52] There is just a hint of the supernatural in this story, which occurs at its very end, when Cribben, intruding upon the residence of a disagreeable homesteader, is spooked by the sudden appearance of a spectral figure and suffers a fatal heart attack.

"Uncle Isaiah" evinces a similar suspicion of government bureaucracy, though the setting has been transposed to a decaying city suffering from rampant crime and corruption. An honest dry cleaner, Daniel Kinnaird, is approached by mobsters who demand that he pay them a bribe, which he cannot afford to do. In desperation, he turns to the semi-mythical "Uncle" of the title, a shadowy character in family lore who spent time in a mental asylum for "homicide by reason of temporary insanity."[53] In this story, too, Kirk refrains from an outright depiction of supernatural events. However, it is strongly suggested that Uncle Isaiah is not quite of this world, having already passed into the next one. He is less coy about such matters in what is, perhaps, the highlight of the first collection, "Sorworth Place," which dates from 1952.[54] A world-weary captain and holder of the Military Cross, Ralph Bain, bored and with time to kill in rural Scotland, gets himself invited to tour the magnificent old house after which the story is named. There, he meets its owner, Ann Lurlin, a young widow who is

---

[50] Unless otherwise indicated, bibliographic details regarding Kirk's fiction are taken from Charles C. Brown, *Russell Kirk: A Bibliography* (Wilmington, DE: ISI Books, 2011): 133-36.
[51] "Kirk Stories Have Varied Backgrounds," review of *The Surly Sullen Bell*, by Russell Kirk, *Beaumont Enterprise*, 6 January 1963.
[52] Kirk, *The Conservative Mind*, 420.
[53] Russell Kirk, "Uncle Isaiah," in *Ancestral Shadows: An Anthology of Ghostly Tales*, ed. Vigen Guroian (Grand Rapids, MI: Eerdmans, 2004), 37.
[54] Originally, "Old Place of Sorworth," and also included in *The Princess of All Lands*.

described in typically Kirkian fashion as "most beautiful, in an antique fashion."[55] Even as Bain grows to love her, he learns that she lives in fear of the thought that her long-dead husband will someday come back to fetch her from the grave. On the first anniversary of his death, Bain agrees to watch over her, during which he is confronted by a strange figure with a "sagging face" and "mildewed" suit, a dead man walking.[56] In an act of heroism that earns him his own form of immortality, Bain sacrifices himself to destroy the thing once and for all.

Two stories in this collection differ from the others—and from almost everything else that Kirk wrote—in ways worth noting. "Skyberia" is another that was published in the productive year of 1952. The title refers to the "dry uninhabited uplands" that surround Mecosta, as Kirk explains in an article originally published in 1987 in *Michigan Living*.[57] Unlike "Behind the Stumps" or "Uncle Isaiah," "Skyberia" does not feature even the slightest trace of supernatural or ghostly elements; it is perhaps the only work of fiction Kirk ever wrote about which that can be said. Two hunters, Clements and Robertson, lose themselves in the backwoods of Michigan. They stumble upon a family of scavengers who somehow manage to eke out a living from the inhospitable lands that surround their farm. The patriarch of the Williamses, Samuel, is a fundamental dispensationalist who is convinced that the Second Coming is at hand. God, he warns them, is "going to burn us and He's going to starve us, but He'll keep us men ... There's a time coming when people in the cities will look for rats and cats to eat, and there'll be none."[58] The story ends with him declining to assure Clements and Robertson that city folk such as them will be spared God's wrath. Kirk's antipathy towards urban living is plainly evident, as well, in 1957's "Lost Lake." Technically, this is not a story at all but a first-hand account of Mecosta folklore and history, written in Kirk's own voice. The numerous references to witches, séances, and ghostly occurrences might have suggested its inclusion in a collection of fiction.

The Princess of All Lands features stories published during the 1950s, 60s, and 70s and includes several that can also be found in the previous anthology. It, too, was favorably received by contemporary reviewers, with Wendy Bousfield

---

[55] Russell Kirk, "Sorworth Place," in *Ancestral Shadows*, 183.
[56] Ibid., 193.
[57] Russell Kirk, "Mecosta County: Where the Country Spirit is Alive and Well," *The Russell Kirk Center*, https://kirkcenter.org/kirk-essay-mecosta-county/.
[58] Russell Kirk, "Skyberia," in *The Surly Sullen Bell* (New York: Fleet Publishing Corp., 1962): 140-41.

in the *Library Journal* praising the "allusiveness" of Kirk's "uncanny tales."[59] The new stories, "Saviourgate," the title story, and "There's a Long, Long Trail A-Winding," all reveal Kirk's growing interest in metaphysical questions about time and the afterlife. There is also a marked increase in his willingness to blend fact and fiction by using real people and events in his stories. "Saviourgate" features the return of Ralph Bain, now serving as host to a harried businessman who thinks he has a train to catch, not realizing that he is already dead. As a reward for having given his life to save another, Bain now enjoys a timeless existence, with access to his favorite memories from his past life—including his walks on the moors with Ann Lurlin. "The Princess of All Lands" is based on a real-life kidnapping attempt of Kirk's wife, Annette, as recounted in his memoirs.[60] A young mother driving home through the wastes of Michigan one Halloween day picks up a teenage hitchhiker. As it turns out, the girl has a gun, and the attempted act of charity soon turns into an abduction. Though the real-life incident ended happily enough for Annette, the story climaxes with the young mother, Yolande, confronting the girl's father and brother. The whole family is revealed to be cursed spirits, the ghosts of a group of notorious rapists and murderers, whom Yolande, a mystic, succeeds in exorcising.

Like "The Princess of All Lands," "There's a Long, Long Trail A-Winding" is at once both highly intimate and allegorical, recasting familiar people and places in a mythopoeic framework that allows Kirk to explore universal themes related to sin, suffering, and redemption. This story, David G. Hartwell writes, "epitomizes the overtly allegorical mode in contemporary horror ... Kirk's body of work in this mode made him the C. S. Lewis of the supernatural genre in our day."[61] The main character, Frank Sarsfield, is based on the Kirks' long-time "burglar-butler," Clinton Wallace.[62] Sarsfield, who has been in and out of prison all his life, stumbles upon an empty house one day while trying to find shelter from a blizzard. He decides to make himself at home for the time being, writing letters to his sister and former confessor that demonstrate well the skill with narrative voices, which Kirk puts to even better use in his second novel, *A Creature of the Twilight*. Sarsfield experiences several dreams or waking fantasies, which suggest that he has a history with the family of the house in which he is staying and a particularly close relationship with the youngest of the three daughters, Allegra. The story ends with Sarsfield saving them from a

---

[59] Wendy Bousfield, "The Princess of All Lands (Book Review)," *Library Journal* 104, no. 17 (1979): 2119, *Health Source: Nursing/Academic Edition*. I consider Kirk's use of allusions in the next chapter.
[60] Kirk, *The Sword of Imagination*, 359-65.
[61] David G. Hartwell, introduction to "There's a Long, Long Trail a-Winding," in *The Dark Descent*, ed. David G. Hartwell (New York: Tor, 1987), 59.
[62] Kirk, *The Sword of Imagination*, 350-55.

violent gang of escaped convicts that has broken into the house, though he is fatally wounded in the process. While crawling around outside, he discovers a tablet inscribed with a dedication to himself; the suggestion is that Sarsfield, who is dead, has been reliving incidents from his life as part of the penance he must pay before being accepted into Heaven.

The final volume of stories published during Kirk's lifetime is *Watchers at the Strait Gate*, which offers several new tales in addition to reprints from the earlier collections. Of the former, one of the more interesting is "The Peculiar Demesne of Archvicar Gerontion," which marks the final appearance of Kirk's most celebrated character, Manfred Arcane. Arcane has already appeared in a few stories and serves as the protagonist of *A Creature of the Twilight* and its sequel, *Lord of the Hollow Dark*.[63] The titular "archvicar" is the dealer of a psychotropic drug known as *kalanzi*, whose identity Arcane assumes as part of a plan to take down the leader of a dangerous, diabolical cult. By the late 70s, Kirk had become confident enough as a writer of fiction to indulge his metaphysical interests without feeling the need to disguise what he was doing as allegory. On the surface, the plot of this story—which involves Arcane being chased around a surreal, incorporeal landscape by a "corpse-candle" of light—is something of a head-scratcher. However, it faithfully replicates the "dramatic synthesis of terror and spiritual transcendence" Kirk had achieved in *Lord of the Hollow Dark*, to which it serves as a prequel.[64] A more cheerful spin on these themes is offered by Kirk in one of his last and best works of short fiction, "An Encounter by Mortstone Pond." A young boy grieving the loss of his parents experiences a timeless moment with his embittered future self, resulting in a measure of comfort for both. Person describes it as one of Kirk's "most keenly personal" stories, the closing paragraphs of which offer a nice overview of the author's "metaphysic."[65] Not for nothing is it the concluding tale in the most recent collection of his stories, which was published in 2004 as *Ancestral Shadows: An Anthology of Ghostly Tales*.

If Kirk's fiction, in general, has been neglected by scholars and readers, that is especially true of his three novels, only one of which—the first—remains in print today. *Old House of Fear*, released in 1961 by Fleet, is described by the author as a "Gothick romance, conforming to the canons of Ann Radcliffe as described by Walter Scott: an antique genre, forgotten."[66] It is, as Kirk's

---

[63] See Chapter 9 for an extended discussion of Arcane's genesis and evolution throughout Kirk's career.
[64] Don Herron, "Russell Kirk: Ghost Master of Mecosta," in *Rediscovering Modern Horror Fiction I*, ed. Darrell Schweitzer (Berkeley Heights, NJ: Wildside Press, 1999), 35.
[65] Person, *Critical Biography*, 129.
[66] Kirk, *The Sword of Imagination*, 250.

description suggests, a curious hybrid. Part adventure story, part Brontëan romance, it features a villain straight out of Chesterton: a loquacious Marxist with a demonic "third eye" who serves as a precursor for both Arcane and his arch-nemesis in *Lord of the Hollow Dark*. Kirk took pride in noting that the success of this book led to a temporary resurgence in popularity for Gothic fiction, though it would be unfair to dismiss it simply as a throwback. As Person notes, despite the obvious influence of Radcliffe, Scott, Horace Walpole, and others, Kirk offers a lively and modern take on the genre, mixing foggy moors and dilapidated castles with contemporary social and political commentary. His characters, moreover, are fully realized, "three-dimensional beings who possess the depth, quirks, and growth reminiscent of [those] crafted in the best of modern literature."[67] Kirk was in his early 40s when *Old House of Fear* was published. In it, one discerns many of his early passions, from his love of Scottish culture to his interest in the supernatural, as well as his loathing of "radical social reformers" such as the novel's antagonist, Dr. Edmund Jackman. Like all Marxists, Jackman longs to "see society forced into a single mold, characterized by central administration, rule through executive decree, uniformity of life, and eradication of all personal and local distinctions."[68]

Jackman and his goons are opposed by Hugh Logan, a quick-thinking lawyer who has been charged with arranging the purchase of a small island in Scotland. Logan is cast from quite a different mold than most of Kirk's male protagonists. Unlike Arcane, for instance, and unlike Kirk, Logan is more athletic than scholarly, though he does have a talent for acting that eventually comes in handy. Even before arriving in Scotland, he is forced to contend with a variety of sinister figures who seem determined to prevent him from accomplishing his mission. When Logan finally makes it to Carnglass, he discovers that the whole island, including the dilapidated castle after which the novel is named, has fallen under the control of Jackman. There is no sign of Lady MacAskival, with whom Logan had been sent to negotiate, though he does meet her much younger and happily prettier niece, Mary, a "tiny beauty" with "flaming glory of red hair."[69] Working together, they devise a plan to dislodge Jackman from the premises while engaging in the expected amount of flirtatious banter. "The story is a romantic romp," notes Birzer, "but, unlike most of Kirk's short stories, it offers nothing truly original in terms of philosophy or theology."[70]

---

[67] Person, *Critical Biography*, 139.
[68] Russell Kirk, *Concise Guide to Conservatism* (1957; repr., Washington, DC: Regnery, 2019), 40. This book was originally published by Devin-Adair as *The Intelligent Woman's Guide to Conservatism*.
[69] Russell Kirk, *Old House of Fear* (1961; repr., Grand Rapids, MI: Eerdmans Publishing, 2007), 77.
[70] Birzer, *American Conservative*, 310.

Old House of Fear is an entertaining read but lacks some of the thematic complexity that defines Kirk's mature work as an author of fiction.

His versatility is readily evident from the shift in tone and style of his second novel, a devastating political satire aimed at American colonialism and misguided humanitarianism in the developing world. The book is set mainly in Hamnegri, a fictional kingdom in Africa that is being wracked by civil war. On one side stands the "Progressives," a party of Marxist-Leninists supported by Russia that has deposed and killed the rightful ruler of the country, Sultan Ali. They are opposed by the "Legitimists," nominally headed by Ali's son, but really under the control of the redoubtable Manfred Arcane, who maintains order through the use of his battle-hardened mercenaries, the "Interracial Peace Volunteers." Caught in the crossfire is a group of American diplomats and volunteers hoping to exploit the situation for the benefit of either their wallets or consciences. Kirk has little sympathy for either, suggesting that the former are not nearly so wise as they think themselves and the latter not as useful. In a recent article about *A Creature of the Twilight* published online by the Kirk Center, John Wilson argues that the novel has much to reveal about Kirk's political views, especially regarding his consistent opposition to foreign intervention:

> The United States [Kirk believed] was uniquely favored but not the triumphal end of Western Civilization. Its independence, a prescriptive and propositional circumstance, was framed by a constitutional system that at its heart and by its nature limited the authority of some men over others. It would last only so long as prudence prevailed over ideology; only so long as its reach did not exceed its grasp."[71]

Kirk saw our involvement in wars throughout Southeast Asia, Latin America, and the Middle East as proof that, as he'd feared and warned against in his role as prophet, prudence had, indeed, already lost out to ideology.

From his base in the northern city of Haggat, Arcane dominates the story. He narrates several chapters himself and is a frequent subject of interest in those recounted by others. Kirk skillfully employs a variety of speakers in this largely epistolary book, reflecting well its mix of violence, chaos, and intrigue. And yet, whether writing as the sophisticated Arcane, the naïve Mary Jo Travers, or jaded newspaper correspondents, his ear for dialogue rarely fails. "I'm going to come right out and ask Manfred to establish Civil Rights in Haggat," Travers confides

---

[71] John Wilson, "A Foreign Policy for (Probably Not Very Many) Americans," *The Russell Kirk Center*, 3 March 2009, https://kirkcenter.org/essays/a-foreign-policy/.

in a letter to her mother.[72] In just a sentence, Kirk reveals how hopelessly out of depth this Peace Corps volunteer with a PhD in "communication skills" is in the Machiavellian world of international politics. The reader learns about the progress of the war from a variety of sources, such as newspaper clippings and radio broadcasts issued by the radical Progressives or top-secret diplomatic messages sent between officials of the American State Department, which have somehow been intercepted by the resourceful Minister without Portfolio. Gradually, it emerges that Arcane has succeeded in luring his rivals into a final confrontation at the fords of the Krokul River, from which he emerges utterly triumphant. Through the involvement of some ex-Nazis who attempt to blackmail Arcane, Kirk hints at the larger forces at play in this forsaken struggle over land and oil. "Vengeance ... is empty enough. To exact, in cold blood, agony for agony, a man must be *altogether* mad. Yet justice must be done somewhere here below, and crimes against the innocent must not pass unpunished."[73] Ultimately, the responsibility for ensuring justice within a community, Kirk insists, rests with individual members of that community, not their governments.

Lord of the Hollow Dark, the last of Kirk's novels, was published in 1979. It is hardly a stretch to suggest that its lack of success might have played a role in his decision to abandon long fiction thereafter and devote himself more to his political and social efforts. His description of it is highly suggestive of both its great ambition and frustrating lack of marketability. Kirk called it "in form a Gothick romance, by intent a symbolic representation of the corrupting cults that had come up from underground in the latter half of the twentieth century."[74] To the author's credit, form and content are perfectly matched in this work, with allusions to everyone from Dante, Vergil, and Milton combining to create a suitably moody atmosphere for the (literally) diabolical proceedings that unfold. But the novel came and went without generating much interest from readers; according to Kirk, the American public "had supped so long on literary horrors that their taste had become depraved" and no longer constituted a market he wished to write for. "Like his literary mentor Walter Scott, he might convivially consume ... such small resources as he possessed. Yet because there was in the beginning the Word, he would not abuse words."[75] A revised edition was published in 1989, containing the same text but adding "Balgrummo's Hell" as a prologue and a short acknowledgments section at the

---

[72] Russell Kirk, *A Creature of the Twilight: His Memorials* (New York: Fleet Publishing Corp., 1966), 80.
[73] Ibid., 316.
[74] Kirk, *The Sword of Imagination*, 433.
[75] Ibid., 434.

end. Like *A Creature of the Twilight*, *Lord of the Hollow Dark* has long been out of print.

The two books do not share much else in common. They are linked by the dominating presence of Arcane, now older though still capable of occasional feats of daring. He has been summoned to Balgrummo Lodging, a dilapidated Scottish castle, at the behest of his boss, Mr. Apollinax, an occultist who promises his followers eternal life through Gnostic ceremonies known only to him. In addition to Arcane and his clique, many of whom are carried over from his adventures in Hamnegri, the gathering also includes Marina, a former nun and single mother; Sweeney, an architect with a forged diploma; and Ralph Bain, adrift again in another of his timeless moments. At the insistence of Apollinax, all of the characters are given names taken from poems by T. S. Eliot. Planning for the ceremony begins immediately, and Sweeney, with the occasional help of Arcane or Bain, is sent to explore the treacherous tunnels underneath the Lodging. Formerly, there had existed an extensive weem or *souterrain* beneath the castle, which had been the site of various pagan and Christian rituals and which Apollinax believes to be especially conducive to his plans.

On Ash Wednesday, he summons his followers for a Ceremony of Innocence, during which it is revealed that the timeless existence he had promised them is predicated upon the sacrifice of Marina's baby as an offering to Satan. Instead of heavenly bliss, they are to spend eternity stuck in the Weem, restless spirits like those who died there before them. At the last moment, Arcane successfully confounds Apollinax's plans, escaping with others into the tunnels and eventually finding a way out through the other side. Dantean overtones are obvious in this allegorical representation of the journey to overcome sin and achieve salvation, which defines the life of every Christian on earth. As the last of Kirk's novels, *Lord of the Hollow Dark* serves as a good distillation of many of the themes and techniques he had developed as a writer of fiction for the past 30 years. *Old House of Fear* is little more than a fun romance filled with exotic characters—"Bolshevik mystics, Irish republicans, and an enchanting ingénue."[76] Something of the highly-allusive style of *Lord of the Hollow Dark* is evident in *A Creature of the Twilight*, which, of all Kirk's fiction, offers perhaps the best approximation of his political views. But only Kirk's last novel grapples with the ultimate questions of good and evil that were at the heart of everything he wrote and the way he tried to live his own life. If Arcane is supposed to represent Kirk's alter ego, then it must be the spiritual triumph he enjoys in this

---

[76] "Nothing to Fear," *The New Criterion* 38, no. 2 (2019): 3.

final novel that best reflects how his author preferred to think of himself. There is something of a wizard and prophet in both.

Chapter 2

Kirk's Inimitable Style

Readers new to Russell Kirk's work will soon become acquainted with the distinguishing features of his style. They will learn, for instance, that he is fond of repetition, often employing the same words and phrases from his favorite authors, such as Edmund Burke or T. S. Eliot, in multiple texts. He frequently begins sentences with the words "Why" or "Aye" and favors elaborate, even Latinate sentence structures. But perhaps the most characteristic feature of Kirk's style, which is especially prevalent in his fiction, is the high number of allusions packed into each page. Almost all authors allude, either overtly or subtly, to their predecessors and influences, but few American authors of the twentieth century can hope to match Kirk in either frequency or breadth. In his third novel, *Lord of the Hollow Dark*, he manages to combine an extended riff on the poems and plays of Eliot with the cosmological outlook of Dante, resulting in a brooding "mystical romance" that has been hailed for its "nearly perfect narrative flow and unified mythology."[1] Aside from the references to Eliot and Dante, Kirk alludes in this single text to almost one hundred different individuals and works spanning 2000 years of Western civilization! His second novel, *A Creature of the Twilight*, is no less densely-packed with references to classical antiquity, English literature, and the Bible.

There are so many allusions in Kirk's novels that one cannot help but wonder whether there is any rhyme or reason to it all. Is the frequent barrage of quotes meant only to show off his considerable learning, or is there a reason that Kirk either alludes to the specific authors he does or alludes to them so often? I believe that both of these questions can be answered in the affirmative, and I propose that what these sources share in common is a keen sense of the moral imagination, which Kirk equates with the normative and prescriptive end of humane letters. Great literature exists, he insists, "to teach us what it means to be genuinely human."[2] In these authors, Kirk sees his fellow conservators and guardians of the "permanent things" that form the basis of Western culture.

---

[1] Birzer, *American Conservative*, 371.
[2] Russell Kirk, "The Moral Imagination," in *The Essential Russell Kirk*, ed. George A. Panichas (Wilmington, DE: ISI Books, 2007), 209.

Allusions provide Kirk with an opportunity to demonstrate his affinity for them, and his strong desire to do so helps to explain why he feels the need to allude to them so often. In sum, allusions serve as a way for Kirk to emphasize the inherently conservative nature of his fiction. In this chapter, I offer a quantitative and qualitative analysis of Kirk's allusive style, examining both the frequency and source of his allusions, as well as their intended literary effects. Although this style is evident in his short and long fiction, I shall focus mainly on the latter, both because his novels have received less attention from critics and readers and because it is especially prominent in them. I begin with a discussion of Kirk's views regarding the writing and interpretation of literature—in other words, his literary theory.

Kirk's Literary Theory

Like his exemplars, Burke and Eliot, Kirk was a writer who also theorized about writing. Their respective approaches to criticism nevertheless reflect similar views about the larger role of literature in society. Burke's best-known contribution to aesthetics is represented by his theory of the sublime, an attempt to "expand the European consciousness beyond sectarian interests to an awareness of obligations and commitments to an open-ended and ever-expanding community of humanity."[3] His arguments about how the sublime differs from the beautiful and how the former may be achieved by writers of fiction were a major influence on the subsequent development of the Romantic and Gothic movements, as I discuss in Chapter 6. Eliot, for his part, wrote several essays that deal with aesthetic issues. Still, one that proved especially influential on Kirk was "Tradition and the Individual Talent," which first appeared in 1919 in *The Egoist* and was included the next year in Eliot's *The Sacred Wood*. In admiring even the most talented authors, Eliot explains, we often assume that there is something completely new or original about their work, which serves as proof of their genius. In fact, if we were somehow able to approach that author "without this prejudice, we shall often find that not only the best, but the most individual parts of his work may be those in which the dead poets, his ancestors, assert their immortality most vigorously."[4] In words that anticipate many of Kirk's statements about the purpose of art, Eliot also

---

[3] Matthew W. Binney, "Edmund Burke's Sublime Cosmopolitan Aesthetic," *Studies in English Literature, 1500-1900* 53, no. 3 (2013): 644-645, *Gale Academic OneFile*. Burke discusses the sublime, primarily, in *A Philosophical Enquiry into the Origin of Our Ideas of the Sublime and Beautiful* (1757), but also mentions it in *Reflections on the Revolution in France*/ The latter, of course, was also a major influence on Kirk.

[4] Eliot, T. S. "Tradition and the Individual Talent," in *Selected Essays: 1917-1932* (New York: Harcourt, Brace and Company, 2014), 4.

describes the link between tradition and "the historical sense," by which an author is compelled to write "not merely with his generation in his bones, but with a feeling that the whole of the literature of Europe from Homer and within it the whole of the literature of his own country has a simultaneous existence and composes a simultaneous order."[5] In his remarks about this essay, Kirk noted that the poet's talent "was not to be revolutionary … It is no paradox, he said in substance, to be at once an innovator and a reactionary."[6] Those same words apply equally to his intentions as a writer of fiction, of course.

Essentially, Burke and Eliot form the bedrock of his literary theory. From the former, Kirk borrows the idea of a "moral imagination": "that power of ethical perception which strides beyond the barriers of private experience and momentary events … [and which] aspires to the apprehending of right order in the soul and right order in the commonwealth."[7] Though he had been an early supporter of the American colonists' struggle for independence, Burke sharply criticized the violent actions of the French revolutionaries, whom he regarded as "immoderate in extreme,"[8] and a danger to peace and stability throughout Europe. In *Reflections on the Revolution in France*, he warns against the danger of trying to overthrow the established order of society, as the French revolutionaries aspired to do:

> But now all is to be changed. All the pleasing allusions, which made power gentle and obedience liberal, which harmonized the different shades of life, and which, by a bland assimilation, incorporated into politics the sentiments which beautify and soften private society, are to be dissolved by this new conquering empire of light and reason. All the decent drapery of life is to be rudely torn off. All the superadded ideas, furnished from the wardrobe of a moral imagination, which the heart owns, and the understanding ratifies, as necessary to cover the defects of our naked shivering nature, and to raise it to dignity in our own estimation, are to be exploded as a ridiculous, absurd, and antiquated fashion.[9]

By moral imagination, Burke seems to have in mind a kind of mental faculty through which certain "superadded ideas" are expressed that are common to

---

[5] Ibid., 5.
[6] Kirk, *Eliot and His Age*, 50.
[7] Kirk, "The Moral Imagination," in *The Essential Russell Kirk*, 207.
[8] Peter Berkowitz, "The Liberalism of Edmund Burke," *Policy Review*, no. 176 (December 2012 / January 2013): 54, *Academic Search Premier.*
[9] Burke, *Reflections on the Revolution in France*, 75-76.

civilized persons. These ideas include non-rational feelings such as piety, prejudice, and prudence, which serve as "emotional attachments" that "bond us to society," also forming the basis of our duties to that society.[10] Without them, we would be stripped down to bare, "naked shivering" nature, a state devoid of culture, order, and freedom. Burke links the moral imagination with "the spirit of religion ... along with a whole system of manners" that, for all intents and purposes, constitutes the basis of the Judeo-Christian heritage.[11] Burke only uses the phrase once, in passing, but Kirk more than made it his own; it appears in dozens of essays, books, and letters he wrote over the years and defined his sensibilities as a writer, critic, and moralist.

For Kirk, the moral imagination is an essential feature of all worthwhile literature. It is that ethical, moral, or normative concern one finds expressed in the great works of Plato and Dante, Flannery O'Connor, and Ray Bradbury. It is what, specifically, distinguishes *conservative* writers from their liberal or radical counterparts. In his introduction to *The Portable Conservative Reader*, Kirk cites approvingly Paul Elmore More's distinction between the "controlling power of the imagination," as found in conservative art, with "the liberal's lack of imagination and the radical's misplaced confidence in human nature."[12] Elsewhere, in tandem with Irving Babbitt and Eliot, he contrasts the moral imagination of Burke with the "idyllic" imagination of Jean Jacques Rousseau and the "diabolic" imagination of Thomas Hardy, D. H. Lawrence, and others. The diabolic imagination, Kirk frets, was particularly ascendent during the latter half of the twentieth century.[13] Basically, the moral imagination is what Kirk himself attempted to promote through his public speaking and writing. "My endeavor is to help to refurbish what Edmund Burke called 'the wardrobe of a moral imagination.' When the moral imagination is enriched, a people find themselves capable of great things; when it is impoverished, they cannot act effectively even for their survival, no matter how immense their material resources."[14] He wrote those words to explain his intentions in *Enemies of the*

---

[10] Lauren Hall, "Rights and the Heart: Emotions and Rights Claims in the Political Theory of Edmund Burke," *The Review of Politics* 73, no. 4 (Fall 2011): 610, https://www.jstor.org/stable/41345995.

[11] Kirk, "The Moral Imagination," in *The Essential Russell Kirk*, 208.

[12] Russell Kirk, ed., Introduction to *The Portable Conservative Reader* (Penguin Books, 1982), xxxviii.

[13] Russell Kirk, *Redeeming the Time* (Wilmington, DE: ISI Books, 1996), 73. This posthumous collection contains essays Kirk delivered as lectures to the Heritage Foundation between 1980 and 1994.

[14] Russell Kirk, *Enemies of the Permanent Things: Observations of Abnormality in Literature and Politics* (1984; repr., Providence, RI: Cluny Media, 1984), 2.

Permanent Things, which was published in the 1980s, but they just as easily describe everything he wrote or spoke before then.

His careful reading of Eliot, meanwhile, suggested to him the idea of there being certain enduring principles, or "permanent things," which we inherit from our predecessors and have the duty of passing on to the next generation. "Conservatism is too often conservation of the wrong things," Eliot had written in 1939's *The Idea of a Christian Society*, "liberalism a relaxation of discipline; revolution a denial of the permanent things."[15] Although Eliot does not seem to have used the term often, Kirk believed the preservation of those things to be his friend's *raison d'être*. "Lifelong, Eliot had contended against the spirit of the age. He made the poet's voice heard again and thereby triumphed; knowing the community of souls, he freed others from captivity to time and lonely ego; in the teeth of winds of doctrine, he attested the permanent things."[16] Certainly, he regarded that as being true of himself. In a letter written in 1987 to Henry Regnery (who had published *The Conservative Mind* in 1953), Kirk confessed, "What I have been undertaking, ever since I first was published nationally when I was sixteen years old, is the defense of what T. S. Eliot called 'the permanent things.'"[17] These values, norms, and standards, he adds, have been "the concern of the poet ever since the time of Job, or ever since Homer …"[18] In sum, Kirk argues that poets, playwrights, and other writers of humane letters have an important role to play in the conservation and transmission of the core values of Western society. Thus, the permanent things might be described as the end or aim of the moral imagination: the latter is intended to guide the reader to the former.

Perhaps this helps to clarify Kirk's fondness for allusion. Before offering a quantitative analysis of their use in his fiction, it might be helpful to define the term more precisely. When used in a literary sense, allusions may be defined as a reference, "echo," or adaptation of an earlier author by a later one.[19] The successful use of an allusion relies on the assumption that "there is a body of knowledge that is shared by the author and the reader and that therefore the reader will understand the author's referent,"[20] though certain authors, including Eliot, make that a more difficult task due to their deliberate use of obscure references. Samuel Johnson, the great lexicographer whom Kirk names as one of

---

[15] T. S. Eliot, *The Idea of a Christian Society* (1939; repr., New York: Houghton Mifflin Harcourt, 2014), 102.
[16] Kirk, *Eliot and His Age*, 355.
[17] Kirk to Henry Regnery, 6 December 1987, in *Letters*, 273.
[18] Ibid., 209.
[19] Gregory Machacek, "Allusion," *PMLA* 122, no. 2 (2007): 526.
[20] *Merriam-Webster's Encyclopedia of Literature*, 1st ed., s.v. "allusion."

his "ten exemplary conservatives,"[21] offers this definition: "A reference to something supposed to be already known; a hint; an implication."[22] Johnson's explication suggests an idea with which Kirk would have undoubtedly agreed: that the best allusions do not merely point backward in time but are rife with "implication" for past, present, and future. A carefully chosen allusion, in other words, will do much more than simply make the author look smart or well-read: it serves a dialogic purpose, bringing the author and his readers into conversation with the older text. Consider the reference to Shakespeare's sonnet in the title of his short story, "The Surly Sullen Bell." Although the characters at one point do read the poem aloud, providing the author with a convenient excuse for using the phrase in his title, Kirk's main reason for doing so is to foreshadow Nancy Schumacher's fate through the imagery of her death knell being rung from the church steeple:

> No longer mourn for me when I am dead
> Than you shall hear the surly sullen bell
> Give warning to the world that I am fled
> From this vile world with [vilest] worms to dwell.[23]

The reader may not pick up on the reference right away since, at the time of the recital, all seems to be going well between Nancy and Frank Loring, the great love of her life, whom she has not seen in many years. After he realizes that her husband is slowly poisoning her, his subsequent actions reveal the kind of enduring love that is memorialized in Shakespeare's poem. Even from a simple allusion, much wisdom may ensue.

Kirk's use of allusions to promote the moral imagination contrasts sharply with how contemporary writers and theorists often conceptualize them. Reflecting the rise of post-structural criticism in the latter half of the twentieth century, allusions have come to be regarded by many as "destructive verbal devices" that symbolize "corruption" and resistance against the sources to which they refer.[24] Instead of encouraging conversation, allusions used this way tend to promote suspicion or even the outright rejection of authors whose views or

---

[21] Kirk, *The Politics of Prudence*, 67-68.

[22] Samuel Johnson, *A Dictionary of the English Language*, 2nd revised ed. (London: William Pickering, 1828), 25, *Google Books*, https://www.google.com/books/edition/A_D ictionary_of_the_English_Language/z3kKAAAAIAAJ?hl=en&gbpv=1&bsq=allusion.

[23] William Shakespeare, "Sonnet 71," in *The Riverside Shakespeare*, ed. G. Blakemore Evans (Houghton Mifflin: Boston, 1997), lines 1-4, 1856. The editors prefer Q's variant spelling of "vildest."

[24] Laszlo K. Gefin, "False Exists: The Literary Allusion in Modern Fiction," *Papers on Language & Literature* 20, no. 4 (1984): 433, EBSCO*host*.

identities have fallen out of favor—including some of the most important voices in the Western canon. "Prominent in the poststructural climate of opinion," M. H. Abrams observes, "is an explicit opposition to the established grounds, standards, and procedures in all provinces of Western intellection."[25] The authors Kirk alludes to most often, by contrast, are not those he wishes to overthrow in a misguided attempt to assert his ego. They are, instead, authors he most admires and desires to emulate. Almost all of his allusions are positive and dialogic ones. As he writes in *Enemies of the Permanent Things*:

> Great works of literature join us in an intellectual community. And the ethical cast of enduring humane letters, working upon the imagination, is as normative as is religious doctrine or political principle. Humane literature teaches us what it means to be a man. Homer and Hesiod; Herodotus and Thucydides; Sophocles and Plato; Vergil and Horace; Livy and Tacitus; Cicero and Seneca; Epictetus and Marcus Aurelius; Dante, Petrarch, Erasmus, Shakespeare, Cervantes, Goethe, and all the rest—these have formed the mind and character of Americans as well as of Europeans.[26]

References to these authors, and many others besides, abound in his fiction. Even if they occasionally seem gratuitous, they serve as a constant reminder of Kirk's aims as a conservator of the permanent things. For Kirk, an allusion is a fundamentally conservative act. Indeed, as I have mentioned, it may be the most conservative act a writer of fiction can undertake. I turn now to an examination of the quantitative aspects of Kirk's allusions, focusing on his three novels.

A Quantitative Analysis of Kirk's Allusions

As I have noted, Kirk's frequent use of allusion is one of the most distinctive features of his writing style. From his first to last novel, there is a steady increase both in the overall number of allusions and in the variety of sources to which he refers. Of course, any attempt to quantify allusions in a given work is limited by one's ability to recognize them as such, as well as the difficulty of determining whether the author actually intended an allusion, as William Irwin observes.[27] With those caveats in mind, I count at least thirty distinct allusions

---

[25] M. H. Abrams, "On the Transformation of English Studies: 1930-1995," *Daedalus* 126, no. 1 (Winter 1997): 118.
[26] Kirk, *Enemies of the Permanent Things*, 25.
[27] William Irwin, "What Is an Allusion?" *Journal of Aesthetics & Art Criticism* 59, no. 3 (2001): 289, EBSCO*host*.

in *Old House of Fear*, with most being obvious enough to make it clear that Kirk intended them to be taken as such. Most are to a core group of authors: Shakespeare, Rudyard Kipling, and Robert Burns. The number of allusions nearly triples in *A Creature of the Twilight*, with Kirk adding Alfred Tennyson and John Milton to his list of favorites. Shakespeare remains the most frequently-cited author in this novel, however, with direct and indirect references to at least half a dozen of his plays. The number of allusions in *Lord of the Hollow Dark*, finally, easily surpasses 100 and includes sources as disparate as the nineteenth-century Polish poet and political activist Adam Mickiewicz to common nursery rhymes of England and America. But his most important source in this "elaborate allegorical novel,"[28] as I discuss in Chapter 8, is T. S. Eliot. As I have mentioned, all of the main characters in this book are given pseudonyms taken from Eliot's poems and plays.

Repeatedly, Kirk insists that the roots of American culture can be found in three major sources: the Old and New Testaments, the social and philosophical ideas of the Greeks and Romans, and the great inheritance of literature, language, and law inherited from the British. Accordingly, one would expect him to allude most often to the Bible, classical authors such as Homer or Vergil, and major English writers, including Shakespeare and Milton. Indeed, his novels contain dozens of references to Scripture, with about an equal split between the Old and New Testaments.

Table 2.1. Allusions to the Bible in Kirk's novels

	Old Testament	New Testament
Old House of Fear	0	3
A Creature of the Twilight	8	9
Lord of the Hollow Dark	16	18
Totals	24	30

The Book of Psalms is cited repeatedly in both *A Creature of the Twilight* and *Lord of the Hollow Dark*, with the verses sometimes rendered in Latin in the latter. Genesis and the Prophetic books are Kirk's other major sources from the Old Testament, to which, curiously, he does not seem to refer at all in *Old House of Fear*. There are allusions to the Gospels of all four Evangelists in every novel,

---

[28] W. Wesley McDonald, *Russell Kirk and the Age of Ideology*, Columbia, MO: University of Missouri Press, 2004), 130.

however. Matthew and Luke are cited more often than Mark and John; there are also a few references to Paul's letters to Timothy and the churches of Corinth and Rome. Kirk's preference for an English translation of the Bible seems to be the Authorized King James Version, which, it is worth noting, he goes out of his way to single out as worthy reading material in a proposed curriculum for high school students from 1981.[29]

The wisdom of the ancients is well represented in Kirk's novels through multiple allusions to Greek and Roman poets, philosophers, and historians. In *Old House of Fear*, as in several non-fiction works, Kirk quotes some obscure lines from a lost tragedy, later repeated by Cicero: "When I am dead, let the earth be mixed with fire."[30] The Greek historian Polybius, the author of *The Histories*, is a favorite of Kirk's and is mentioned or quoted on at least four separate occasions in *A Creature of the Twilight*.

Table 2. 2. Allusions to Greeks and Roman Authors

	Greeks	Romans
Old House of Fear	1	0
A Creature of the Twilight	11	0
Lord of the Hollow Dark	9	5
Totals	21	5

Polybius is known for his attention to detail in politics and warfare and for arguing that every country progresses through a historical cycle involving the different forms of government known to the ancient Greeks, ranging from monarchy to ochlocracy (i.e., government by mob rule),[31] all of which helps to explain his popularity in this dark satire of international affairs. Kirk's second and third novels are full of allusions to Greek mythology, with the stories of Persephone, Iphigenia, Sisyphus, and the Sirens all drawing attention to the rich interplay of themes and symbols in these texts. *Lord of the Hollow Dark* contains a half-dozen references to the Minoan Minotaur and his labyrinth, which, despite being a Greek myth, is best known to us through a pair of works

---

[29] Kirk, *The Roots of American Order*, 443.
[30] Robert W. Sharples, *Peripatetic Philosophy 200 BC to 200 AC: An Introduction and Collection of Sources in Translation* (Cambridge: Cambridge University Press, 2010), 114.
[31] David Inglis and Roland Robertson, "From Republican Virtue to Global Imaginary: Changing Visions of the Historian Polybius," *History of the Human Sciences* 19, no. 1 (2006): 6, *Sage Premier*, doi: 10.1177/0952695106062144.

more closely associated with the Roman tradition: Plutarch's *Parallel Lives* and Ovid's *Metamorphoses*. Juvenal, Catullus, and Horace are other Romans, or Greco-Romans, explicitly alluded to by Kirk. By far, though, the Latin author cited most frequently is Vergil, whose *Aeneid* is directly quoted several times in *Lord of the Hollow Dark*—often in the original language.

I have already mentioned some of the British authors favored by Kirk, including Shakespeare and Eliot. Excluding the Bible, he alludes more to these two than to any other source.

Table 2. 3. Allusions to Shakespeare and Eliot

	Shakespeare	Eliot
Old House of Fear	3	0
A Creature of the Twilight	14	0
Lord of the Hollow Dark	7	38
Totals	24	38

Each garner between two to three dozen references. There are slightly more allusions to Eliot overall than to Shakespeare, though the former is only referenced in a single novel, whereas the latter is alluded to or quoted in all three. I will discuss Shakespeare more later in this chapter and focus only on the references to Eliot in *Lord of the Hollow Dark* here. The most frequently cited works by Eliot in this book are *The Waste Land*, "The Hollow Men," and "Burnt Norton," with at least five references to each. In addition, several poems are alluded to more than once: "Gerontion" and "East Coker" three times and the following at least twice: "Whispers of Immortality," "Mr. Apollinax," "The Love Song of J. Alfred Prufrock," "Little Gidding," and "Ash Wednesday." A few lines from "Sweeney Agonistes" are quoted and paraphrased repeatedly throughout the novel, most often during the troubling dreams experienced by one of the characters. All of these texts reflect Eliot's growing unease with certain trends in Anglo-American society, especially the drives towards increased capitalism and liberalism, which, he believed, had the potential to undermine "the stability of communities conforming to the order of nature and pursuing the

Good."[32] These worries, of course, were shared by Kirk, who warns about them in various essays.[33]

There are multiple allusions to a handful of British authors throughout Kirk's novels. His interest in them can hardly be a surprise; he wrote a whole book, after all, dedicated to exploring *America's British Culture*, in which he argues that the British influenced this country in "four major ways," starting with our shared language "and the wealth of great literature in that language."[34] Two of his novels are set mainly or entirely in Scotland, and that country's leading intellectuals are well-represented in Kirk's fiction.

Table 2. 4. Allusions to British authors

	Burns	Milton	Scott	Tennyson	Carroll
Old House of Fear	7	1	4	0	0
A Creature of the Twilight	1	3	1	5	1
Lord of the Hollow Dark	0	3	3	1	6
Totals	8	7	8	6	7

Robert Burns, an "unifying and iconic representation" of Scottish identity whose birthday is still celebrated as a national holiday,[35] is quoted or alluded to over half a dozen times in *Old House of Fear* and at least once in *A Creature of the Twilight*. Sir Walter Scott, meanwhile, is one of the rare authors Kirk alludes to in every novel. He is especially fond of quoting a line from "The Call" that refers to "one crowded hour of glorious life."[36] Milton is another poet Kirk turns to repeatedly, with around half a dozen references to *Paradise Lost* scattered

---

[32] James Matthew Wilson, "Conservative Critics of the Bourgeoisie," *Modern Age* 55, no. 3 (2013): 20, accessed 18 May 2019, EBSCO*host*.
[33] See, e.g., "The Drug of Ideology" and "The Humane Learning of Wilhelm Röpke," both collected in *The Essential Russell Kirk*, 348-64 and 543-49.
[34] Russell Kirk, *America's British Culture* (London: Routledge, 1993), 11.
[35] Corey E. Andrews, "Venders, Purchasers, Admirers: Burnsian 'Men of Action' from the Nineteenth to the Twenty-First Century," *Scottish Literary Review* 2, no. 1 (2010): 103, EBSCO*host*.
[36] Tom B. Haber, "The Chapter-Tags in the Waverley Novels," *PMLA* 45, no. 4 (1930): 1142, *JSTOR*, doi: 10.2307/457832. As Haber explains, this poem is actually by Thomas Osbert Mordaunt, but was attributed to Scott for many years. It is unclear whether Kirk was aware that the lines were not by Scott, especially since some of the characters identify Scott as the author of this poem.

across all three of his books. Various works by Alfred Tennyson are alluded to almost as often; Lewis Carroll and Rudyard Kipling follow closely after, with about five references each. The poems of William Wordsworth, finally, are quoted or alluded to at least four times: those of John Keats and W. B. Yeats, three. Poetry is one of the only forms of literature in which Kirk did not, himself, dabble, yet it is clear enough that he read and enjoyed quite a bit of it.

The Literary Effects of Kirk's Allusions

Clearly, allusions are an important aspect of Kirk's style. This is especially true of his last two books, though one can certainly trace the development of that style through his short stories, which tend to become more thematically complex and referential over time. (In general, those featuring Manfred Arcane are as packed with allusions as any of his novels.) I turn now to a qualitative analysis of Kirk's allusive style: an exploration, in other words, of the myriad advantages it affords the author. What literary effects is he able to achieve by referring so often to so many different sources? First, as has been mentioned, there is a dialogic aspect to many of Kirk's allusions. Through a careful reference to some beloved source, he attempts to bring the reader into conversation with that source and with himself. Like Burke, Sir Philip Sidney, and Plato, Kirk insists that writers of fiction have as much—if not more—responsibility for instructing their readers as they do for keeping them entertained. "Literature, in short, was and is intended to persuade people of the truth of certain standards or norms ... The very phrase 'humane letters' implies that literature is meant to teach us the character of human normality."[37] Some of these truths may best be conveyed by authors who are dead or writing in languages that are completely unknown to the reader. Through allusions, a conservative author can guide his reader to these enduring sources of wisdom, providing a clear example of the moral imagination in action.

The instructive potential of Kirk's allusive style deserves closer attention. A pivotal scene in *Old House of Fear* contains what at first appears to be a casual reference to the Bible. Having fallen into the hands of the evil scientist Edmund Jackman, the protagonist, Hugh Logan, has every reason to believe that he will never leave Carnglass Island alive. He is alone and unarmed, whereas Jackman has at his command at least a dozen armed men. And yet, while staring into Jackman's eyes, Logan suddenly recalls a line from Jesus' Sermon on the Mount. The whole thing reads as follows: "But if thine eye be evil, thy whole body shall be full of darkness. If, therefore, the light that is in thee be darkness, how great

---

[37] Russell Kirk, "Teaching Humane Literature in High Schools," in *The Essential Russell Kirk*, 434-36.

is that darkness!"[38] Jesus' words have an obvious ethical and normative bent, and Logan takes them as confirmation that Jackman's spiritual corruption has grown so great as to become a liability. "It was just possible that he might prove a match of Edmund Jackman now," Kirk writes, "though the odds were against him."[39] And that is exactly what ends up happening: despite heavy odds, Logan goes on to win the game of chess they had been playing, as well as the larger philosophical battle at stake between the two. From Logan's example and from the allusion Kirk uses to draw our attention to certain aspects of his situation, the reader learns about the importance of persevering in the face of impossible odds. Just because the lesson is a simple one does not make it unworthy of the telling.

Often throughout Kirk's novels, multiple allusions are proximally linked, resulting in a greater potential for edification. For example, *Lord of the Hollow Dark* begins with an allusion to an important work by Dante that takes on additional significance when considered in the light of subsequent references to other authors. One of the main characters, Marina, has just arrived at Balgrummo Lodging in the hopes of learning from a spiritual guru who styles himself Mr. Apollinax. She recalls what he said to her when they met: "This is the commencement of your *vita nouva*. All the triviality, all the shame of your past life is to be washed away …"[40] The reference here to Dante is probably meant to come across as shallow and pretentious; Apollinax, after all, only means the words in their literal sense. What Marina does not yet realize is that Dante's idea of a "new life" could not be further from what Apollinax has in mind. Dante's poem, romantic and yet fully rational, teaches us that "embracing divine love need not entail the abandonment of human love" and that only through the kind of love symbolized and embodied by Beatrice can we overcome our sinful natures and desires.[41] Apollinax, by contrast, preaches the debasement of love, through hedonistic rituals and "ecstasy of the animals."[42] Dante's new life will lead us to Heaven; Apollinax's straight to Hell.

To ensure that the reader does not mistake his point, Kirk follows up this first subtle allusion to Dante with another to Eliot just a few pages later. Marina and her traveling companion, Sweeney, are greeted at the mansion by Arcane. He

---

[38] Matt. 6:23 (KJV). Logan recalls only the second part of this verse: "And if thy light be darkness, how great shall be thy darkness."
[39] Kirk, *Old House of Fear*, 136.
[40] Russell Kirk, *Lord of the Hollow Dark* (New York: St. Martin's Press, 1979), 2.
[41] Tristan Kay, "Redefining the 'matera amorosa': Dante's *Vita nova* and Guittone's (anti-)courtly 'canzoniere,'" *Italianist* 29, no. 3 (2009): 394, EBSCO*host*, doi: 10.1179/026143409 X12584559181732.
[42] Kirk, *Lord of the Hollow Dark*, 253-54.

bids them welcome to "a draughty house, under a windy knob," which neither of the characters recognizes as a quote from Eliot's "Gerontion."[43] The reference proves rather provocative in the light of later events. The older man who narrates this poem, after all, faces the same crippling indecision that haunts Marina, a former nun who is unable to reconcile reason and passion in response to an increasingly war-torn and materialistic world. She left the convent after getting pregnant; likewise, he no longer feels connected to the old traditions and religious beliefs upon which he formerly relied:

> Signs are taken for wonders. "We would see a sign!"
> The word within a word, unable to speak a word,
> Swaddled with darkness.[44]

"This inability to act in the shadow of violence, except by propagating more violence, is the very essence of Gerontion's plight," Jamie Wood observes. "For Gerontion can neither move, fight, believe, conclude, nor love."[45] He and Marina respond to their paralysis in exactly opposite, but equally futile, ways: she by embracing passion, he by spurning it in favor of reason. Lacking Dante's conception of a divine love that is both fully rational and passionate, neither can hope to escape the wayward path onto which they have strayed.

Both Dante and Eliot are among the most frequently cited authors by Kirk, and the proximity of the two allusions seems indicative of a strong desire to bring the great poets into conversation with one another. From this dialogue, the reader can learn a great deal about, among other things, the dangers of false prophets and ideologies. But not all of Kirk's readers are religious, let alone Catholic; for whatever reasons, many would be unwilling to accept the tutelage of Dante or Eliot in this matter. But Kirk has not finished the lesson yet. Just a few paragraphs after the allusion to Eliot, one of Arcane's closest confidantes, Madame Sesostris, warns Marina against associating with anyone else at the mansion: "A word to the unwary, if you please: cherish the Archvicar. Stay as close to him as you may. Those young men and women below stairs in this house—*O tempora, O mores!*"[46] The phrase is by Cicero, the Roman orator and lawyer whom Kirk frequently quotes and names as one of his "ten exemplary conservatives."[47] It is often used in the present as an expression of surprise or

---

[43] Ibid., 4.
[44] Eliot, *The Complete Poems and Plays*, 37 ("Gerontion").
[45] Jamie Wood, "'Here I Am': Eliot, 'Gerontion,' and the Great War," *Biography: An Interdisciplinary Quarterly* 41, no. 1 (2018): 134, EBSCOhost, doi: 10.1353/bio.2018.0011.
[46] Kirk, *Lord of the Hollow Dark*, 6.
[47] Kirk, *The Politics of Prudence*, 64-65.

dismay regarding changing habits, especially in regard to a supposed decline in morals. Against this decline, Cicero stresses the importance of an orderly disposition in both body and mind: "decorum is a 'perceptible' aspect of every virtuous act …"[48] In other words, he insists upon a conservative respect for tradition and the customs and virtues cherished by our ancestors, as opposed to the latest fads. Through this allusion, Kirk offers his readers a final lesson on how to avoid falling into the errors of Apollinax, Gerontion, and young Marina.

Aside from their educational function, allusions also serve as an organizing principle within the novels. Linking these allusions thematically in the manner described above allows Kirk to return to key themes multiple times while preserving a heightened sense of unity and cohesion. An example of this can be seen in the myriad references to cataclysmic destruction that recur throughout *A Creature of the Twilight*, which begins with an allusion to the *Seven Against Thebes*, a tragedy by Aeschylus that opens in the midst of chaos. The city, long the scene of horrors in ancient Greece, teeters once again on the brink of violence: "besieged by the army of Polyneices and defended by his brother Eteocles; the chorus, women of Thebes, are in a state of panic, which Eteocles has at all costs to allay …"[49] That violence, as any reader of Greek tragedy knows, will only end after further bloodshed. The allusion implies that a similar price will have to be paid to bring peace to Hamnegri. Additional references to the Book of Revelations, *Julius Caesar* and *Macbeth*, Wagner's *Götterdämmerung*, and Yeats's "The Second Coming" further illustrate the destabilizing effects of Western policy in Africa. These allusions, spoken by different characters and in vastly different contexts, nevertheless enable Kirk to maintain a sense of order even in the fundamentally disordered world of the novel.

Kirk's first and third books are also arranged thematically around certain authors. The most frequently quoted in *Old House of Fear* and *Lord of the Hollow Dark* are Robert Burns and T. S. Eliot, respectively. Even before Logan arrives at Carnglass Island, there are several conversations about Burns and his work. Midway through the novel, the main love interest, Mary MacAskival, sings some of his ballads in full, songs that, as Josephine Dougal observes, "draw on the natural landscape of Scotland not only as a setting but also as a key metaphor for love and lost love."[50] Kirk, too, employs Scotland as a metaphor, with the allusions to Burns serving as a thematic link that connects

---

[48] Nancy Sherman, "Of Manners and Morals," *British Journal of Educational Standards* 53, no. 3 (2005): 278, JSTOR, https://www.jstor.org/stable/3699243.
[49] H. D. F. Kitto, "The Greek Chorus," *Educational Theatre Journal* 8, no. 1 (March 1956): 2, *JSTOR*, doi: 10.2307/3203909.
[50] Josephine Dougal, "Popular Scottish Song Traditions at Home (and Away)," *Folklore* 122, no. 3 (2011): 292, *JSTOR*, https://www.jstor.org/stable/41306603.

the first pages of the novel to the last, despite the variety of locations in which it is set, as well as the number of characters and themes that enter and depart at regular intervals. This is especially important in the longer and more complex *Lord of the Hollow Dark*. Though set entirely in a single location and featuring a smaller group of characters, the journey upon which they embark is far vaster, perhaps, than can be measured. Theirs is an allegorical journey that will take them over the ground, trodden only by a select few, including Dante. As Birzer notes, Balgrummo Lodging is a maze-like castle "saturated with the supernatural, good and evil, over time. Some believe it purgatorial; others believe it a gateway to hell."[51] The various references to Eliot serve as waypoints by which the characters and reader may find their bearings. One of the final scenes in the novel, for instance, takes place in a rose garden that seems deliberately intended to evoke a key passage in the closing lines of *Four Quarters*. For Eliot and the characters in Kirk's story, the garden symbolizes (among other things) our uncertain status between "the temporal world ... and human perceptions of that world,"[52] which in the story has been dramatically altered following the characters' experiences at Balgrummo Lodging.

No author is accorded such importance in *A Creature of the Twilight*. As a result, the novel can, at times, feel more sprawling and episodic than the other two. About midway through this dense and sprawling satire, however, Kirk begins to cite repeatedly Shakespeare and *Macbeth*, in particular. He starts with a reference to one of the play's most famous lines, as spoken by the witches in Act I, Scene I: "Till the hurly-burly's done, till the battle's lost or won." Throughout the rest of the novel, Kirk continues to draw from progressively later parts of the play. After another fifty pages, for instance, one finds a reference to Act II, Scene 2: "Zingu doth murder sleep, and so shall sleep no more." This is followed, after another forty pages, by an allusion to Act III, Scene 4: "Stand not upon the order of thy going, but go." Finally, in the closing pages, Kirk quotes Macbeth's elegiac soliloquy about the "sear and yellow leaf."[53] The traitorous Scottish king, "careless of his beauty, profligate in the expenditure of those virtues central to his identity as a person,"[54] makes for a sharp contrast with the dying Arcane (who soon recovers). But on a structural level, the allusion simply reinforces the idea that the climax of the novel has passed, and that it will soon be ending. The allusions

---

[51] Birzer, *American Conservative*, 373.
[52] William Kevin, "Dialect of the Tribe: Modes of Communication and the Epiphanic Role of Nonhuman Imagery in T. S. Eliot's *Four Quartets*," *Harvard Theological Review* 108, no. 1 (Jan. 2015): 104, doi: 10.1017/S001781601500005X.
[53] Kirk, *A Creature of Twilight*, 147-317.
[54] Michael Bristol, "Macbeth the Philosopher: Rethinking Context," *New Literary History* 42, no. 4 (2011): 658, *JSTOR*, https://www.jstor.org/stable/41328990.

to *Macbeth* in *A Creature of the Twilight* serve as organizing principles for at least half of the book.

Kirk and Shakespeare

Kirk's interest in Shakespeare is worth exploring in greater detail, however, especially since it reveals so much about his literary theory and the high esteem in which he held the British playwright. As I have noted, after Eliot, Shakespeare is the most frequently cited author in Kirk's books. Unlike Eliot, he is mentioned in all three novels, which suggests something of his overall importance to Kirk.

Table 2. 5. Allusions to Shakespeare

	Julius Caesar	Macbeth	Othello	Henry V	Hamlet
Old House of Fear	1	0	1	0	0
A Creature of the Twilight	4	6	1	1	1
Lord of the Hollow Dark	0	1	1	2	2
Totals	5	7	3	3	3

Based on the sheer number of mentions, Kirk must have been especially fond of *Macbeth*: he refers to it at least half a dozen times in his last two books. *Julius Caesar* is next, with five references, followed by *Henry V* with four. *Othello* and *Hamlet* share fourth place, with three apiece. Finally, there are the plays that Kirk refers to only once: these include *A Midsummer Night's Dream* and *As You Like It*. One cannot help but note the apparent lack of interest in comedies and romances; regardless of which plays, exactly, one would place into these two genres, neither is alluded to much. Kirk's partiality to tragedy and history, on the other hand, can hardly surprise. His life's mission, to "conserve the best of Western civilization and enrich the ideas of the world,"[55] is, after all, essentially a historical one. Likewise, the stalking ghosts, cackling witches, and prophetic soothsayers who populate Shakespeare's tragedies and histories must have appealed to him as a fan and author of Gothic fiction.

Kirk alludes to Shakespeare at least twice in *Old House of Fear*. Early in Logan's journey to Scotland, he reads from a pamphlet written by the Reverend Samuel Balmullo, who relates the story of a local who drowned in an underground dungeon, a death he compares to "[w]hat the Duke of Clarence suffered in a

---

[55] Bradley J. Birzer, "The Permanence of Humanism," *Modern Age* 59, no. 2 (2017): 54.

butt of Malmsey."⁵⁶ The allusion here to Clarence's death in *Richard III* mainly serves to highlight the literary pretensions of this amateur folklorist (1.4).⁵⁷ Later, after arriving in Scotland, Logan meets Edmund Jackman, a Marxist revolutionary and occultist. Logan pretends to be a high-ranking member of Jackman's party and succeeds in gaining his trust. While showing Logan a set of carved ancient chessmen, Jackman paraphrases one of Iago's most famous lines from *Othello* (1.3.339-41): "You have not visited the British Museum? Once, like Marx, I went there daily. But I presume it is all *l. s. d.* [pounds, shillings, and pence] with you, Mr. Logan. 'Put money in thy purse, and yet again, put money in thy purse.'"⁵⁸ This allusion is more revealing, as Jackman's attempt to mock Logan for being interested solely in financial matters provides, instead, an important clue about his sinister character and intentions.⁵⁹

The number of allusions to Shakespeare rises dramatically in *A Creature of the Twilight*. Its hero, Manfred Arcane, is especially fond of quoting the playwright, often for no other reason than to luxuriate in the musicality of his words. On two separate occasions, for instance, he echoes Oberon's impish greeting of Titania in *A Midsummer Night's Dream* (2.1.60), revising it only slightly to reflect his own, more agreeable intentions towards the comrades he is addressing: "Well met by moonlight!"⁶⁰ Shortly before the climactic Battle of the Krokul Fords, upon which both his life and the fate of the country depend, Arcane pens a long missive to the young Peace Corps volunteer who has fallen in love with him, Mary Jo Travers. A recent PhD student, Travers came to Africa out of a sincere desire to do well by its inhabitants, only to discover that she and her fellow volunteers are hopelessly out of their league and have likely caused more harm than good in the long run. While admonishing her (and the large body of Americans she represents) not to be so eager to involve herself in the affairs of others, Arcane gently dissuades her from pursuing any further romantic interest in him. "Hearkening literally to the maxims of your diplomats, leave Africa to the Africans—and hie thee to the nursery. You are meant to be the mother of children, not the nurse of nations …"⁶¹ By changing a few words in Hamlet's famously cryptic message to Ophelia (3.1.120), Arcane introduces a

---

⁵⁶ Kirk, *Old House of Fear*, 36.
⁵⁷ Quotes from Shakespeare's plays in this chapter are taken from *The Riverside Shakespeare*.
⁵⁸ Kirk, *Old House of Fear*, 88.
⁵⁹ Shakespeare is also referred to, by name, early in *Old House of Fear*, when one of the characters recalls having seen Logan perform as Cassius in a production of *Julius Caesar* (p. 11). This does not qualify as an "allusion," however, so the incident is not listed in the table above.
⁶⁰ Kirk, *A Creature of the Twilight*, 33, 245. On p. 33, the full quote is, "Well met by moonlight, caballeros!"
⁶¹ Ibid., 229.

more playful tone into his otherwise serious letter, thereby cushioning the twin blows of his rejection of Travers and his critical advice to her.

By far, the most frequently alluded to plays in Kirk's second novel are *Macbeth* and *Julius Caesar*. The former is somewhat unexpected, given that this is one of his rare works of fiction without any mention of the supernatural. Most of the allusions to *Macbeth* consist of punning jokes made by Arcane, like the passing reference to *Hamlet* noted above. I have already discussed a few of them earlier in the chapter since the repeated allusions help to impose a sense of order on the novel's polyphonic plot. Late in the book, Arcane delivers a rousing speech to his troops that features an astonishing number of allusions, with dozens occurring over the span of about four pages. His brazen attempt to plagiarize his way toward oratorical brilliance draws from a wide range of sources, including the Bible, ancient Greek and Roman historians, and, of course, Shakespeare. Indeed, most of the references to *Julius Caesar* in the novel occur in this single passage, as Arcane exhorts his forces through words spoken by both Caesar and Marc Antony (2.2.32-33, 3.2.75-77). Several lines are borrowed from Antony's "masterful" speech before the mob at Caesar's funeral,[62] which is especially fitting since Arcane faces a rhetorical situation of equal complexity and danger (not to mention an audience of comparable gullibility).

Arcane returns as the protagonist of *Lord of the Hollow Dark*. He is part of a small group of outsiders who, for one reason or another, have found themselves involved in the strange proceedings at Balgrummo Lodging. Though slowed by old age and less physically imposing than in his days as master of Hamnegri, Arcane's wry, sardonic humor still sparkles, and he is as fond as ever of the well-chosen allusion. Eliot and Dante are Kirk's preferred sources in this metaphysical tale of divine justice and salvation, but there are numerous references to Shakespeare, as well. After meeting Arcane, who has disguised himself as the cult leader's loyal acolyte, one of the characters recalls, imperfectly, Hamlet's words following his encounter with the ghost of his father (1.5.108): "A man may smile and smile, and be a villain still."[63] Having revealed his true identity, Arcane must rouse his motley assortment of followers and prepare them for the arduous physical and spiritual dangers that await them. He looks for inspiration to *Henry V*, long recognized as one of Shakespeare's most patriotic and inspirational works (3.1.1, 4.3.60). "'Once more into the breach, dear friends!' [Arcane] flourished his heavy stick. 'We contend against

---

[62] Gary M. Weier, "Perspectivism and Form in Drama: A Burkean Analysis of *Julius Caesar*," *Communication Quarterly* 44, no. 2 (1996): 254, doi: 10.1080/01463379609370013.

[63] Kirk, *Lord of the Hollow Dark*, 126.

the Lord of This World.'"⁶⁴ In the end, only his small band manages to make it out of the castle alive, feeling very much like those "happy few" who stood with Henry on St. Crispian's. Once again, the allusions are more than just gratuitous demonstrations of learning, either on the part of Arcane or his author. In his journey from Africa to Scotland, the one-time "father of shadows" and ruler of thousands must learn to embrace a new role as the spiritual shepherd of half a dozen souls. His transformation reveals a similar growth in wisdom and maturity as Prince Hal does in spurning Falstaff in favor of his responsibilities as king.

The Permanent Things ... and Ghosts

Not for Kirk is the facile aesthetic of "art for art's sake," by which art is conceived of as being "independent from prevailing social mores and divorced from the notion of moral utility that underlies them."⁶⁵ He insists, instead, that writers have as much responsibility for responding to the major issues of his day as any academic or politician. "The survival of any culture, or the material fabric of civilization, requires vigorous imagination and readiness to sacrifice. By dullness and complacency are intellectual and social orders undone."⁶⁶ Throughout his life, Kirk sought to prevent the triumph of "dullness and complacency" in the twentieth century, writing countless articles and books and lecturing widely in defense of the permanent things. But he also brought his moral imagination to bear on the literary front through stories and novels that grappled with many of the same issues discussed in his social and political works. Somewhat unexpected, most of these works are examples of Gothic fiction, a venerable genre that includes supernatural elements not often associated with conservatives or politics in general. What do Kirk's ghosts, witches, and avenging spirits have to teach us about the permanent things? In my next chapter, I consider the answer to this question and trace some of Kirk's key influences in the Gothic tradition.

---

[64] Ibid., 133.
[65] Elisabeth Ladenson, *Dirt for Art's Sake: Books on Trial from* Madame Bovary *to* Lolita (Ithaca, NY: Cornell University Press, 2007), 29.
[66] Kirk, *The Sword of Imagination*, 228.

Chapter 3

The Gothic Tradition in England and America

The start of Gothicism in literature is typically dated to the publication of *The Castle of Otranto* by Horace Walpole in 1764.[1] I will have more to say about Walpole and his baffling book in Chapter 6, in which I trace the influence of Edmund Burke on the Gothic and conservative movements, which both began at about the same time and feature some overlapping figures, themes, and motivations. My interest in this chapter is in Kirk's relation to the broader Gothic tradition that Walpole initiated: who were the key influences on his work, and what kind of Gothic fiction did he actually write? Fortunately, Kirk's own words provide us with a useful starting point for answering such questions. In his memoirs, he describes his first novel, *Old House of Fear*, as "conforming to the canons of Ann Radcliffe as described by Walter Scott."[2] He refers to *Lord of the Hollow Dark*, his third and last, in almost identical terms, as a "mystical romance, conforming faithfully to the canons of the Gothick tale as expounded by Walter Scott in his memoir of Ann Radcliffe."[3] Radcliffe was an English novelist who wrote several influential novels during the late eighteenth century, in which she mingled psychological intensity with supernatural themes and established many of the now-familiar conventions of the genre. Among her many successors was the Scottish poet, novelist, and historian Scott, whom Kirk acknowledged as a major influence on his own life and work.[4] Closer to home, I believe that Kirk was chiefly inspired by the work of Nathaniel Hawthorne, an important figure in early American literature and the Romantic movement in that country.

As his frequent allusions suggest, however, Kirk was familiar with a wide range of authors, and there are many others worth mentioning as potential influences on his approach to Gothic fiction. These include the Inkling, Charles Williams; M. R. James, master of the antiquarian ghost story; Washington Irving,

---

[1] See, e.g., E. J. Clery, "The Genesis of 'Gothic' Fiction," in *The Cambridge Companion to Gothic Fiction*, ed. Jerrold E. Hogle (Cambridge: Cambridge University Press, 2002), 21.
[2] Kirk, *The Sword of Imagination*, 250.
[3] Kirk, dedication in *Lord of the Hollow Dark* [ii].
[4] See the previous chapter for a discussion of the numerous allusions to Scott in Kirk's books.

arguably the first American to achieve international success as a writer; and Flannery O'Connor and Ray Bradbury both of whom Kirk knew personally and deeply admired. But Radcliffe, Scott, and Hawthorne each left an indelible imprint on Kirk's Gothicism, as is evident in the many thematic, structural, and even stylistic parallels that can be observed between their work and his. The quality of Kirk's stories may not always match the lofty standards set by his forebears, but they prove, nonetheless, that he deserves a place within their ranks. Before discussing these rather disparate influences on his work, it may be worth considering what Kirk had to say about his intentions as a writer of Gothic fiction. His most important statement to that effect can be found in "A Cautionary Note on the Ghostly Tale," an oft-anthologized essay first published in 1962 as an afterword to his first collection of short stories, *The Surly Sullen Bell*. In 1984, Kirk revised and expanded this essay to serve as a preface for his final anthology, *Watchers at the Strait Gate*. For the sake of convenience, I shall refer to these two versions of the essay as A (1962) and B (1984).

Gothic Fiction and the Moral Imagination

Some of the differences between versions A and B are quite substantial, though the two essays cover much of the same ground. Version A begins with a lament over the decline of religious belief in America, which Kirk blames on the shift in emphasis from religious belief to science that has occurred since the Enlightenment. The supernatural concerns of Gothic fiction have given way, accordingly, to the fantastic ones of *science fiction*, a fine genre in its own right. Yet humans have an inherent need for the transcendent, Kirk argues, which science (and science fiction) can never fully satisfy. The irony is that although no one has ever seen a Martian or flying saucer, recorded history offers numerous examples of those who claim to have seen a ghost. "Scholars have analyzed soberly such appearances," Kirk adds, "from Father Noel Taillepied's *Treatise on Ghosts* (1588) to Father Herbert Thurston's *Ghosts and Poltergeists* (1955). *The Journal of the Society for Psychical Research* has examined painstakingly, for decades, the data of psychic manifestations."[5] In short, the supernatural has been subjected to as much critical scrutiny as any other subject. And it has never been conclusively disproved by scientific methods.

But can we be sure that will always be the case? Kirk seems to have regarded the contemporary interest in psychic phenomena as an encouraging development despite its potential to explain away formerly unknowable things. We may have lost the religious justification for ghosts, poltergeists, and

---

[5] Russell Kirk, "A Cautionary Note on the Ghostly Tale," *The Russell Kirk Center*, 19 March 2007, https://kirkcenter.org/kirk/a-cautionary-note-on-the-ghostly-tale/. This will be my source for the "A version" of this essay.

revenants, he admits. Still, now people have a (pseudo-scientific) reason for believing in them, and it is unlikely that further research into the mind will ever be able to provide a fully satisfactory explanation for whence they come. In any case, the uncertain status of the supernatural offers certain advantages for writers of Gothic fiction since (unlike science fiction authors) they do not have to worry about whether the things they write about will eventually be proven false. The ghostly tale, Kirk argues, "can piece together in some pattern the hints which seem thrown out by this vision or that haunting or some case of second sight. It can touch keenly upon the old reality of evil—and upon injustice and retribution."[6] Here, Kirk touches upon one of his motivations for writing Gothic stories: to explore themes such as evil, divine justice, and retribution. As I shall discuss below, they are ones he shares with Nathaniel Hawthorne.

The next few paragraphs offer a good indication of the kind of Gothic writers Kirk admired. He mentions literary authors who only dabbled in the genre and those known primarily for writing in it. Among the former are Daniel Defoe, Sir Walter Scott, Samuel Taylor Coleridge, Guy de Maupassant, and Edith Wharton. The latter includes M. R. James, Algernon Blackwood, and Arthur Machen. Kirk acknowledges that many Gothic authors, including Walpole and Charles Dickens, write mostly to entertain or reassure their readers. There is certainly a time and place for that, for instance, when gathered with family around a roaring fire during the holidays. Still, the twentieth century has given rise to enough horrors and depravities that such old-fashioned ghost stories may seem antiquated. Those who would write Gothic fiction in the present would do well to look, instead, to the examples of George Macdonald and C. S. Lewis, who "employ the ghostly and the supernatural means in letters to a moral and theological end."[7] The best Gothic stories, Kirk insists, are instilled with the moral imagination; they begin with a healthy respect for the reality of evil but relegate that evil to its proper place in a universe guided by divine providence. He cites Robert Hugh Benson's *The Light Invisible* (which Kirk mistakenly attributes to A. C. Benson) and W. B. Yeats' *Mythologies* as examples of Gothic works that illustrate this truth.

Kirk next offers a surprising observation. "I venture to suggest that the more orthodox is a writer's theology, the more convincing, as symbols and allegories, his uncanny tales will be."[8] Given that he was still in 1962 several years away from his formal conversion to Roman Catholicism, one wonders what Kirk would have made of his own published stories according to this criterion (especially

---

[6] Ibid.
[7] Ibid.
[8] Ibid.

since most of his early ones lack supernatural elements entirely, let alone an ethos that could be equated with any "orthodox" theology.) Nevertheless, he asserts, contemporary Gothic authors must engage in some way with the Christian tradition if they hope to write something of lasting value beyond mere shock entertainment. After criticizing Freud and the positivists for their hostile attitudes towards the transcendent, Kirk warns the aspiring Gothic author against the tendency to moralize. There is also a danger in not taking one's creations seriously—in not sharing some of the fear one hopes to impart to one's readers. In closing, Kirk reminds us that the Gothic tradition is old-fashioned and even conservative and that it is important not to try to modernize it too much. Though rather disorganized, version A offers a clear enough sense of what Kirk thought about the writing of Gothic fiction at the start of his career.

Twenty years later, Kirk would revisit these ideas while preparing his final collection of stories. Version B begins on a suitably reflective note, with the author noting the long years that have elapsed since the writing of his earliest ones. He repeats a quote by M. R. James that he had used in the final paragraph of version A before clarifying his motivations as an author. "I did not write [these stories] to impose meaningless terror upon the innocent ... What I have attempted, rather, are experiments in the moral imagination."[9] It is worth noting that he had not used the phrase "moral imagination" at all in version A; perhaps the mature Kirk had a clearer sense of what he hoped to accomplish as a writer than when he was first starting. He may have undergone a slight change in literary taste, as well. Aside from M. R. James and Sheridan Le Fanu, the earliest writers he mentions in version B are a group of prominent Christians associated with the Inklings movement at Oxford in the early twentieth century. "All important literature has some ethical end," Kirk writes, "and the tale of the preternatural—as written by George Macdonald, C. S. Lewis, Charles Williams, and other masters—can be an instrument for the recovery of moral order."[10] Of course, Kirk had by then been a Catholic for several decades.

The following paragraphs are taken with only slight alterations directly from version A. Kirk discusses the freedom enjoyed by writers of Gothic fiction to explore topics that can never be made obsolete by modern science and repeats his warning against moralizing. The same stories about Samuel Johnson and Le Fanu are referenced to support his assertion about the importance of taking the supernatural seriously, though transported from their place at the end of version A. Some new material follows: first, Kirk mentions a letter by George Orwell in which he describes seeing a ghost once in a cemetery in England.

---

[9] Kirk, "A Cautionary Note on the Ghostly Tale," in *Ancestral Shadows*, 402.
[10] Ibid., 403.

Orwell dismisses the incident as a possible hallucination, but Kirk is not so sure that that is not a distinction without a difference. The anecdote replaces a similar one told in version A about Ford Maddox Ford. Next, Kirk considers how psychic and psychological research into the supernatural has failed to progress much beyond the initial, tepid speculations made by Sigmund Freud and his followers. I have noted Kirk's lifelong interest in keeping himself informed of the latest scientific developments, and his intelligent discussion of the differences between Carl Jung and Freud here reveals how much he was still learning even in his mid-sixties. However brilliant some of the advances of science have been in the past two decades, Kirk remains untroubled by the prospect of the supernatural being conclusively debunked.

Kirk then turns to the question of why he wrote so much Gothic fiction during his life. One reason, he says, is that he aspired "to help extract the stuffing from the keyhole," to shed some light on the difficult metaphysical questions that lie at the heart of the human condition.[11] Kirk notes that he could have written about any number of real-life encounters with the supernatural, but such tales are not as effective at conveying the true nature of these experiences as fiction. He then repeats points made in version A: that there is a great deal of evidence throughout history to support belief in things like ghosts or angels, which can neither be confirmed nor denied empirically. At the same time, we must be cautious regarding claims involving the fantastic: more often than not, that bump in the night is being caused by the wind rather than a spectral visitor.

In closing, Kirk acknowledges the influence of many of the same authors mentioned in the middle of version A, beginning with Daniel Defoe; this time, however, and rather curiously, he replaces E. T. A. Hoffmann, Maupassant, and F. Marion Crawford with the Sitwells, a trio of siblings who enjoyed varying levels of artistic success throughout the twentieth century.[12] In general, the latter version of "A Cautionary Tale" seems to offer a more concise and organized overview of Kirk's attitude towards the Gothic. It is less strident in tone and more focused on defining and defending Gothic fiction than on criticizing broad cultural or scientific trends. Perhaps the most significant difference between the two is in version B's relative lack of interest in religion. Kirk does not repeat his remarkable assertions about the superiority of ghostly tales that are grounded in theological orthodoxy and the Christian tradition. Still, he does end version B with a clear echo of the petition from the "Hail Mary," an important Catholic prayer: "Pray for us scribbling sinners now and at the hour

---

[11] Ibid., 405.
[12] In descending order of age, these are Edith, Osbert, and Sacheverell Sitwell.

of our death."[13] The same line is referenced in T. S. Eliot's "Ash Wednesday,"[14] which Kirk probably intends to allude to, as well.

Key Influences: Radcliffe, Scott, and Hawthorne

"A Cautionary Note on the Ghostly Tale" offers a good starting point for understanding Kirk's approach to the Gothic. But to understand the kind of Gothic writer he was, or aspired to be, one must also consider his major influences within the genre. By his admission, these include Anne Radcliffe and Sir Walter Scott. Radcliffe was born in London in 1764, the same year that *The Castle of Otranto* was published. Her father was a haberdasher or seller of small articles of clothing such as buttons and ribbons; he and his wife had important family connections, however, extending even to the royal family, and Radcliffe was raised in a comfortable, supportive environment.[15] She married at 23 and published her first book two years later. *The Castles of Athlin and Dunbayne* did not prove a great success, but her subsequent offerings, including *The Romance of the Forest* (1791), *Mysteries of Udolpho* (1794), and *The Italian* (1797), all managed to capitalize on the growing public appetite (especially among female readers) for stories set in exotic locales featuring supernatural elements and a bit of horror. As with Walpole's *The Castle of Otranto*, Radcliffe's books can make for difficult reading today: most are far too long, and they vary wildly in tone from lurid to tediously descriptive. Yet, during her lifetime and for many years after, her work was highly regarded by both critics and readers. "She was far and away the best-selling English novelist of the 1790s," biographer Robert Miles notes, "the most read, the most imitated, and the most translated."[16] Though her novels were often described as "romances" by her contemporaries, reflecting the conventional use of that term to describe novels with supernatural or unrealistic elements, Radcliffe played a key role in establishing some of the basic conventions of what we now call Gothic fiction.

For example, many of her books are set in dilapidated castles or ruined churches replete with secret dungeons and winding underground tunnels—the kind of setting, in other words, that is now considered *de rigueur* for any self-respecting ghostly tale. But it is important to note that they are only *partly* set there; most, in fact, involve a great deal of journeying back and forth between these Gothic locales and the villages, towns, and cities of the normal or real

---

[13] Ibid., 406.
[14] Eliot, *The Complete Poems & Plays*, 90 (*Ash Wednesday*).
[15] Rictor Norton, *Mistress of Udolpho: The Life of Ann Radcliffe* (London: Leicester University Press, 1999), 13.
[16] Robert Miles, *Ann Radcliffe: The Great Enchantress* (Manchester: Manchester University Press, 1995), 8.

world. For instance, in *The Mysteries of Udolpho*, the main character, a female orphan named Emily, does not arrive at the titular castle until Volume 2, Chapter 5, almost a third of the way into the novel. Before then, she accompanies her father on a long trek through southern France and the Pyrenees, which Radcliffe describes with remarkable skill, especially considering that she never visited the region herself! Nevertheless, her contemporaries often remarked upon the picture-like quality of her descriptive passages, which were often compared to paintings. It has long been a critical convention "to describe [her] writing as a gallery of watercolors in black and white print, adept at stimulating in the reader's eye the very images which nature or fancy had presumably imprinted upon the author's."[17] The varied settings also serve a useful narrative function; for by delaying the arrival of her (normally female) protagonists into the Gothic realm, Radcliffe is able to foreshadow some of its supernatural, grotesque, or bizarre elements while heightening the dramatic effect of their eventual entrance into it. *The Romance of the Forest* likewise begins and ends in the safe, bustling city of Paris, far from the haunted abbey at its center.

Radcliffe's distinctive treatment of the supernatural is worth mentioning here. She is acknowledged today as a pioneering figure in the "explained supernatural," a strain of Gothic fiction in which no ghosts appear, and supernatural or mysterious events are later revealed to have perfectly ordinary causes. Inspired by contemporary debates over aesthetics, she distinguished between horror and terror; only the latter, she believed, can lead the reader to the sublime. "The horror-Gothic writer is keen on local effect, surprise, a series of impacts," Michael Schmidt summarizes, "where the terror-Gothic writer sustains and cranks up a single passion toward a resolution ..."[18] An early passage in *Romance of the Forest* demonstrates her basic method. A group of travelers seeking shelter at an abandoned abbey are suddenly disturbed by unusual noises emanating from deep within its walls. The tension rises over several paragraphs as the characters speculate about potential sources of the unsettling sounds, ranging from vengeful spirits to a gang of much-dreaded *bandetti* (local outlaws) lying in wait for them. A brave soul ventures forth to investigate, only to return with the happy news that the noises were due to "nothing but owls and rooks,"[19] a type of crow. Likewise, the main character in *Mysteries of Udolpho* spends much of the book convinced that she has seen a corpse, which is later revealed to have been a wax figure. The ultimate effect of these last-minute revelations and reversals, Adam Miller explains, is "at best a

---

[17] Jayne Lewis, "'No Color of Language': Radcliffe's Aesthetic Unbound," *Eighteenth-Century Studies* 39, no. 3 (2006): 381, *JSTOR*, https://www.jstor.org/stable/30053478.
[18] Michael Schmidt, *The Novel: A Biography* (Cambridge, MA: Harvard University Press, 2014), 172.
[19] Anne Radcliffe, *Romance of the Forest* (Philadelphia: J. B. Lippincott & Co., 1865), 25.

vague disappointment and at worst a feeling of having been duped by cheap, gothic tricks."[20] Even sympathetic readers of Radcliff, such as Walter Scott, expressed dismay at her habit of explaining away supernatural phenomena.[21]

One would hardly expect that Kirk, who believed in ghosts from a very young age, would be willing to follow her example in this regard. And yet, he did just that, at least in his early fiction, inviting the obvious question of why a Gothic author who believes in ghosts would fear to use them in his stories. Perhaps Radcliffe's success with the "explained supernatural" helps to explain his flirtation with the same in tales such as "Behind the Stumps," "The Surly Sullen Bell," and "What Shadows We Pursue," all of which were published during the early 1950s. All of these stories make effective use of Gothic tropes but decline to attribute them to supernatural causes. As I noted in Chapter 1, only "Behind the Stumps" allows for the possibility that there might be something going on in the story that science or reason cannot fully explain. This also describes his approach to the Gothic in *Old House of Fear*. Despite all the talk of bogles and half-man, half-goat monsters stalking the moors of Carnglass, Hugh Logan encounters nothing scarier there than a lunatic Marxist and some explosives. In 1963, Kirk married Annette Courtemanche and converted to Catholicism; from that point on, he would never again write a story or book that does not offer clear and unmistakable evidence of a genuine belief in the supernatural.

There is, in fact, scant evidence of Radcliffe's direct influence on Kirk. In his descriptions of *Old House of Fear* and *Lord of the Hollow Dark*, after all, he does not cite her canons or conventions as having directly inspired the novel, only those canons *as described/expounded* by Walter Scott. This implies that Kirk was less familiar with Radcliffe's work than he was with Scott's analysis of it. Indeed, given the lack of references to Radcliffe in Kirk's essays, letters, and memoirs, that is probably the case. By Scott's "memoir" of Radcliffe, he probably means the *Lives of the Novelists*, an idiosyncratic survey of contemporary literature that was published in 1821. A chapter is devoted to Radcliffe, whom Scott acknowledges as an important figure in establishing the respectability of Gothic romance, despite his reservations about the quality of some of her work. Perhaps his comments on *The Sicilian Romance* left a lasting impression upon Kirk, for they describe so well the overall tone he was able to achieve in his initial, full-length foray into Gothic fiction: "Adventures heaped on adventures, in quick and brilliant succession, with all the hair-breadth charms of escape or

---

[20] Adam Miller, "Ann Radcliffe's Scientific Romance," *Eighteenth Century Fiction* 28, no. 3 (2016): 528-29, doi: 10.3138/ecf.28.3.527.

[21] Katherine Ding, "'Searching After the Splendid Nothing': Gothic Epistemology and the Rise of Fictionality," *ELH* 80, no. 2 (2013): 560-61, *JSTOR*, https://www.jstor.org/stable/24475517.

capture, hurry the reader along with them, and the imagery and scenery by which the action is relieved are like those of a splendid Oriental tale."[22] Scott also praises her skill at descriptive passages involving landscapes, which is a highlight of Kirk's first novel, too. In any case, even if Kirk never read any of Radcliffe's books, the parallels between his work and hers noted above may not be entirely coincidental. Radcliffe had her school of followers, after all, and her books were so widely read and imitated[23] that he is sure to have been exposed to her conventions even before learning of them from Scott.

Scott was born in 1771, just a few years after Radcliffe, and was proficient in a wide range of genres, including epic poetry, historical fiction, drama, and, of course, Gothic romance. His most enduring works include the long narrative poems *The Lay of the Last Minstrel* (1805) and *The Lady of the Lake* (1810), along with the novels *Ivanhoe* and *The Bride of Lammermoor* (both 1819), the latter of which was adapted into a well-known opera by the Italian composer Gaetano Donizetti. Kirk was especially fond of Scott's Waverley series of historical novels, which cover a period of about eight hundred years in European history, with settings as varied as the rugged highlands of Scotland and the bustling capital of the Byzantine Empire, Constantinople. "By the 1820s," observes Peter Garside, "it was a critical commonplace that Scott was the founder of a new historical fiction, superior in several ways to conventional historiographical modes, whose formula was now immediately transferable to other national identities."[24] Kirk regarded him as a foundational figure in Scottish and European letters and an important influence not only on his writing but on the whole of his life. "I began to read Sir Walter Scott when I was twelve or thirteen, and I think I learned from the Waverley novels … more of the varieties of character than ever I have got since from the manuals of psychology."[25] Kirk devotes an entire section of *The Conservative Mind* to Scott, whom he praises for promoting the thought of Edmund Burke through imaginative means. His appreciation of the Waverley series comes through quite clearly here.[26]

Unsurprisingly, then, Scott's influence on Kirk's approach to Gothic fiction can be traced in ways both small and large. "The Tapestried Chamber" offers evidence of the former; it was one of three stories contributed by Scott to a

---

[22] Walter Scott, *The Lives of the Novelists* (London: Oxford University Press, 1906), 305.
[23] Katherine Bowers, "Ghost Writers: Radcliffiana and the Russian Gothic Wave," *Victorian Popular Fictions* 3, no. 2 (2021): 156-57, doi: 10.46911/TVCT9530. Bowers points out that there was a trend in Russia of attributing random books to her famous name.
[24] Peter Garside, "Popular Fiction and National Tale: Hidden Origins of Scott's Waverley," *Nineteenth-Century Literature* 46, no. 1 (1991): 31, doi: 10.2307/3044962.
[25] Kirk, *Enemies of the Permanent Things*, 50.
[26] Kirk, *The Conservative Mind*, 114-24.

literary annual published in 1828. It concerns General Browne, recently discharged from the Revolutionary War in America, who spends a night at the castle of an old friend, Lord Woodville. He insists on leaving the next day and, after some prodding from Woodville, eventually confesses the reason for his hasty departure: the previous night, he had seen the ghost of a woman dressed in old-fashioned clothing, whose face was distorted by "the fixed features of a corpse," a "diabolical countenance" that frightened him into a prolonged stupor.[27] The story is genuinely scary and quite unlike anything Kirk ever wrote, except in one important detail: the main character, Browne, shares enough similarities with one of Kirk's most important literary creations to suggest a possible link between the two. Like Browne, Ralph Bain is introduced (in 1952's "Sorworth Place") as a former soldier who recently returned from war, who has been touring the British countryside for the past several months and now finds himself in a small, undistinguished town. Browne is "an officer of merit, as well as a gentleman,"[28] and much the same could be said of Bain, who holds the prestigious Military Cross, awarded for bravery in battle. Both have an eye for architecture, which matches Kirk's interest in the subject. Early in their respective stories, Browne and Bain are struck by the appearance of a nearby castle, which they decide to investigate similarly, first questioning residents, then heading over for a closer view of their own. Browne and Bain's names are also quite similar, obviously.

Kirk may have also been influenced by Scott's tendency to use a framing device with his Gothic stories: in other words, to begin or end with a brief scene that has little direct bearing on the rest of the plot. Though narratively digressive, they enable him to indulge in a bit of social criticism or historical commentary without interrupting the flow of the ensuing story. "Wandering Willie's Tale," for example, starts with a lengthy description of some of the troubles arising from the 1688 Glorious Revolution and its aftermath, which has little relevance to the blind fiddler's tale about his grandfather's attempts to pay off his rent through worldly and otherworldly means. It does, however, provide Scott with an opportunity to reflect upon one of his favorite themes: his "Jacobite enthusiasm, a recurrent thread in the fabric of his texts."[29] Similarly, in the opening paragraphs of "The Fortunes of Martin Waldeck," the reader learns about the recent expulsion of a Catholic friar who had infuriated the locals of a medieval German town by preaching against their demonic superstitions. He

---

[27] Walter Scott, *The Talisman, My Aunt Margaret's Mirror, The Tapestried Chamber* (New York: Funk and Wagnalls Company, 1900), 354.
[28] Ibid., 346.
[29] Kathryn Sutherland, introduction to *Redgauntlet*, by Walter Scott (Oxford: Oxford University Press, 2011), viii.

reappears in the closing pages but plays no role in the main adventures of the titular character and is hardly needed to reinforce the story's simple moral, which is, at any rate, explained in the final line: "Thus were the miseries attendant upon wealth, hastily attained and ill employed, exemplified in the fortunes of Martin Waldeck."[30] Why mention the friar at all, then? Scott was a member of the Scottish Episcopal Church, a Protestant, but his works express an ambivalent, if not generally positive, attitude towards the Catholic Church. He also had a major influence on several figures in the Oxford Movement, a group of Anglican clergy that converted to Catholicism in the nineteenth century,[31] and it is likely that the inclusion of the friar in "Martin Waldeck" simply reflects some of his sympathy towards his country's former, pre-Reformation faith.

The point is Scott could have easily trimmed these scenes and characters without affecting the success of his stories as Gothic narratives. In fact, doing so would have arguably improved them in that regard since the digressions impair his ability to provoke sublime feelings in the reader—long recognized as a major goal of Gothic writers, as Scott knew well from his reading of Edmund Burke, John Milner, Uvedale Price, and, of course, Radcliffe.[32] His decision to keep them anyway hints at a possible affinity with a central tenet of traditional conservatism, oft-espoused by Kirk: that authors have a responsibility not only to entertain but also to educate and inform their readers. Kirk certainly regarded Scott as a fellow proponent of the moral imagination, naming him one of his ten "exemplary" conservatives who sought to instill traditional principles through his fiction.[33] In any case, many of Kirk's stories begin similarly, with a scene or (more often) descriptive passage that may be superfluous to the plot but supports his didactic intentions. In "There's a Long, Long Trail A-Winding" and "Ex Tenebris," he spends the opening paragraphs reflecting upon the decline of rural lifestyles. In "The Surly Sullen Bell" and "The Invasion of the Church of the Holy Ghost," his attention is drawn, instead, to the devastating impact of urban blight. "Saviourgate" begins with a few paragraphs that allow Kirk to vent his

---

[30] Walter Scott, *The Antiquary*, ed. Nicola Watson (London: Oxford University Press, 2009), 262.

[31] Peter Gorday, "'He Recited in a Low Voice the Splendid Hymns of the Roman Church': Sir Walter Scott and Catholic Romanticism in the Thought of Henri Bremond," *Logos: A Journal of Catholic Thought & Culture* 25, no. 4 (2022): 89, doi: 10.1353/log.2022.0030.

[32] Catherine Henry Walsh, "The Sublime in the Historical Novel: Scott and Gil y Carrasco," *Comparative Literature* 42, no. 1 (1990): 34, doi: 10.2307/1770311. Walsh points out that Scott kept a copy of Price's *Essay on the Picturesque* on his bookshelf. I discuss Burke's theory of the sublime and its influence on the first Gothic novel by Horace Walpole in chapter six.

[33] Kirk, "Ten Exemplary Conservatives," in *The Essential Russell Kirk*, 36.

frustration over changes in the Catholic Church that he blamed on the Second Vatican Council of 1965. In his best work, Kirk follows Scott's lead in keeping his social or historical commentary on the margins of the story. Occasionally, as in "The Last God's Dream," they overwhelm it, resulting in a less satisfactory read.

But Scott's influence on Kirk extends beyond characterization or narrative structure. As a historian, a conservative, and a patriot, Kirk must have admired Scott's success in promoting his country's history and culture through his fiction. He looked to the past with a nostalgic eye, contrasting the natural beauty and high romantic ideals of medieval Scotland with the dull and increasingly urbanized world in which he and his readers lived.[34] Interspersed throughout his prose were some of the traditional songs and ballads he picked up during his many tours of the Highlands and other remote places. Though capable of sustaining only a hardscrabble sort of existence, these were fertile grounds for the moral imagination, full of unforgettable legends and snatches of folklore that would furnish many an idea for a story, as they would do the same, centuries later, for another outside visitor named Russell Kirk. Along with Robert Burns, Scott played a central role in shaping contemporary attitudes towards his nation and its people:

> [W]hile he resisted political nationalism, Scott was a great proponent—and, some have argued, an inventor—of Scottish cultural nationalism. Having lived and worked in the Scottish Borders for years, Scott drew particularly on the traditions of the region in sketching his sense of "Scottishness." He harnessed the natural and cultural histories of the Borders as sources of Loyalist fidelity, repurposing stories of clan conflicts in wild spaces as tales of honor, chivalry, and "authentic" allegiances between people and their lived landscapes.[35]

Scott's Gothic fiction played a key role in his literary efforts to shape his readers' impressions of Scotland. As much, if not more, of these stories' appeal tends to come from their use of unfamiliar dialects, exotic songs, and cultural artifacts as from the odd ghost or witch that haunts their pages.

---

[34] This is an oversimplification of Scott's broad and varied output, of course, but pertains especially to the Waverley novels. For an overview of critical attitudes towards this series, see Ian Duncan, "Primitive Inventions: Rob Roy, Nation, and World System," *Eighteenth Century Fiction* 15, no. 1 (2002): 81-84, doi: 10.1353/ecf.2002.0061.

[35] Julia C. Obert, "Yes Scotland?: The Political Ecologies of the Borders in Walter Scott's Minstrelsy of the Scottish Border and Lay of the Last Minstrel, and in Contemporary Scottish Poetry," *Scottish Literary Review* 11, no. 2 (2019): 81, *Project MUSE*, https://muse.jhu.edu/article/741712.

Critics have long remarked upon the prominent use of Gaelic or Scots dialect within Scott's stories. These languages are closely associated with the traditional communities dwelling in the Highlands, the Hebrides, and other rural places, in contrast to English, which had come to displace them as the *lingua franca* for educated, upper-class Scots. In the Waverley novels, explains Alexander Welsh, Scott "regularly assigned a high style to his protagonists and historical personages, and a low style (usually dialect) to the lower ranks of society and the comic characters (who are usually one and the same)."[36] The use of dialect represents an obvious way for Scott to promote Scottish culture through his fiction, and it would have struck his readers as colorful or exotic. Even when he uses dialect as comic relief, Scott is careful to ensure that the joke is as much at the expense of those who do not understand it as of those who do. Early in *Waverley*, for instance, the young hero finds himself accompanied by a gruff Highlander with little knowledge of English. After asking for an estimate of the length of their remaining journey, he receives the following, incomprehensible reply: "Ta cove was tree, four mile; but as Duinhé-wassel was a wee taiglit, Donald could, tat is, might—would—should send ta curragh."[37] Edward Waverley wisely decides against insisting upon a translation, hoping that the man's meaning will become clear enough on its own—as it eventually does. Though he often limits his use of dialect to dialogue in his historical novels, Scott also wrote stories like "Wandering Willie's Tale" that are told entirely in Scots.

Perhaps this helped to inspire some of the linguistic experimentation undertaken by Kirk in many of his Gothic tales. Following Scott's lead, he employs what one can only assume it is supposed to represent a rural Michigan dialect in several stories. In 1957's "Lost Lake," a personal essay about Mecosta County, Kirk discusses the colorful local inhabitants, including the Van Tessels, who have a characteristic way of speaking: "I jes' love to make bread ... Your han's allays so nice an' white after."[38] "The Princess of All Lands," published in 1979, is set partly in the derelict town of Pompeii, Michigan. Its main character encounters a trio of evil spirits who sound much like the Van Tessels. "Lissen to the lady talk," says one. "Jest lissen to her! Real lady, all right, all right, but she won't be for long. Mercy! We'll twitch her tricks that ain't so ladylike."[39] Like Scott, Kirk tends to reserve dialect for lower-class characters. Unlike Scott, he does not limit himself to local dialects or those from rural Michigan but experiments

---

[36] Alexander Welsh, "Contrast of Styles in the Waverley Novels," *NOVEL: A Forum on Fiction* 6, no. 3 (1973): 219-20, *JSTOR*, https://www.jstor.org/stable/1344834.
[37] Walter Scott, *Waverley, Or 'Tis Sixty Years Since* (London: J. M. Dent & Co., 1906), 156.
[38] Russell Kirk, "Lost Lake," *Southwest Review* 42 (1957): 322.
[39] Kirk, "The Princess of All Lands," in *Ancestral Shadows*, 175.

with several others, including New York street slang and even Scots. "The Reflex-Man in Whinnymuir Close," from Kirk's final collection of fiction in 1984, is surely one of the oddest Gothic stories he ever wrote. In the manner of Sheridan Le Fanu, M. R. James, and Scott, it is presented as a manuscript recovered from a random pile of papers found in a locked chest. It tells the story of a witch who summons her dead brother's *doppelgänger*, the "Reflex-Man" of the title. Perhaps reflecting its ultimate source of inspiration, all of the characters talk in Scots dialect. The story is also filled with snatches of English poetry and quotes from the Bible, in the manner of much of Scott's fiction.

Indeed, songs, poems, and ballads are some of the most effective means by which he introduces his readers to Scottish culture. Almost any Waverley novel can be used to illustrate Scott's fondness for music, which dates to the very start of his literary career and the publication of the first volume of the *Minstrelsy of the Scottish Border* in 1802. Scott had spent several years traveling through the country's border region collecting material for this anthology of traditional ballads, working closely with John Leyden, James Hogg, Charles Kirkpatrick Sharpe, and others.[40] The experience provided him with extensive knowledge of Scotland's folklore and superstitions, which he was able to put to good use in his fiction. *The Bride of Lammermoor* demonstrates how music, poetry, and song remain prominent even in his mature Gothic works. Each chapter begins with an epigraph, which is usually attributed to a Scottish poet or folk song, as is the case with the lines that open Chapter 7:

> Now, Billy Bewick, keep good heart,
> And of thy talking let me be;
> But if thou art a man, as I am sure thou art,
> Come over the dike and fight with me.
>   Old Ballad.[41]

Within the story, characters frequently burst into song: the unfortunate Laird of Bucklaw (eventual husband of the titular bride, who stabs him on their wedding night) is especially fond of humming or quoting bits of songs during conversation. Even random characters, such as the old forester who accompanies Bucklaw on a hunt in chapter 9, cite "an old woodman's rhyme" as proof that the horns of a deer are not to be taken lightly.[42] Detailed descriptions of musical

---

[40] Lucy Macrae, "'A vast o' bits o' stories:' Shortreed, Laidlaw, and Scott's *Minstrelsy of the Scottish Borders*," *Scottish Literary Review* 7, no. 2 (2015): 96, *Academic Search Complete*.
[41] Walter Scott, *The Bride of Lammermoor* (Edinburgh: A. L. Burt Company, 1857), 47.
[42] Ibid., 70.

performances and poetry readings are not rare occurrences in the Waverley series.

Kirk may have credited Radcliffe's "canons" for having inspired the writing of *Old House of Fear*, but the substantial number of songs and poems recited in the book result in its feeling more, at times, like a continuation of the Waverley series than anything else. The first chapter, for instance, features a long discussion between Hugh Logan and his employer, Duncan MacAskival, that ends with the two exchanging couplets from a story and poem by Rudyard Kipling ("With Any Amazement" and "The Winners," respectively). In Chapter 3, Logan recalls a few lines from "The Call" by the Scottish poet Thomas Osbert Mordaunt, which he mistakenly attributes to Scott. The book reaches its lyrical climax in Chapter 8, during a long dinner scene involving Logan and Mary MacAskival, a young Scottish lass. The characters recite parts of various poems by Robert Burns before Mary is convinced to sing several stanzas from a popular Scottish folk song, "Charlie is My Darling." The "Charlie" mentioned in its title refers to Charles Edward Stuart, son of the deposed James II, who had ruled England, Ireland, and Scotland (as James VII) until the Glorious Revolution of 1688. Supporters of the House of Stuart were known as "Jacobites," after the Latin version of James' name.[43] Jacobinism is, as I have noted, a recurring theme throughout Scott's work; he was often accused of harboring Jacobite sympathies and even wrote a novel in 1824 (*Redgauntlet*) that explores the ramifications of a fictional Jacobite uprising.[44] By featuring one of their anthems so prominently in *Old House of Fear*, Kirk only invites further comparisons of it to a Waverley novel. In fact, he probably had some Jacobite sympathies himself. In "The Reflex-Man in Whinnymuir Close," the noble Ian Inchburn is depicted riding off to his death in service of the same "Bonnie Prince" immortalized in the song.[45]

In the final appraisal, Kirk's admiration for Scott only leads him so far as a Gothic author in his own right. Whereas Scott was able to distinguish himself partly by devoting his works to the promotion of Scottish culture, Kirk was neither prolific nor focused enough to establish himself as a regional or national author. He wrote some two dozen stories and three full-length novels; some are set in unspecified locations, others in rural Michigan or St. Louis, and still others in Scotland. His depiction of these places is always convincing, and few readers of *Old House of Fear* or "The Reflex-Man in Whinnymuir Close" will

---

[43] Peter Widdowson, *The Palgrave Guide to English Literature and Its Contexts 1500 - 2000* (London: Palgrave Macmillan, 2004), 41.
[44] Tara Ghoshal Wallace, "Historical *Redgauntlet*: Jacobite Delusions and Hanoverian Fantasies," *Romanticism* 21, no. 2 (2015): 152, doi: 10.3366/rom.2015.0225.
[45] Kirk, "The Reflex-Man in Whinnymuir Close," in *Ancestral Shadows*, 350.

doubt the genuine enthusiasm that compelled him to write so much about his ancestral homeland. Yet, heart excepted, Kirk was not actually Scottish—he was an American, more specifically a Michigander, and it was to the backwoods of his home state that he ought to have looked more often for inspiration. If anything, he should have followed Scott's lead more closely and tried to establish himself as a local Midwestern author. Or he could have learned from the example of Hawthorn, who also had a strong influence on his Gothic fiction and was, like Scott, closely associated with a specific region.

Hawthorne was born in 1804 in Salem, Massachusetts, one of the earliest American colonies and long notorious as the namesake of the "Salem Witch Trials," which had begun about a century prior and led to the deaths or persecutions of hundreds of innocent individuals. One of his grandfathers was a leading figure in the trials, which may have been a factor in Hawthorne's decision to change his name (from Hathorne) during his early twenties.[46] He enjoyed notable success with two collections of stories: *Twice-Told Tales* in 1837 and, almost a decade later, *Mosses from an Old Manse*. But it was the 1850 publication of *The Scarlet Letter* that guaranteed Hawthorne his lasting reputation. The book remains a classic of American literature. It explores many of the themes that would occupy him throughout his career, including New England history and the region's struggle to come to terms with its Puritan past. He followed it up the next year with *The House of Seven Gables*, in many ways an improvement upon its predecessor, and, in 1852, *The Blithedale Romance*, his last, completed full-length work. Like Radcliffe and Scott, he did not regard his stories as examples of "Gothic" fiction but referred to them, instead, as "romances." He articulated his literary theory in a series of prefaces attached to his four novels. The one written for *The House of Seven Gables* offers perhaps his most comprehensive view of the genre. "When a writer calls his work a Romance, it need hardly be observed that he wishes to claim a certain latitude, both as to its fashion and material, which he would not have felt entitled to assume had he professed to be writing a Novel."[47] This is more or less in keeping with the traditional view of a "romance" as a novel featuring supernatural or realistic elements.

---

[46] Brenda Wineapple, *Hawthorne: A Life* (New York: Random House, 2004), 63. Wineapple dates Hawthorne's name change to 1825, though she doesn't attribute it specifically to Hawthorne's desire to distinguish himself from his infamous grandfather, the witch-hunter, Colonel John Hathorne. On p. 75, though, she notes his "animosity toward an ancestral name (Hathorne)."

[47] Nathaniel Hawthorne, Preface to *The House of Seven Gables*, in *The Best of Hawthorne*, ed. Mark Van Doren (New York: The Ronald Press Company, 1951), 399.

Although Kirk does not cite Hawthorne as a direct influence on his fiction, he does devote considerable attention to him in Chapter 7 of *The Conservative Mind*, "New England Sketches." Hawthorne's great achievement in letters, Kirk argues, was to restore "to the American mind that doctrine of sin which [Ralph Waldo] Emerson and his school so studiously ignored." On the next page, he restates the point: "He influenced American thought by his perpetuation of the past and by his expression of the idea of sin."[48] If the best Gothic fiction can be characterized as having an awareness of the reality of evil, as Kirk asserts in "A Cautionary Note on the Ghostly Tale," then it stands to reason that it must acknowledge as well humanity's fallen or sinful nature, since that (according to Catholic doctrine) is what leads us to commit evil acts in the first place.[49] Hawthorne was more familiar with the Protestant / Puritan take on sin and evil, which, if anything, is even more insistent upon the pervasiveness of sin at both the individual and societal levels. As Tracy B. Strong asserts, "The sense of sin was central to the Puritan sense of community."[50] Without question, *The Scarlet Letter* represents his fullest treatment of this complex theme. Among its many other lessons, it reveals how a single sin can affect the members of a small community in various ways. Some are overtly marked by that sin, and others bear it secretly. But even a child cannot escape its wages. "In giving her existence, a great law had been broken; and the result was a being, whose elements were perhaps beautiful and brilliant, but all in disorder ..."[51] Thus Hawthorne on Pearl, the innocent child conceived out of wedlock.

But Hawthorne's interest in sin, as Kirk reminds us, extends to nearly everything he wrote. His protagonists tend to suffer from a moral or spiritual malaise that isolates them from others and drives them to dangerous extremes in search of satisfaction. They "approach the limits of the known and the accepted, in some cases ... transgressing the boundaries with painful, even fatal consequences."[52] Kirk would describe such characters quite accurately as suffering from a disordered soul, though the specific sin through which that disorder manifests itself varies. In *The Scarlet Letter*, Dimmesdale is haunted by guilt and hypocrisy, but many of Hawthorne's stories are built entirely around such figures. In "The Birth-Mark," for example, a brilliant scientist loses everything in the vain pursuit of physical perfection. Tormented by his failure to

---

[48] Kirk, *The Conservative Mind*, 250-51.
[49] *Catechism of the Catholic Church*, 2nd ed. (New York: Doubleday, 1994), 403.
[50] Tracy B. Strong, "Hawthorne, the Politics of Sin, and Puritanism," *Telos* 178 (2017): 127, doi: 10.3817/0317178121.
[51] Nathaniel Hawthorne, *The Scarlet Letter* (New York: Penguin Books, 2003), 81.
[52] David Stouck and Janet Giltrow, "'A confused and doubtful sound of voices': Ironic contingencies in the language of Hawthorne's Romances," *Modern Language Review* 92, no. 3 (1997): 562-63, doi: 10.2307/3733384.

assist a dying colleague, a young soldier in "Roger Malvin's Burial" finds himself unable to integrate back into society or enjoy the love of his devoted wife and child. Then, there is the titular figure in "Young Goodman Brown," who has a demonic experience one evening in the woods outside of Salem Village. Despite being uncertain as to whether it was real or just a dream, he decides to abandon Christianity altogether in favor of a bitter cynicism that poisons his relations with family and friends alike. "And when he had lived long," the story concludes, "and was born to his grave a hoary corpse, followed by [his wife] Faith, an aged woman, and children and grandchildren, a goodly procession, besides neighbors, not a few, they carved no hopeful verse upon his tombstone, for his dying hour was gloom."[53]

As Kirk discusses in *The Conservative Mind*, Hawthorne was something of a political and social reactionary who resisted the reforming zeal of his day. Though opposed to slavery, he dreaded the onset of the Civil War, even penning an essay in 1862 in which he criticized its ecological and social devastation and dared to ask whether the price of victory might not prove too high. "No human effort," he writes, "on a grand scale, has ever yet resulted according to the purpose of its projectors. The advantages are always incidental. Man's accidents are God's purpose. We miss the good we sought and do the good we little cared for."[54] The publication of this article in *The Atlantic Monthly* shocked many readers. Still, the sentiments expressed in it can hardly have come as a surprise to careful readers of Hawthorne's fiction. In several stories, he condemns those who seek to overturn the established order of things without giving due consideration to the long-term consequences of their actions. Kirk notes several examples of such tales by Hawthorne, including "Hall of Fantasy," "The Celestial Railroad," and "Earth's Holocaust," which describes the effort of several would-be reformers to rid the earth of all sources of evil. After burning newspapers, medals, and liquor, they proceed to more innocent luxuries such as coffee and works of art. "The truth was that the human race had now reached a stage of progress so far beyond what the wisest and wittiest men of former ages had ever dreamed of that it would have been a manifest absurdity to allow the earth to be any longer encumbered with their poor achievements in the literary line."[55] Hawthorne's sarcasm cannot mask his genuine loathing for radical changes made under the guise of "progress." In *The Blithedale Romance*,

---

[53] Nathaniel Hawthorne, "Young Goodman Brown," in *Hawthorne: Tales and Sketches* (The Library of America, 1996), 289.
[54] Nathaniel Hawthorne, "Chiefly About War Matters," *The Atlantic Monthly*, July 1862, https://www.theatlantic.com/magazine/archive/1862/07/chiefly-about-war-matters/306159/.
[55] Nathaniel Hawthorne, "Earth's Holocaust," in *Hawthorne: Tales and Sketches*, 898-99.

he aims at the leaders of a utopian community, who "attempt to form a new society, and, through it, a new kind of Man ..."[56] He understood that thinking well, having spent a year at a communal farm outside of Boston shortly before his marriage.

"[A]s a rule," observes Matthew Schmitz, Kirk's villains "were the chosen enemies of the mid-century right."[57] Yet many of his stories involve characters who resemble the archetypes favored by Hawthorne. Kirk, too, offers several lessons on the dangers of self-destructive obsessions. In "Fate's Purse" and "What Shadows We Pursue," he explores the poisonous effects of greed on familial relations. "The Surly Sullen Bell" involves a megalomaniac so consumed by his grandiose schemes for world domination that he has no time for the beautiful, loving wife who adores him. Nor does Kirk spare the crusading social reformers of his day, whom he targets in "Behind the Stumps," "Ex Tenebris," and his first and third novels. Despite his warning to avoid moralizing in "A Cautionary Note on the Ghostly Tale," most of his stories end in a fairly didactic manner, with the wicked punished through supernatural means and the status quo restored. "Kirk combated Modernity through an understanding of the formative nature that literature brings to society," explains Sean Hadley. "He engaged the imagination through the proposal that there is something of value in the world of old. As a conservative writer, he put forth stories that recognized that the scale of human life must be weighed in eternity."[58] Hawthorne, by contrast, tends to treat his sinful characters with more sympathy, often declining to subject them to the justice of either God or man. On a related note, and in keeping with the grand tradition of Radcliffe and Scott, most of Hawthorne's stories do not take a firm stance on the existence of the supernatural. Overall, though, there are enough similarities between the two to suggest that Hawthorne was an important influence on Kirk's approach to the Gothic, perhaps only secondary to Scott.

These similarities are perhaps most apparent in *The House of Seven Gables*, which foreshadows many themes that would later be explored by Kirk and offers an excellent model of how to address conservative issues through Gothic fiction. The novel is set in an old mansion that was based on a real building in

---

[56] Harvey L. Gable, "Inappeasable Longings: Hawthorne, Romance, and the Disintegration of Coverdale's Self in the *Blithedale Romance*," *New England Quarterly* 67, no. 2 (1994): 267, doi: 10.2307/366081.
[57] Matthew Schmitz, "The Haunting of Russell Kirk," *First Things*, December 2023, https://www.firstthings.com/article/2023/12/the-haunting-of-russell-kirk.
[58] Sean Hadley, "Russell Kirk and Reenchanting the Political Imagination," *Voegelin View*, 16 September 2023, https://voegelinview.com/reenchanting-the-political-imagination-russell-kirk/.

Salem, Massachusetts, which Hawthorn describes in loving detail in the early chapters. One is reminded of Kirk's abiding interest in architecture and the memorable houses that are featured in so many of his stories, such as the Old House of Fear or Balgrummo's Lodging, which are also inspired by real-life examples. *The House of Seven Gables* centers around the Pyncheon family, who were once prominent in the area but have long since fallen on hard times. Through their struggles to adapt to the changing world around them, Hawthorne comments implicitly upon the decline of traditional lifestyles and social distinctions in New England. In the opening chapters, he introduces the reader to the home's current resident, Hepzibah Pyncheon. An elderly spinster, she has been forced by poverty into business as a shopkeeper, a line of work that she regards as degrading due to her sex and patrician ancestry. Instead of mocking her pretensions, which conflict with the democratic and commercializing thrust of American culture, Hawthorne presents her as a tragic heroine: "poor" and "immemorial," a "lady" in every traditional sense of that word, who rightfully scorns the inferior label of working-class "woman" that would be foisted upon her by others, including her progressive-minded lodger, Holgrave.[59] With its aristocratic leanings and nostalgic depiction of past, simpler times, the novel may be the most socially conservative work ever written by Hawthorne—it is certainly his most Kirkian.

Art and Order

Had he been more prolific, Kirk may have eventually succeeded in making a name for himself, either as a writer of conservative Catholic fiction or as a master of Michigan ghost stories. From his limited output, it is clear that he learned much from his predecessors in the Gothic tradition, especially Scott and Hawthorne. At the same time, he worked hard to establish his style and thematic interests, which were drawn from the social and political issues he often addressed as a prominent public figure. Above all, Kirk was concerned with the loss of order, which he believed to be a danger to both the individual and the state. This danger was compounded, moreover, by a growing tendency to rely on an ever-expanding government bureaucracy to solve problems better handled at the local level. As Person observes, Kirk was "no friend of governmental intrusiveness, legally coerced standardization, excessive taxation, or other agencies and actions that strain and (in time) destroy the voluntary associations of community."[60] He even wrote a book on the *Roots of American Order*, in which he examines order and its decline not only in present-day

---

[59] Nathaniel Hawthorne, *The House of the Seven Gables* (Signet Classics, 1961), 40. Hepzibah's discussion with Holgrave occurs in the next chapter (3).
[60] Person, *Critical Biography*, 4.

North America but throughout history and around the world. In the next chapter, I explore how he addresses this important theme in his fiction.

Chapter 4

Order in the Soul and Commonwealth

Eric Voegelin was a German professor and philosopher who is hailed by some as "the most important political scientist of the [twentieth] century."[1] He had a major influence on Russell Kirk, as noted by the latter's biographers,[2] as well as by Kirk himself. In his memoirs, Kirk credits Voegelin with helping to convince him of the link between religious belief and social stability.[3] Kirk also devotes a chapter to Voegelin in his 1969 collection of essays, *Enemies of the Permanent Things*, in which he discusses Voegelin's views of Plato. Both authors, Kirk writes, remind us "that order in society is possible only if there is true order in individual souls; and that there cannot be order in souls unless those souls, in some degree, know the author of their being and His intention for them."[4] In a revealing aside, Kirk points out the imaginative basis of Plato's thought, which is so unlike that of Aristotle and many of their successors in the analytical tradition. "Plato writes in symbol, for there is no other way in which transcendent knowledge can be expressed..."[5] This is an apt description of Kirk's intention in writing fiction. Like Plato, he, too, often found it necessary to resort to "symbol" to convey the transcendent truths represented by the permanent things. Some of his stories and novels, including "Saviourgate," "Watchers at the Strait Gate," and *Lord of the Hollow Dark*, are basically elaborate allegories in which the characters and events represent ideas that would be difficult to express through more literal means.

In this chapter, I consider what Kirk teaches us about order through symbol— that is, through the symbolic framework of his fiction. As one might expect of a topic on which he wrote and lectured so often through the years, order is a prominent theme in many of his stories and novels. It is, in fact, with the *decline* of order that Kirk is primarily concerned with: he believed it to be one of the most pressing issues facing modern-day conservatism. He distinguishes between order in the soul, as it relates to individuals, and order in the state or "commonwealth," which concerns larger communities or even whole

---

[1] Barry Cooper, *Eric Voegelin and the Foundations of Modern Political Science* (Columbia, MO: University of Missouri Press, 1999), xi.
[2] See, e.g., Birzer, *American Conservative*, 196-201.
[3] Kirk, *The Sword of Imagination*, 474.
[4] Kirk, *Enemies of the Permanent Things*, 344.
[5] Ibid.

countries. These are intricately linked, he claims, "For the order of society is merely the order of souls writ large; there cannot be a good society without individual goodness of heart; and that goodness of heart is possible only when human beings perceive, with Socrates, that man is not the measure: God is the measure."[6] In his stories and novels, Kirk reflects upon the loss of both kinds of order, suggesting that only through a renewal of religious faith and the widespread cultivation of virtue can order in the community be preserved. In states that have slipped far into disorder, hope for renewal must be placed in those few men and women of high principle and character who remain. Above all, he concludes, we must guard against the "leveling schemes" of contemporary progressives, who are willing to sacrifice the natural and God-given rights of the individual to the centralized, leviathan state in a misguided attempt to enforce social equality.[7] Thus, on the topic of order, Kirk demonstrates the potential of fiction to express or convey moral imagination: it is not necessary to consult his fiction to understand what he is trying to say when he talks or writes about this subject, but doing so can help to illustrate his meaning. I shall begin with Kirk's views on "order in the soul," which he considers in numerous stories and is also a major theme in his second and third novels.

Order in the Soul

Kirk's views on order in the soul reflect the clear, though by no means always positive, influence of Enlightenment thinkers such as Jean-Jacques Rousseau, Thomas Hobbes, and Edmund Burke. In contrast to Rousseau, who asserts that "Man was born free" and that his natural goodness was corrupted by society,[8] Kirk argues (with Hobbes) that we need government to provide a "check" or restraint upon our appetites. Without such laws as can be guaranteed and protected by the state, we would descend quickly into chaos and violence. "Burke knew," he writes approvingly, "that just under the skin of modern man stirs the savage, the brute, the demon."[9] An orderly soul is a self-restrained and virtue-seeking one. It embraces the regulating influence of the conscience. It strives to achieve that Aristotelian mean predicated upon the avoidance of excessive thoughts and behavior, which Kirk equates with "moderation, or balance, in

---

[6] Ibid., 326.
[7] Kirk, *The Sword of Imagination*, 124-27. A similar process, he believed, had already befallen England.
[8] Jean-Jacques Rousseau, *The Social Contract*, trans. Christopher Betts (Oxford: Oxford University Press, 1994), 45.
[9] Kirk, *The Conservative Mind*, 39.

private life and public."[10] There is, furthermore, a strong correlation between orderly souls and faith. That is not to say that all good men and women are religious or that all believers are good, but, in general, Kirk concurs with T. S. Eliot that having some faith is healthier for both the individual and the community.[11] Even before his conversion to Catholicism, Kirk regarded Christianity as being especially conducive to order in the Western soul. In a letter written in 1942, he laments his inability to accept the truth of the Christian faith, citing its "great weight of authority" on the "chief authorities" that had inspired his outlook, including Samuel Johnson and John Randolph of Roanoke.[12] Decades later, but still before his formal conversion, he was asked to remove all references to Christianity from a proposed collection of his writings on "The Common Inheritance of America and Europe." Kirk declined to do so on the grounds that the resulting text would represent nothing less than "historical falsification."[13]

An orderly soul is not given to us at birth, and it cannot be legislated into existence. Instead, the desire to pursue virtue must be implanted in us by others, especially our family and teachers. Kirk, himself, never forgot the lessons learned during long walks with his grandfather, Franklin Pierce, who taught him about such important matters as "the notion of Progress, and the iniquities of Richard III, and the desire for immortality, and the significance of dreams …"[14] an intelligent and observant child, Kirk absorbed the values of his "'pilgrim and Bible-reading ancestry.' He learned the civic virtues that a New England culture valued."[15] He always had a close relationship with his parents and labored to ensure that his children would grow up in a loving environment filled with responsible adults who could provide exemplary models for their behavior. Hence, the breakdown of the family unit throughout the twentieth century was an especially worrisome development for Kirk, as it was for many other conservatives. In *The Quest for Community*, published the same year (1953) as *The Conservative Mind*, Robert Nisbet laments the decline of the family as a unifying force and source of comfort in an increasingly fractured and alienating world:

> But in ever-enlarging areas of population in modern times, the economic, legal, education, religious, and recreational functions of the

---

[10] Kirk, *The Roots of American Order*, 90.
[11] Kirk, *Eliot and His Age*, 56.
[12] Kirk to William C. McCann, 1 June 1942, in *Letters*, 21.
[13] Kirk to W. T. Couch, 14 July 1959, in *Letters*, 85.
[14] Kirk, *The Sword of Imagination*, 10.
[15] Gleaves Whitney, "Russell Kirk: The Wizard of Mecosta," *Michigan History* 102, no. 4 (August 2018): 31.

> family have declined or diminished. Politically, membership in the family is superfluous; economically, it is regarded by many as an outright hindrance to success ... On all sides we continue to celebrate from pulpit and rostrum the indispensability to economy and the State of the family. But, in plain fact, the family is indispensable to neither of these at present. The major processes of economy and political administration have become increasingly independent of the symbolism and integrative activities of kinship.[16]

"Institutions decay when they are deprived of function," Kirk summarizes. "[T]hus, Mr. Nisbet proceeds to show, the family is disintegrating before our eyes not because of 'sexual maladjustment' and 'family tensions' ... but because it has been deprived of its old economic and educational advantages."[17]

Of course, not everyone is blessed with the sort of stable, supportive home life that Kirk enjoyed as a youth in Plymouth, MI. Those who happen to be born in an environment less congenial to the ordering of souls can still be saved through education—provided, of course, that one's teachers are, themselves, concerned with the right things: i.e., the cultivation of virtue and the defense of the permanent things. Education was a topic on which Kirk frequently expounded; it is the subject of several books he wrote and something he often discusses in his shorter works. Education was "[a]t the forefront of Kirk's myriads of interests," John M. Pafford observes, adding that Kirk "did not simply gnash his teeth and bewail what had happened to education; he believed that change for the better was possible and had a number of specific improvements."[18] In sum, Kirk argues that the "essential aim, and the chief benefit, of formal education is to make people intelligent and good."[19] The latter quality (goodness) is obviously concerned more with the ordering of the student's soul rather than the growth of his intellect. It is especially neglected by institutions of higher learning today, which tend to be dominated by the influence of progressives such as Paolo Freire or John Dewey, who espouse what might be called a collectivist pedagogy, or the view that "school should assume many of the socializing functions once performed by the family, the workplace, and the community."[20] Fortunately, Kirk encountered just enough

---

[16] Robert Nisbet, *The Quest for Community* (1953; repr., Wilmington, DE: ISI Books, 2010), 52-53.
[17] Russell Kirk, *Beyond the Dreams of Avarice: Essays of a Social Critic* (1956; repr., Peru, IL: Sherwood Sugden & Company, 1991), 92-93.
[18] John M. Pafford, *Russell Kirk* (New York: Bloomsbury, 2013), 48-50.
[19] Kirk, *Concise Guide to Conservatism*, 71.
[20] Lee Edwards, *Educating for Liberty: The First Half-Century of the Intercollegiate Studies Institute* (Washington, D.C.: Regnery Publishing, 2003), 9.

of the right sort of teachers at Michigan State, Duke University, and, especially, St. Andrews to prevent his straying from the path upon which he had been set by his family.

Still, it is not uncommon for parents and educators alike to neglect their respective duties to the young. Many children are raised by those who care little for the pursuit of virtue, either because they know little about it themselves or do not believe it to be as important as other, more easily quantifiable learning objectives. Others are sent to learn from cynical professors who insist that it is their primary responsibility not to direct their students in the contemplation of the permanent things but to engage "in seditious sabotage within the ranks of the university" and "call everything into question, including higher education."[21] As Kirk knew well, children subjected to both a poor upbringing and a "sham" education will inevitably turn out bored and disruptive; such were the college radicals who first appeared on campuses during the 1960s and 70s and later began teaching at them.[22] Millions more of their peers, having no real interest in or aptitude for higher education, are thrust out of the classroom without ever having learned that human beings were made to do more than just eat, sleep, and work. In a vain attempt to inject some meaning into their lives, they indulge their baser instincts, turning from virtue to vice. These contemporary Prufrocks, wracked with sin and ideological sickness, are those whom Kirk portrays as victims of a disorderly soul and whom he frequently casts as villains in his fiction. Unlike Hawthorne, who also wrote Gothic tales involving such characters, Kirk always ensures that his end either with their reformation—or, more often, with their punishment.

One of the primary causes of disorder in the modern soul, Kirk believed, is the kind of "covetous desire" associated with the Tenth Commandment: namely, the sins of greed, avarice, and envy. These are the root of "theft, robbery, and fraud," the Catholic Church declares, as well as major causes of "violence and injustice," and tend to arise in those who cannot learn to properly restrain their appetites.[23] Kirk, a Catholic convert, was especially critical of avarice, "the intense and inordinate desire for money and temporal goods" that goes beyond mere greed or envy[24] and which is characteristic of those for whom the pursuit of material

---

[21] Michael Joseph Franciscon, "Political Sociology and Anthropology in Education: A Manifesto for Subversive Education," *New Proposals: Journal of Marxism and Interdisciplinary Inquiry* 1, no. 2 (2008): 6, https://doaj.org/article/dcc7425711754626939ba553364d3622.
[22] Kirk, *The Sword of Imagination* 408-17.
[23] *Catechism of the Catholic Church*, 2534-35.
[24] David W. T. Brattston, "Avarice and Greed," *Catholic Insight* 15, no. 3 (2007): 39. Kirk frequently refers, disparagingly, to wealth "beyond the dreams of avarice."

goods has become obsessive and self-destructive. For his part, Kirk was famously frugal, boasting of his ability to subsist in college on a single "substantial" meal per day[25] and preferring to live in rural Mecosta rather than any of the glittering coastal capitals, such as one might expect to find a public intellectual of his caliber. At the same time, his attitude towards money can hardly be described as miserly: both of his major biographers are quick to note Kirk's generosity with others, some of whom he loaned money directly[26] or provided with a place to stay during times of hardship.[27] Thus, it is safe to say that Kirk was no hypocrite in denouncing greed, nor can one be surprised to see him denounce it with such fervor in so many of his stories. For Kirk, greed is more than just a major character flaw: if left unchecked, it has the potential to destroy one's very soul in quite a literal sense.

Such is the unfortunate lesson learned by the hapless criminals portrayed in stories such as "Uncle Isaiah" and "Balgrummo's Hell." The former features a low-rent gangster as its antagonist, a "tall and swarthy man" who dresses in "an expensive suit of loud check" and walks with a swagger.[28] After bribing his way out of prison, Costa decides to recoup some of the money from his hard-working, lower-class neighbors. Vain and rapacious, he is lured to a fatal interview with the titular "Uncle"—related to one of Costa's victims—by the promise of a hefty payout. Costa is not seen or heard from again; presumably, he would have been better off staying in prison, which is, after all, only a metaphorical kind of Hell compared to the real thing. In a similar fashion, the thief who breaks into the home of a bedridden Scottish laird in "Balgrummo's Hell" has no worse intention than to steal some of the rare and expensive artworks hidden therein. Instead, he ends up meeting the lord of the manor, who had flirted with and lost his soul to demonic forces years ago. In Hogan, he has found some company for the long afterlife of suffering that awaits them both.

Given that some of his stories feature truly reprehensible characters, neither Hogan nor Costa can be regarded as particularly wicked or even deserving of Hell. Both are blinded by greed, however, and fail to recognize the metaphysical danger into which their sin has betrayed them. These stories illustrate Pafford's observation about the moral dimension of Kirk's fiction well: "Some of [his] stories were downright scary, but they never were twisted or warped so that evil triumphed and the reader was left frustrated. Nor were they amoral tales which

---

[25] Kirk, *The Sword of Imagination*, 37.
[26] Birzer, *American Conservative*, 421.
[27] Person, *Critical Biography*, 13.
[28] Russell Kirk, "Uncle Isaiah," in *Ancestral Shadows*, 47.

Order in the Soul and Commonwealth 71

eschewed making judgments."[29] Kirk is always quick to pronounce judgment on those, especially, whose only concern in this life is with profit.

Greed can also be dangerous to those for whom money is merely a means to an end, something that will enable them to indulge in other, more depraved vices. This describes the unrepentant ex-con, Butte, in the aptly named "Lex Talionis." He is sick in heart and soul, a rapist and murderer who is unwilling to extend even the sort of professional courtesy normally accorded by one thief to another. For twenty grand and, more importantly, "all the dope an' whiskey an' women that money buy," he is willing to give up his immortal soul. He even wonders, jokingly, "Why, what in hell's worth gettin' but them three things?"[30] As it turns out, Hell is exactly what Butte ends up receiving in exchange for his sordid crimes. The group of degenerates in "The Cellar of Little Egypt" prove just as willing to sell their souls for a small "heap" of silver dollars, which they waste on liquor and gambling. Their leader, Dan Slattery, is described as "an animal, with a beast's quickness and a beast's suspicions;" his second-in-command is a Native American who beat up his mother so badly she was left disabled for life.[31] These are not good men, in other words, driven to desperate acts, but those whose souls have become so transfigured by greed that they are beyond saving and fit only for divine vengeance. In Kirk's fiction, Ray Andrew Newman notes, "the mysterious workings of a loving God come alive for the reader."[32] But for the wicked, those workings are often not so mysterious. Greedy characters, such as Butte and Slattery, may be able to lord it over their fellow humans for a while but will always end up receiving their just rewards.

Aside from greed, many of Kirk's characters suffer from what might be called a type of "ideological" sickness of the soul. This is graphically illustrated in the figure of the obstinate census taker, Cribben, from Kirk's first published story, "Behind the Stumps." Cribben's ideology is neither religious nor philosophical, but his single-minded devotion to duty, which he pursues even at the peril of his own life, is no less symptomatic of a disordered soul. Like the "Planning Officer" S. G. W. Barner in "Ex Tenebris," Cribben is little more than a puffed-up bureaucrat who thinks he knows what is good for everyone else and has the power to enforce his distorted vision on others. These crusading government officials, whether British or American, care nothing for the permanent things;

---

[29] Pafford, *Russell Kirk*, 129.
[30] Kirk, "Lex Talionis," in *Ancestral Shadows*, 93.
[31] Ibid., 125.
[32] Ray Andrew Newman, "Deliver Us from Evil: An Introduction to Russell Kirk's Supernatural Fiction," Order No. EP74662, University of Nebraska at Omaha, 1998, in *Proquest Dissertations & Theses Global*, https://search-proquest-com.ezproxy.fhsu.edu/docview/1706289457?accountid=27424, 45.

they are, by default, diametrically opposed to them since it is on the ruins of enduring values and ancient belief systems that they intend to erect their perfectly planned societies. In fact, they cannot tolerate even ruins to stand, as Barner thinks to himself: for "Ruins are reminiscent of the past; and the Past is a dead hand impeding progressive planning."[33] In writing these stories, Kirk attempts to raise awareness about the dangers posed by such misguided figures to themselves and others. "The 'moral imagination' Kirk seeks to cultivate," writes Alex Meregaglia, "is respect for the past and a disdain for progressive plans that impersonally impose a grand design on others without accounting for tradition, or, for that matter, what is best for those it is forced upon."[34] The avenging ghosts who terrorize Cribben, Barner, et al. are a common Gothic trope, which Kirk (unlike many of his predecessors) did not hesitate to confirm as supernatural or provide a theological justification for. Drawing from the Catholic tradition, he presents them as spokesmen for the demons who will be waiting to greet Cribben and his fellows in Hell, provided they do not amend their ways.

At least Cribben, Barner, and their ilk have good intentions. They can claim to be acting in the best interests of the public welfare and perhaps even manage to succeed in convincing themselves that that is the case. This is hardly true of all ideologues, however. As any student of history knows, some become so sure of the superiority of their beliefs that it causes them to look down upon others or even, in the worst cases, to decide that those who refuse to share those beliefs ought to be destroyed outright, as "enemies of the state," "counter-revolutionaries," etc. Such was the case with the most notorious ideologues of the twentieth century, in whose names hundreds of millions perished … and it is true, as well, of the antagonist in one of Kirk's best stories, "The Surly Sullen Bell." Unlike Cribben and Barner, Godfrey Schumacher does not care much about his personal or professional obligations as a husband and college professor. He is fully committed, instead, to his personal philosophy: "a startling blend of psychiatry and quasi-Yoga, spiced with something near to necromancy and perhaps a dash of Madame Blavatsky."[35] Schumacher is "playing God," as James Panero notes,[36] secretly poisoning his wife in a bizarre attempt to prove the superiority of his moral system. Restraint, Schumacher declares, "is for spiritual weaklings … Strength is everything upon the physical

---

[33] Kirk, "Ex Tenebris," in *Ancestral Shadows*, 5.
[34] Alex Meregaglia, "An Introduction to the Short Stories of Russell Kirk: 'Not Written for Children,'" *The Imaginative Conservative*, 15 March 2011, https://theimaginativeconservative.org/2011/03/introduction-short-stories-russell-kirk-not-for-children.html.
[35] Kirk, "The Surly Sullen Bell," in *Ancestral Shadows*, 54.
[36] James Panero, "The ghosts of Russell Kirk," *The New Criterion* 37, no. 5 (January 2019): 28.

plane, and that's just as true, really upon the spiritual—the moral—plane."[37] He succeeds in killing his wife, but the moment his scheme is exposed, Schumacher decides to take his own rather than match his fancied strength against those of the police and criminal justice system. The examples of Hitler and Stalin are enough to suggest what sort of mischief this coward may have caused had his ambitions for great authority not been frustrated at an early age.

Kirk offers an even clearer picture of the ideologically disordered soul in his first novel, *Old House of Fear*. Its villain, Dr. Edmund Jackman, sounds at first like a typical Marxist: "In the coming world ... there will be no rank and no class," he tells Hugh Logan at their first meeting. "And intellect will have its rewards."[38] Jackman and his gang have seized control of Carnglass Island as part of an ill-conceived scheme to track and destroy missile sites located in the Hebrides. They refer cryptically to Party overlords in Paris or Brussels and mistake the novel's hero for one of their representatives. Jackman, who has fought for communist causes in Spain and Romania, thinks this current assignment in Scotland is somewhat beneath him and has allowed his attention to stray from economic and political theory into other, more occult areas. In any case, like so many Marxists, it is not a theory that truly motivates Jackman but a lust for power and domination over others. "I don't think he is interested in women as most men are," reports Mary MacAskival of Jackman. "He is in love with power and terror. He wants me only because with me he could have Carnglass for a while longer and because I have money. And, I suppose, because he enjoys crushing other people's minds."[39] In summary, Jackman is simply a more successful version of Godfrey Schumacher and has the higher body count to show for it.

As intimated above, Jackman's soul is not just disordered in the ideological sense. There is yet one more type of disorder Kirk warns about in his fiction, which is related to his lifelong interest in the occult. Even before his conversion to Christianity, he believed that there were demonic forces at work in the world and that it was up to each of us to learn how to recognize the very real dangers they posed. "The preternatural seemed to be part and parcel of the nature of things at Mecosta," he recalls early in his memoir. "[I] was early inoculated against the darkness at the bottom of the stairs."[40] Before seeing how this type of disorder plays out in the soul of a villain like Jackman, it might be worth considering how Kirk portrays it as a threat even to those with otherwise good intentions. In "The Princess of All Lands," for example, Yolande barely escapes

---

[37] Kirk, "The Surly Sullen Bell," in *Ancestral Shadows*, 64.
[38] Kirk, *Old House of Fear*, 87.
[39] Ibid., 123.
[40] Kirk, *The Sword of Imagination*, 22.

her encounter with the malignant spirits of a family of rapist murderers. Presumably, she is only targeted by them because of her "virtue," a power she has long cultivated that enables her to heal others, communicate with the dead, and perform other preternatural feats.[41] Young Janet Kenly in "The Reflex-Man in Whinnymuir Close" has similar abilities, which she uses to summon a *doppelgänger* of her brother and the ghost of her deceased husband. Though Janet means well and is far from the kind of witch feared by Hawthorne's ancestors, Kirk makes it clear in the story that, by merely dabbling with such forces from "the next world," she risks the fate of her immortal soul.[42] Only through sincere repentance and prayer do both of these characters avoid the dismal fate suffered by Jackman and others.

"Some mediums are charlatans," Kirk wrote in 1967, "but others possess genuine if inexplicable and dangerous power. I advise no one to meddle with the next world who is not very strong of mind and heart."[43] Unlike Yolande and Janet, Jackman disdains to heed this sensible advice; in private, Mary hints to Logan that he has been trying to summon the spirit of her dead uncle.[44] Being weak in "mind and heart," he risks falling prey to forces he cannot possibly understand, let alone control. Kirk suggests that Jackman's interest in the occult arises almost as a natural consequence of his belief in Marxism, that the political and supernatural kinds of disorder afflicting his soul are inexorably linked. "You're a Party intellectual," Jackman tells Logan, "and the Party believes it knows all things. Yet in some matters, the Party is blind … In the nights, it is Hell that is real, and the Party is a sham."[45] Having grown dissatisfied with his initial worldview, Jackman thinks he has found another, even better one, though it is only, in truth, more abstract, superficial, and dangerous than the first. In the end, perhaps out of a desire to increase the book's marketability, Kirk shies away from a full depiction of the spiritual disorder afflicting Jackman's soul. His reluctance was noticed even by early reviewers of the novel, such as one in *Time* magazine, who writes, "For all the apparent ectoplasm floating about it, the *Old House of Fear* is haunted not by ghosts but by the shadow of the welfare state."[46] The hint of spiritual disorder is there in Jackman,

---

[41] Kirk, "The Princess of All Lands," in *Ancestral Shadows*, 159.
[42] Kirk, "The Reflex-Man in Whinnymuir Close," in *Ancestral Shadows*, 339 and 350.
[43] Russell Kirk, "Bishop Has Perfect Faith in the Séance," *Progress-Index*, 13 October 1967, 6, quoted in Bradley J. Birzer, *Russell Kirk: American Conservative* (Lexington, KY: University Press of Kentucky, 2015), 286.
[44] Kirk, *Old House of Fear*, 104.
[45] Ibid., 139.
[46] "Secret Life of Russell Kirk," review of *Old House of Fear*, by Russell Kirk, *Time*, 7 July 1961, 70.

but it remains just that: a hint. Only in Kirk's last novel does he commit to offering a more complete view of the spiritually disordered soul.

In fact, the characters in *Lord of the Hollow Dark* provide a comprehensive picture of all types of disorders that can afflict the soul, according to Kirk. Unlike his other books and most of his stories, the action takes place over a short length of time (the week leading up to Ash Wednesday) and in a single, enclosed setting (a mansion in Scotland). The limited environs offer the author an excellent opportunity to explore the effects of disorder among a small group of individuals. Aside from Arcane and his coterie, almost everyone in the novel suffers from a disorder of one kind or another. Sweeney, the rapist architect, shamelessly admits that he has only sought employment with Apollinax due to his lust and greed: "I take [his] cash, but I don't buy his game."[47] The young single mother, Marina, abandoned her vows as a nurse after falling in love and getting pregnant. Ever since, she has been engaged in the same fruitless search for meaning that characterizes the spiritually disordered soul. The others are an odd mix of adulterers, abortionists, and pornographers; unlike Marina and Sweeney, they are not merely misguided but fundamentally, irredeemably, wicked. All have come to Scotland at the behest of Mr. Apollinax, the "evil protagonist of this gothic tale ... an occultist with diabolical ambitions,"[48] whose knowledge of, and mastery over, dark forces make Jackman and Schumacher look like amateurs.

In return for their patronage, Apollinax promises his followers a chance to enjoy their own everlasting "timeless moments," a phrase borrowed from T. S. Eliot that signifies, in short, eternal life.[49] Eliot had been granted an imperfect vision of the afterlife, Apollinax claims, grasping something of its nature but totally mistaken as to the best means for achieving it. Instead of the self-denial and asceticism demanded of Christians, Apollinax encourages his followers to indulge their every whim. "There shall be no sublimation of desire; we shall acknowledge desire honestly, embrace it, and so be freed."[50] He is a Satanist in the literal sense of the word: one who worships Satan, who knows that God exists but chooses, deliberately, to turn his face away from Him and embrace His enemy instead. On Ash Wednesday, Apollinax intends to offer a Black Mass in honor of the devil, whom he calls by several different names, including Kronos, "Time the Devourer," and "Lord of this World."[51] The Mass will climax with a ritual involving the sacrifice of Marina and her baby, whose deaths are needed

---

[47] Kirk, *Lord of the Hollow Dark*, 17.
[48] McDonald, *Russell Kirk and the Age of Ideology*, 130.
[49] I explore this theme more fully in the next chapter.
[50] Kirk, *Lord of the Hollow Dark*, 96.
[51] Ibid., 217.

to summon the troubled spirit of the last Lord Balgrummo. Arcane and his friends see that the first part of Apollinax's scheme comes to ruin, though they are unable to prevent him from calling forth Balgrummo's ghost. As with all who meddle in such matters, however, Apollinax soon discovers that he has no power over the dark forces of this world or the next. "Having believed he could assume the guise of Time the Devourer, the horrified Apollinax is swept into the abyss of time for which he had claimed to yearn for so long."[52] Ironically, he succeeds in achieving his long-desired timeless moment, but it is sure to be one of unending torment.

The disorder that affects Apollinax's soul is much greater than in any other character, as if Kirk had been building towards it in his earlier stories and novels. One suspects that, had Jackman actually come face-to-face with the ghostly denizens of the Old House of Fear, he would have immediately repented of his interest in the demonic and returned to his original folly, Marxism. Schumacher's plans seem more foolish than dangerous, and his suicide at the end of the story suggests that he lacked the nerve to expand his desire for domination over others beyond the immediate circle of his wife and their mutual friends. Apollinax has far more sinister and destructive ends in mind: not only is everyone at the party to be slaughtered or left for dead in the Weem, but he intends to repeat the process all over again, with twice as many victims, at his next retreat in California.[53] The implication is that, though originating as a disorder in the soul, Apollinax's ideological and demonic illness could continue to grow and, like an infection, spread throughout the rest of society, becoming yet another contributing factor to the nation's decay. Of course, Kirk did not really believe organized Satanism to pose an existential threat to Western culture: he called the novel "a symbolic representation of the corrupting cults that had come up from underground in the latter half of the twentieth century."[54] Unfortunately, the cults themselves were all too real—as was the disorder they caused. One has only to consider the recent example of a song and music video by Lil Nas X featuring the blatant use of Satanic imagery, which scholars are falling over themselves to explain and praise as a genuine attempt to critique "Christianity itself and its repressive nature,"[55] to see that there are many in the present day who could stand to learn from the example of Apollinax.

---

[52] Person, *Critical Biography*, 128.
[53] Kirk, *Lord of the Hollow Dark*, 316.
[54] Kirk, *The Sword of Imagination*, 433.
[55] Andrew R. Chow, "Historians Decode the Religious Symbolism and Queer Iconography of Lil Nas X's 'Montero' Video," *Time*, 30 March 2021, https://time.com/5951024/lil-nas-x-montero-video-symbolism-explained/.

Order in the Commonwealth

Early in 1990, Kirk was asked to contribute to a symposium on the future of conservatism by Adam Meyerson, editor of *Policy Review*. Kirk responded with a list of strategic priorities, touching on everything from foreign to economic affairs. Even after spending a lifetime writing and thinking about them, he still had much to say about social issues such as corruption or the urgent need for community. He also took the opportunity to comment upon an old *bête noire* of his: the ugliness of American cities. "Our cities," Kirk writes, "with few exceptions, have become more dismal and dangerous than those created by any other civilized people, and that within the past three or four decades. The causes of this unhappy phenomenon have been complex; the remedies must be complex."[56] For decades, Kirk had railed against the appearance of American cities, which he believed to be symptomatic of a deep rot in society. Even in *The Conservative Mind*, he could not resist a short digression on the negative influence of the automobile ("a mechanical Jacobin"), which he blamed for its proclivity to "disintegrate and stamp anew the pattern of communication, manners, and city-life in the United States ..."[57] In a classic essay on "The Architecture of Boredom and Servility," he writes that "the total condition of our urban life and the dreariness of our architecture are not separate phenomena."[58] But, as his response to Meyerson indicates, Kirk was not sure what, if anything, could be done on an immediate political or legislative basis to combat the rising disorder of the American republic. Thankfully, he frequently addresses this question in his fiction, in which he does suggest a few intriguing proposals about what can be done to resist and possibly even reverse these trends.

The signs of social decay are everywhere in Kirk's stories and are not limited to those set only in large cities. His first published work of fiction, "Behind the Stumps," takes place partly in fictional Bear City, a fading town of "[f]alse-fronted dry-goods shops and grocery stores and saloons, built lavishly of second-grade white pine when pine was cheap and seemingly inexhaustible."[59] Having never received much help from the state or federal government, the locals balk at an attempt to conduct a census there: it would mean, for them, only "more blank forms, more trips to the county seat, higher taxation, and intolerable prying into every man's household ..."[60] "Ex Tenebris," likewise, is set in derelict Low Wentford, formerly a small but cheerful village, now reduced

---

[56] Kirk to Adam Meyerson, 1 February 1990, in *Letters*, 317-18.
[57] Kirk, *The Conservative Mind*, 373-74.
[58] Kirk, *Redeeming the Time*, 96.
[59] Kirk, "Behind the Stumps," in *Ancestral Shadows*, 19-21.
[60] Ibid.

to a population of one. Once again, blundering officials from the central government are to blame for the loss of order: most of the former inhabitants have been forced to relocate to a nearby town, trading their supposedly unsanitary and unsafe cottages for dreary apartment blocks in a planned community. In both stories, the violent upheaval of long-standing traditions only begets further violence. For Kirk, there should be nothing surprising about this because it is on those traditions that order primarily depends: "when the state arrogates to itself a complex of responsibilities that formerly were undertaken by church, family, voluntary association, and the private person—why, then the old habits of decency are weakened, and the police constable and [reform school] are required to maintain precariously by compulsion what once was taken for granted in Britain and elsewhere."[61]

As Birzer notes, however, Kirk often draws attention to the blighted landscapes of American cities. "He rightly labeled himself a connoisseur of slums, and he railed against urban renewal and what he frequently called the 'architecture of boredom and servility.'"[62] If the signs of social disorder are easy to overlook in the crumbling towns and villages of middle America, they are impossible to ignore in the great cities of St. Louis or New York, home to so many millions. The former is the setting for at least two of Kirk's stories. In "The Surly Sullen Bell," he wastes no time in setting up the appropriate atmosphere of disintegration and decay. "In St. Louis, they have pounded the Old Town into dust," Kirk writes in the second paragraph. "All along the Mississippi, where the little city of the French and their American successors used to lie, now is a brick-strewn desolation ..."[63] A few pages later, he writes of the downtown area, once prosperous and lovely, now in ruins, and home to only the most wretched members of society: "To this slum of slums crawled down the most pitiful and foul sweepings of the white populace of a great city ... They lit fires on sheet-iron scrap in the bare rooms, and slept wrapped in newspaper or filthy old coats ..."[64] This is no "poverty porn," no exploitative mocking or scolding of the poor for the benefit of the author and his readers. Kirk was fond of St. Louis, the birthplace of T. S. Eliot, and deeply regretted the decline of that once-great city.[65] As always, he insists that the responsibility lies squarely with the "modern

---

[61] Kirk, *The Sword of Imagination*, 126.
[62] Birzer, *American Conservative*, 301.
[63] Kirk, "The Surly Sullen Bell," in *Ancestral Shadows*, 50.
[64] Ibid., 52.
[65] See the description of Eliot's hometown in Kirk, *Eliot and His Age*, 18-21, or the short paragraph on the same in Kirk, *The Sword of Imagination*, 74.

politician and planner," to whom "men are the flies of a summer, oblivious of their past, reckless of their future."[66]

The "Gateway to the West" fares no better in "Lex Talionis." The story begins with a reference to the "wrack and glitter of the old city," in which "the old people and the drunken and the drugged and the desperately poor" are afraid to venture out in the early evening due to spiraling crime rates and an ineffective criminal justice system. The increasing number of "vacant lots," Kirk adds, "a legacy of urban 'renewal,'" have been "abandoned to two-footed predators, who had slim pickings."[67] A similar decline may be detected in the unnamed city—clearly based on New York—in which "Uncle Isaiah" is set. Daniel Kinnaird, the central character, had founded his dry-cleaning business in a thriving, ethnically diverse neighborhood that has clearly seen better days. His is the only building on the block that has survived the relentless forces of modernization with any pride or dignity left intact. "Everywhere else, slum children pounded up and down the stairs, or the old parlors were decorated with chromium and converted into hamburger joints, or the ground-floor façades were knocked away to make room for car-wash garages." The culprit? "Fashionable suburbs, the automobile, and industrialization ..."[68] The locals had little opportunity to prevent these changes since they were implemented from afar by meddlesome social planners such as Cribben and Barner. Like most bureaucrats, they are more concerned with ideology than the practical effects of their decisions. In these stories, the decline of order in the city or state is frequently matched by a concomitant rise in violence, corruption, and social degeneracy.

Hence, the number of tales by Kirk that feature gangs of criminals running amok or even ruling over entire neighborhoods that have been abandoned by the usual sources of law and order. "Uncle Isaiah" is one such tale: Kinnaird is repeatedly warned against going to the police about Costa's attempted extortion because it would only get him in further trouble. "The Invasion of the Church of the Holy Ghost" is another, and was one of Kirk's last published works of fiction, which suggests how important the theme of disorder in the state had become to him in his final years. Its hero is a black priest who has been struggling to conduct his ministry among the downtrodden residents of yet another blighted cityscape: the ghetto of Hawkhill, in which a few "fine old houses still stand ... many more have been burnt by arsonists (often hired arsonists), or have fallen into hopeless ruin."[69] Whatever the original cause of

---

[66] Kirk, "The Surly Sullen Bell," in *Ancestral Shadows*, 50.
[67] Kirk, "Lex Talionis," in *Ancestral Shadows*, 85.
[68] Ibid., 34.
[69] Kirk, "The Invasion of the Church of the Holy Ghost," in *Ancestral Shadows*, 355.

the neighborhood's decline, it has fallen fully into the hands of a local pimp named "Sherm the Screamer" and his crew of deviants. As a taste of their style of justice, Kirk describes a scene in which they break into the house of a man who had testified in court against them and beat up his unsuspecting neighbors, leaving one of them crippled for life.[70] With an array of weapons and explosives at hand, it is clear what they have intended for the brave informer, who nevertheless succeeds in defending himself from their vicious attack. Reading these stories, one is reminded of Kirk's description of Edmund Burke, who knew that "just under the skin of modern man stirs the savage, the brute, the demon."[71] Throughout his fiction, he demonstrates how disorder in the state can result in that savage, brute, and demon heart of man being let loose, with devastating consequences for all. Order in the soul and the commonwealth are, as he frequently reminds us, inseparably linked.

Two of his best stories, "There's a Long, Long Trail A-Winding" and "The Princess of All Lands," are devoted to exploring this theme in detail. Both are among the most personal he ever wrote, with their main characters being drawn from people Kirk was close to in real life. Indeed, it is easy to lose sight of the pointed social criticism contained within each since they are so successful at demonstrating Kirk's ability to blur, if not outright obliterate, the line between fiction and reality—what Robert M. Woods describes as "the artificial lines we construct between this realm and the ultimately authentic world beyond this one."[72] But the copious references to social decay and the unexpected bursts of violence the characters must contend with prove that the loss of order in the state is a primary concern of both. In "Long, Long Trail," a hapless tramp, Frank Sarsfield, wanders through a bleak and frozen Midwestern landscape. "This was depopulated country, its forests gone to the sawmills long before, its mines worked out. The freeway ran through the abomination of desolation." He eventually stumbles into an abandoned town, the general store "boarded up" and the village hall "a wreck." Sarsfield "had never seen a deader village."[73] The picture of decay painted in "The Princess of All Lands" is even grimmer. At one point, the titular heroine, Yolande, finds herself driving through the desolate town of Pompeii, "a shrinking hamlet, with no suggestion of Roman pleasures except the name itself." Eventually, she arrives at "a northern swamp jungle, seemingly impenetrable. This must be

---

[70] Ibid., 363.
[71] Kirk, *The Conservative Mind*, 39.
[72] Robert M. Woods, "The Other Side of the Keyhole: Russell Kirk's Ghost Stories," *The Imaginative Conservative*, 13 February 2012, https://theimaginativeconservative.org/2012/02/other-side-of-keyhole-russell-kirks.html.
[73] Kirk, "There's a Long, Long Trail A-Winding," in *Ancestral Shadows*, 277-78.

some hardscrabble homestead abandoned decades ago, never truly fit for cultivation, now the lair of squatter predators."[74]

Unfortunately, those "squatter predators" are exactly as bad as they sound. Indeed, few of Kirk's stories present criminals as dangerous as the ones in these two. The group of escaped convicts Sarsfield encounters on his last day at Tamarack House seems the very embodiment of evil. "He knew what these men were, the rats and bats of Creepmouse Town: the worst men in any prison, lifers who had made their hell upon earth, killers all of them and worse than killers."[75] It is sufficient for Kirk to merely hint at what they have planned for the ladies they have taken hostage (a young wife and her daughters). Likewise, the family of reprobates waiting for Yolande more than earns their comparisons to various beasts of myth and legend: the casually racist girl who sniffs glue and carries a gun; her brother, "gross and filthy;" and her father, a wicked spirit that had terrorized Yolande throughout her life.[76] "[I]n the end," Ben Reinhold comments, "they are revealed to be—appropriately enough—damned spirits."[77] One year ago, the three had kidnapped, raped, and murdered a young woman before being tracked down and killed themselves by law enforcement. Even in the afterlife, they cannot abandon their evil ways.

These stories remind us that gangs of rampaging convicts and families of criminals do not spring up overnight out of the aether; they are created, in part, by the misguided policies of bureaucrats such as Cribben and Barner. "REMEMBER YOUR FUTURE / BACK THE TOWNSEND PLAN," reads a fading sign Sarsfield comes across in empty, isolated Anthonyville.[78] What was the goal of that plan? Kirk does not elaborate, but it obviously failed to stem the decline of the town. It is highly probable, in fact, that the plan was the very *cause* of that decline in the first place. Perhaps it led to the building of the nearby state prison, which scared away many locals after a successful break-out. Or the "Townsend Plan" may have resulted in the creation of the massive freeway to the east of town that signaled its final demise, as one of the Tamarack children suggests in a letter to her grand-niece.[79] Kirk's point, once again, is that Anthonyville was not destroyed by the indifference or laziness of its residents but by those seeking to impose upon it their collectivist plans. In addition to

---

[74] Kirk, "The Princess of All Lands," in *Ancestral Shadows*, 169-72.
[75] Kirk, "There's a Long, Long Trail A-Winding," in *Ancestral Shadows*, 304.
[76] Kirk, "The Princess of All Lands," in *Ancestral Shadows*, 172.
[77] Ben Reinhard, "The Haunting of America: Russell Kirk's Ghostly Fiction," *The Imaginative Conservative*, 16 March 2020, https://theimaginativeconservative.org/2020/03/haunting-americas-russell-kirk-ghostly-fiction-ben-reinhard.html.
[78] Kirk, "There's a Long, Long Trail A-Winding," in *Ancestral Shadows*, 278.
[79] Ibid., 295-96.

forcing out many of the hard-working inhabitants who had called the place home for generations, these social planners succeeded only in creating an environment fit for the worst elements of society. Unfortunately, they are stronger now than ever before, and the same process continues to unfold in countless neighborhoods, towns, and cities throughout the country.

What Is to be Done?

As I have noted, Kirk was often criticized for not offering practical solutions to the problems he addressed. Even in the twenty-first century, George A. Panichas still felt the need to acknowledge this complaint in his introduction to *The Essential Russell Kirk*.[80] The criticism may seem especially valid of Kirk's fiction since, after all, so many of his plots seem to be resolved by a kind of supernatural *deus ex machina*: the sudden appearance of an avenging ghost, which ensures a happy ending for the good and punishment for the wicked. The 2020s have proven an especially disordered decade in American history, marked by frequent and destructive rioting over civil rights issues and the federal government's confused, ineffectual response to the COVID-19 pandemic. One can see that the problems of order identified by Kirk are very real concerns in the present. And yet, most of us will never be able to call upon kindly, if purgatorial, relatives for protection against organized crime. Nor can we draw from the sort of "virtue" possessed by Yolande when faced with the raw anger of the less civilized. What does Kirk, through the moral imagination, teach us about what should be done in response to the continuing decline of order in the soul and state?

First, he is clear enough about what we should *not* do. In brief, we must be careful to avoid making the same mistake as the French revolutionaries denounced by Burke, who believed fatuously that all of humanity's problems could be solved by the government. The preservation of order is primarily a moral, rather than legislative or political, issue, and "moral systems," as Kirk insisted, "are not constructed readily by social engineers."[81] "A central administration," he adds elsewhere, "or a corps of select managers and civil servants, however well-intentioned and trained, cannot confer justice and prosperity and tranquility and decent conduct upon a mass of men and women deprived of their traditional responsibilities and institutions."[82] At best, the efforts of these social engineers, planners, managers, and civil servants—these real-life Cribbens and Barners—can only lead to mischief, either for themselves

---

[80] George A. Panichas, preface to *The Essential Russell Kirk*, by Russell Kirk (Wilmington, DE: ISI Books, 2007), xxiii.
[81] Kirk, *The Conservative Mind*, 470.
[82] Kirk, *Concise Guide*, 43.

or for others. At worst, they have the potential to destroy entire communities, as anyone who has driven through the urban wastelands of Detroit, St. Louis, or Chicago recently can attest. As John Rodden observes, Kirk was no believer "in utopias or futuristic blueprints for social betterment …"[83] In striving against the loss of order in the soul and state, we must not look to the government for salvation, lest we discover a cure that is even worse than the disease.

Only by first addressing order within the soul can one hope to combat the disorder afflicting others and society at large. For all the otherworldly elements of his fiction, most of Kirk's heroes are ordinary people forced to choose between right and wrong; it is their readiness to acknowledge that such a choice must be made in the first place that distinguishes them from their corrupt or indifferent peers. "Uncle Isaiah" might be named after the deceased, vindictive figure who stalks its pages, but at its heart, there is simple and decent Daniel Kinniard, a hard-working launderer: "the last scion of a respectable old family in Boston's decaying North End … the only man in town with the mettle to defy the local mob boss."[84] Frank Sarsfield, similarly, is a frequently imprisoned, barely literate tramp, but when presented with the opportunity to prove his mettle, he does not hesitate to sacrifice himself to save a group of women and children to whom he is completely unrelated. Finally, of course, there is Manfred Arcane, a "bastard" and "broken creature,"[85] who nevertheless manages to claw his way to the top of a forsaken country in Africa through sheer force of will and ingenuity. Without these individual examples of sacrifice, heroism, and nobility, no one else can be saved, and no kingdoms can be restored.

Order in the soul and commonwealth may be linked, then, but it is clear that the latter is dependent on the former and cannot endure long without it. This lesson is one Kirk repeatedly sought to instill in his listeners and readers, but which is conveyed most vividly, perhaps, in his fiction. The same is true of the subject I shall explore in the next chapter: Kirk's views on time and the afterlife. He was not shy about discussing his eschatology in letters and his memoirs; throughout the latter, for instance, he frequently refers to "timeless moments," a phrase he borrowed from T. S. Eliot. Regardless of how many times he tried to explain how, exactly, they were supposed to work or what he thought happened to our souls after death, one must acknowledge that these are matters that

---

[83] John Rodden, "A Young Scholar's Encounter with Russell Kirk," *Modern Age* 49, no. 3 (2007): 296.
[84] Ben Reinhard, "Russell Kirk's Literary Gentlemen," *The Imaginative Conservative*, 8 April 2020, https://theimaginativeconservative.org/2020/04/russell-kirk-literary-gentlemen-ben-reinhard.html.
[85] Kirk, *A Creature of the Twilight*, 318.

cannot easily be understood through reason alone. Certain metaphysical questions are best explored through symbolic means, using the tropes and conventions available to writers of Gothic fiction. Thus, it is to Kirk's stories and novels that we must turn for a satisfactory explanation of them.

Chapter 5

Timeless Moments

Towards the end of his long life, Russell Kirk found himself corresponding more often with old associates he knew that he was not likely to see again on this earth. In nearly every case, the letters he wrote them are curiously ebullient, as if the impending death of one or the other person was just a temporary inconvenience soon to be overcome by both parties. In 1987, for instance, a month before the death of Jay Gordon Hall, an executive with General Motors whom Kirk had known for decades and considered a "disciple of Cicero" and "friend of the permanent things,"[1] Kirk had written to assure him not to worry too much about the prognoses of his doctors. "We never know, actually, whether or not we will survive for a few more years ... for all we know, you and I may have many more good times together ... Then be of good cheer, Gordon. We do pray for you."[2] Kirk's faith partly explains this attitude; after all, Catholics believe in "the resurrection of the dead" and "life everlasting" as official dogma.[3] Yet even many Catholics, facing their death or that of loved ones, can hardly bring themselves to look upon it with much enthusiasm. We are, after all, only human, and it is only natural for us to fear the unknown.

But Kirk, clearly, was not afraid of dying or of what would happen to him afterward. Even in his final days, he remained alert and productive, discussing current events and making plans to complete the various works-in-progress he had left unfinished.[4] He died, quite literally, with a smile on his face—hardly the impression of a man reluctant to let go of life. I believe that Kirk's unusually optimistic perspective towards death may be explained, in part, by his firm belief in the existence of "timeless moments," at which (as he wrote to Richard Nixon in 1993) "all the good occurrences and things of one's temporal life are eternally present, whenever the soul desires them; and present not merely in recollection, but in all their fullness." Similar, eternally recurring moments are experienced by those condemned to Hell or Purgatory, he adds.[5] Such moments represent points of contact between the material and transcendent worlds, at which the past, present, and future intersect: they

---

[1] Kirk, *The Sword of Imagination*, 226.
[2] Kirk to Jay Gordon Hall, 15 November 1987, in *Letters*, 271-73.
[3] *Catechism of the Catholic Church*, 989-990.
[4] Person, *Critical Biography*, 18-19.
[5] Kirk to Richard Nixon, 28 June 1993, in *Letters*, 352.

determine how (or where) we shall spend eternity and constitute our experience of the same. Timeless moments comprise the main element in Kirk's eschatology, which he discusses frequently in his articles, letters, and memoirs; they are also a recurring theme throughout his stories and novels, as I discuss in this chapter. Before beginning my analysis of timeless moments in Kirk's fiction, I shall trace their development in the thoughts of some of his favorite writers and philosophers.

Timeless Moments, from Plato to Kirk

The most important direct influences on Kirk's conception of timeless moments were T. S. Eliot and the German philosopher Eric Voegelin. Kirk also discussed them with Martin D'Arcy, a Jesuit priest and close family friend. But, as with so many Western ideas, their roots lie much further back, through the medieval Doctors of the Church and the late classical mind of Augustine, all the way to that wellspring of Western thought, Plato. In the *Symposium*, he describes a place "in-between" (μεταξύ, *metaxy*) wisdom and ignorance, mortal and immortal; it is the true home of the transcendent Forms, as well as powerful spirits, such as *Eros* (Love), who exchange messages between human beings and the gods:

> Being in the middle of the two, they round out the whole and bind fast the all to all. Through them all divination passes, through them the art of priests in sacrifice and ritual, in enchantment, prophecy, and sorcery. Gods do not mix with men; they mingle and converse with us through spirits instead, whether we are awake or asleep. He who is wise in any of these ways is a man of the spirit, but he who is wise in any other way, in a profession or any manual work, is merely a mechanic.[6]

The philosopher, Plato explains, endeavors to be a "man of spirit," to achieve a level of consciousness or being that is between the "merely biological existence and the divine, between the beasts and the gods."[7] Plato's concept of *metaxy* influenced the epistemology of classical and medieval thinkers such as Plotinus and Anselm of Canterbury, but it was not until Voegelin wrote about it in the early twentieth century that it began to interest contemporary philosophers.

Voegelin was born in 1901 and fled Germany for the United States in 1938. Having witnessed the rise of Naziism and Stalinism first-hand, he came to

---

[6] Plato, *Symposium*, trans. Alexander Nehamas and Paul Woodruff, in *A Plato Reader: Eight Essential Dialogues*, ed. C. D. C. Reeve (Indianapolis: Hackett Publishing Company, 2012), 202e-203b.

[7] Robert McMahon, "Eric Voegelin's Paradoxes of Consciousness and Participation," *The Review of Politics* 61, no. 1 (1999): 124, https://www.jstor.org/stable/1408650.

believe that the modern world suffered from a form of Gnosticism, that ancient Christian heresy with its emphasis on "salvific knowledge" known only to a select few.[8] Like Kirk, he spent much of his life trying to encourage the preservation of order in both the individual soul and commonwealth. Also, like Kirk, he believed that Western society suffered from a crisis that was, to a large extent, essentially spiritual, or religious, in nature. "The true dividing line in the contemporary crisis," he writes, "does not run between liberals and totalitarians, but between the religious and philosophical transcendentalists on the one side and the liberal and totalitarian immanentist sectarians on the other."[9] In Kirkian fashion, he seized upon a relatively minor term used only a handful of times by Plato (*metaxy*) as a possible solution to the *malaise* afflicting Europe and North America. Our uneasy status *in between* the material and transcendent represents the "thoroughly paradoxical structure of existence ... ever evident to anyone who cared to reflect upon and symbolize it."[10] "Voegelin saw the human being as 'framed' by a series of tensions between the 'beyond and the below,' the finite and the infinite, time and eternity, the human and the divine," Bjørn Thomassen adds. "To try to move outside the *metaxy*... equals for Voegelin a loss of balance, a human hubris (duly signaled in Greek mythology as such), a 'deformation' of both thought and consciousness, with deadly consequences."[11]

While Voegelin hashed out these ideas in his monumental, multi-volume *Order and History*—which remained unfinished at the time of his death in 1985—Eliot was working his way through similar questions about time and transcendence in his post-conversion work, especially *Four Quartets*. Of particular interest for Kirk is Eliot's attempt in this work to reconcile Plato's and Voegelin's views of *metaxy* with Christian theology. Since God created time, the poet reasons, He must, therefore, be outside of it. And if Heaven and Hell mean either total union with or separation from God, then humans must also enjoy a timeless existence once they have died and entered the afterlife. But if temporal distinctions cease to exist for us, if "the end and the beginning were always there, / Before the beginning and after the end. / And all is always now," as Eliot

---

[8] Ismo Dunderberg, *Beyond Gnosticism: Myth, Lifestyle, and Society in the School of Valentinus* (New York: Columbia University Press, 2008), 16.
[9] Eric Voegelin, *The New Science of Politics* (Chicago: Chicago University Press, 1952), quoted in Russell Kirk, *The Essential Russell Kirk*, ed. George A. Panichas (Wilmington, DE: ISI Books, 2007), 176.
[10] Colin Cordner, "The diagnosis of scientism: Eric Voegelin and Michael Polanyi on science and philosophy," *Appraisal* 9, no. 3 (March 2013): 4-5, *Gale Academic OneFile*.
[11] Bjørn Thomassen, "Reason and Religion in Rawls: Voegelin's Challenge," *Philosophia* 40, no. 2 (2012): 243-44, https://www.dx.doi.org/10.1007/s11406-011-9351-4.

writes,[12] what is the significance for us, really, of time? Are past, present, and future not the same, as much for the living as for their immortal souls? Kirk concluded that the only logically consistent answer to such questions was *yes*, adding that the choices we make in the present still matter because they alone have the potential to determine our past and future. "It is the exertion of the will *now* that matters."[13]

To what end should that be directed? The frequent allusions in *Four Quartets* to John of the Cross, a sixteenth-century mystic, suggest one approach, that of what is commonly referred to as apophatic or negative theology. "The goal is the stripping away of all things, both temporal and spiritual, and transcendent union with the ineffable silence of God."[14] On a more practical level, and following in the footsteps of Plato and Voegelin, Eliot recommends that we strive to overcome the artificial restrictions placed upon us by a linear understanding of time. In fact, being made *Imago Dei* or "in God's image," we are not bound by time but share in His immaterial and immortal nature. Throughout *Four Quartets*, argues David Soud, Eliot catalogs some of the transcendent, or timeless, moments enjoyed during his lifetime:[15]

> To be conscious is not to be in time
> But only in time can the moment in the rose garden,
> The moment in the arbour where the rain beat,
> The moment in the draughty church at smokefall
> Be remembered …[16]

Voegelin was delighted to discover in Eliot's work a resemblance to his views: "[E]very point of presence is, as T. S. Eliot formulated it, a point of intersection of time with the timeless. This is the point of presence."[17] From his readings of Voegelin and Eliot, Kirk drew support for his growing conviction that, in any

---

[12] Eliot, *The Complete Poems & Plays*, 175 ("Burnt Norton" V).

[13] Kirk, *Eliot and His Age*, 246.

[14] Elizabeth Anderson, "Burnt and Blossoming: Material Mysticism in *Trilogy and Four Quartets*," *Christianity and Literature* 62, no. 1 (Autumn 2012): 132, doi:10.1177/0148333 11206200107.

[15] David Soud, "'The Greedy Dialectic of Time and Eternity': Karl Barth, T. S. Eliot, and *Four Quartets*," *ELH: English Literary History* 81, no. 4 (Winter 2014): 1384.

[16] Eliot, *The Complete Poems & Plays*, 173 ("Burnt Norton" II).

[17] Eric Voegelin, "Notes on T. S. Eliot's *Four Quartets*," in *The Drama of Humanity and Other Miscellaneous Papers 1939-1985*, ed. Gilbert Weiss and William Petropulous (Columbia, MO: University of Missouri Press, 2004), 34, quoted in Stephen J. Costello, *Philosophy and the Flow of Presence: Desire, Drama, and the Divine Ground in Being* (Newcastle upon Tyne, England: Cambridge Scholars Publishing, 2013), 11.

person's life, there may occur one or more "timeless moments" that recur *ad infinitum* after death, not merely as memories, but in actuality. "The central discovery [of *Four Quartets*], the meaning, is this: through the transcendent consciousness, it is possible to know God, and through Him to know immortality," he concludes.[18]

Kirk credits Fr. D'Arcy with articulating these ideas to him from a more orthodox Catholic perspective. One night, D'Arcy was asked by Annette, Kirk's wife, if she and her husband would still be married after death since, in the Gospel of Luke, Jesus seems to suggest otherwise.[19] Kirk summarizes the priest's response in his memoirs, switching between direct quotes and paraphrases:

> "Heaven is a state," D'Arcy told Annette, "in which all the good things of your life are present to you whenever you desire them"—not in memory merely, not somehow re-enacted, but present, beyond the barriers of time, in all their fullness. Thus husband and wife would experience in eternity, when they should will it, what they had experienced within mundane time, linear time; and human creatures, resurrected, will have perfected bodies.[20]

Much the same, D'Arcy adds, can be said of Hell, "a state of being in which all the evil one has done is eternally present—and there is no escape from it. So it is that human creatures make their destiny, their own Heaven and their own Hell."[21] Kirk was fond of repeating this conversation and did so in several letters, including the ones to Jay Gordon Hall and Richard Nixon already cited in this chapter. Throughout his memoirs, he describes experiencing several timeless moments himself, including a drunken bender through Huntly, Scotland, undertaken as a graduate student, and a morning decades later when he stopped his youngest daughter, Felicia, from eating pebbles at the urging of her older sisters.[22] He suspected that D'Arcy may have influenced Eliot's writing of *Four Quartets*[23] and freely acknowledged the impact of D'Arcy on his own beliefs about the afterlife. In his fiction, the influence of D'Arcy is unmistakable,

---

[18] Kirk, *Eliot and His Age*, 242.
[19] Luke 20:34-35 (KJV): "And Jesus answering said unto them, The children of this world marry, and are given in marriage: But they which shall be accounted worthy to obtain that world, and the resurrection from the dead, neither marry, nor are given in marriage ..."
[20] Kirk, *The Sword of Imagination*, 341.
[21] Ibid.
[22] Ibid., 99-107, 366-68.
[23] Kirk, *Eliot and His Age*, 257-58. See also Kirk to Rev. Martin D'Arcy, 12 July 1971, in *Letters*, 150-52.

as I shall demonstrate in the following pages. I begin with Kirk's portrayal of Purgatory and Hell.

"The Everlasting Moment of Damnation": Purgatory and Hell

In keeping with conventional Christian views of Hell, Kirk depicts it as a state of being in which the souls of unrepentant sinners are sent or kept after death. To be deserving of Hell, one must be more than just a bad person; one must commit a mortal sin and repeatedly refuse to seek absolution for it, though in Kirk's fiction, the latter does not necessarily entail formal confession to a priest. To clarify, mortal sin requires "*full knowledge* and *complete consent*" on the part of the sinner; "If it is not redeemed by repentance and God's forgiveness," the Church declares, "it causes exclusion from Christ's kingdom and the eternal death of hell …"[24] In other words, mortal sin requires one to recognize the action as a sin, understand the consequences of committing it, and choose to do so anyway. One does not necessarily have to be Catholic or even Christian to sin in this way since there is a "natural law" written in our hearts, as St. Paul explains, by which even pagans ought to be able to discern right from wrong.[25] The hapless planning officer in "Ex Tenebris" is a good example of an unrepentant mortal sinner who is not a Christian.

Nonetheless, in declining to show charity towards poor Mrs. Oliver, living alone and harming no one in her abandoned village, S. G. Barner certainly commits a mortal sin. He receives a clear warning to that effect from the ghostly former vicar, Hargreaves, who offers him numerous opportunities to repent before it is too late. "For the sake of a void upon a map, man, would you cast away your hope of salvation?"[26] Barner scoffs in response and is offered yet a final chance to save his soul, which he also rashly declines. There can be little doubt as to what lies in store for him then: "For now is the ax put to the root of the trees, so that every tree that bringeth forth not good fruit, is hewn down and cast into the fire."[27] Our last glimpse of Barner is of him cowering in fear, with Hargreaves' hands around his throat.

Many of Kirk's stories involve sins much graver than Barner's. For instance, the handsome thief in "Bulgrummo's Hell," Rafe Hogan, may seem like an irrepressible scamp whose theft of a few paintings from the mansion of a bed-ridden Scottish laird can hardly be described as a sin worthy of eternal damnation. But in doing so, he commits much worse ones, lying about his

---

[24] *Catechism of the Catholic Church*, 1859.
[25] Rom. 2:15.
[26] Kirk, "Ex Tenebris," in *Ancestral Shadows*, 15.
[27] Ibid.

identity, beating up an innocent night guard, and convincing his accomplice to cheat on her husband. Though not a Christian, Hogan knows that what he is doing in each of these instances is *wrong*. He is formally introduced to Kirk's metaphysics in a conversation with T. M. Gillespie, a lawyer overseeing the care of Lord Balgrummo and his home. Years ago, Gillespie explains, Balgrummo had been involved in some diabolical ceremony that left several people dead, "an everlasting moment of damnation" for which his enforced confinement at home is part of the penance he must pay—in this world and, possibly, the next. "Balgrummo is not merely remembering the events of what you and I call 1913 or even 'reliving' those events," he adds. "No, I suspect it's this: he's embedded in those events like a beetle in amber. For Balgrummo, one certain night in Balgrummo Lodging continues forever."[28]

But greedy Hogan, like Barner before him, lets slip his chance for redemption. He is unimpressed with Gillespie's inexplicable fear of the house he is planning to rob or his reluctance to spend any more time in the enfeebled laird's company than his professional obligations demand. "Between [the laird's sister] Dr. Effie and me on the one side and distant Balgrummo on the other, a great gulf is fixed." Gillispie is grateful for that vast gulf of Time; he adds: "'For if any man's or woman's consciousness should penetrate to Balgrummo's consciousness, to his time-scheme, to his world beyond the world ... then the intruder would end like *this.*' Gillispie, tapping his cigar upon an ashtray, knocked into powder a long projection of gray ash. 'Consumed, Rafe.'"[29] Hogan carries on with his plans, even after recalling Euphemia "Effie" Inchburn's warning that her brother had meddled with powerful forces in the past, through which he still retained the capacity to commit great evil. "They had thought they were raising the Devil *for* Lord Balgrummo. But as it turned out, they raised the Devil *through* Balgrummo and *in* Balgrummo."[30] And, in the ruined chapel, Hogan comes face-to-face with the Devil himself in the guise of Balgrummo. Ray Andrew Newman summarizes Kirk's lesson for the reader: "The thief's sins are real, but he stumbled upon a much more malicious evil and, in its self-created lair, a vile but timeless moment. Hogan could not say he wasn't warned about the dangers ..."[31]

In his introduction to the most recent collection of Kirk's stories, Vigen Guroian observes that a number of them feature "avenging and retributive ghosts" who perform various roles, sometimes serving to "bring mortal terror

---

[28] Kirk, "Balgrummo's Hell," in *Ancestral Shadows*, 80-81.
[29] Ibid.
[30] Ibid., 83.
[31] Ray Andrew Newman, "Avoiding Hell in Russell Kirk's Uncanny Tales," *St. Croix Review*, 2004, http://www.stcroixreview.com/archives_nopass/2004-12/Newman.htm.

upon a principal character" or to "lead characters to penance."[32] These figures, including Hargreaves and Lord Balgrummo, represent a common trope in Gothic fiction, though Kirk does not always employ it in the expected manner. In some of his tales, the vengeful spirit is not a denizen of Hell, as is usually the case, but of Purgatory instead. Kirk was very interested in this stage *in-between* death and the afterlife, during which (Catholics believe) our souls undergo a final purification before entering Heaven. For Kirk, Purgatory is no more of an actual place one must go or be sent to than Heaven and Hell; rather, it is a state of mind that can occur at certain timeless moments in a person's life. How we choose to act at those moments may determine whether we spend eternity in one place or the other. For some imperfect but well-intended sinners, Purgatory offers an opportunity to prove themselves worthy of Heaven by performing a noble, often sacrificial, deed. For example, despite being a notorious figure in Kinnaird family lore, Uncle Isaiah is basically a good man willing to help his overmatched nephew, Daniel Kinnaird, deal with an extorting gangster. Kirk plays coy with Isaiah's true nature, having him speak to Daniel from behind a closed door and delaying his appearance until the very end of the story. His abrupt disappearance after the final confrontation with Costa and the revelation that Daniel never sees his uncle again both support the idea that he has been dead all along and was merely granted a temporary reprieve from Purgatory to perform this act of mercy.

Like Isaiah Kinnaird, the protagonist of "Lex Talionis" has a troubled past. After participating in a bungled robbery, during which an off-duty policeman was shot and killed, Eddie Mahaffy (also known as Monk or Cain) is sentenced to life in prison. And yet, he has a personal code of honor that distinguishes him from the average criminal, as one of his accomplices recognizes: not only does Cain refuse to engage in any violent behavior during the robbery, but he also declines to betray his partners in crime, despite their lying about his culpability on the witness stand. His underlying goodness paves the way for Cain to earn a possible shot at redemption. "There was reserved for Eddie only the possibility of inexplicable infinite mercy and the plea that he had sinned more from folly than from malice."[33] Unlike in "Uncle Isaiah," Kirk does not try to hide the fact that Eddie is dead, having been murdered in prison by a violent gang leader, Butte. As part of his penance, Cain is sent back to confront Butte, who kills an old couple and their niece as soon as he is set free. When it becomes clear to Butte that he has been tricked and that only death—or something worse—awaits him in the cellars of the house in which he left the family's money, he curses Cain: "You go to hell, Monk!" For Butte's sake, Cain confirms what most readers

---

[32] Guroian, introduction to *Ancestral Shadows*, xiii.
[33] Kirk, "Lex Talionis," in *Ancestral Shadows*, 100.

already know or have begun to suspect. "You chose the wrong word: you should have said, 'Purgatory.' But I'm there already, Butte. Hadn't you begun to guess that?"[34]

No character better illustrates the link between timeless moments and Purgatory than Frank Sarsfield, who makes a brief appearance in "Lex Talionis" as Cain's cellmate and is given his starring role in one of Kirk's best-known stories, "There's a Long, Long Trail A-Winding." In a prologue to *The Princess of All Lands*, Kirk explained that "There's a Long, Long Trail" was intended to form one part of a trilogy "with theological or transcendental implications," representing Purgatory; its companions, representing Hell and Heaven, respectively, are "Balgrummo's Hell" and "Saviourgate."[35] Though they differ in several respects, there are enough similarities between Sarsfield and Cain to draw attention to the identical themes in their stories. Like Cain, Sarsfield is an ex-con who has been in and out of prison for most of his life. He, too, is at heart a good man, one who will only resort to violence in extreme circumstances. A psychiatrist who treats Sarsfield in jail observes that he "has no record of aggression while confined, nor in connection with any of the offenses for which he was arrested."[36] Sarsfield and Cain are both religious, though not observant (as was true of Kirk himself). The same doctor describes Sarsfield as "oppressed by a haunting sense of personal guilt. He is religious to the point of superstition, an R. C. [Roman Catholic], and appears to believe himself damned."[37] Sarsfield is prone to robbing the poor boxes of Roman Catholic churches on occasion but enjoys a good relationship with an old priest, Father O'Malley.

Both characters are in Purgatory, but their ultimate fates appear to be quite different. After leading Butte to his well-deserved death, Cain says a quick prayer for the deceased family and then wanders away from the scene, whistling a tune. Presumably, this timeless moment does not, in and of itself, satisfy the demands of his penance, so he will have to await further opportunities to prove himself worthy of Heaven. "There's a Long, Long Trail" ends, by contrast, with Sarsfield dead in the snow; more precisely, it ends with the character *reliving* the timeless moments leading up to his heroic death. In a rambling letter to his sister, Sarsfield inadvertently touches upon some of the finer points of Kirk's theology:

---

[34] Ibid., 104.
[35] Russell Kirk, prologue to *The Princess of All Lands* (Sauk City, WI: Arkham House Publishers, 1979), viii. Kirk also mentions this tripartite structure in a 1976 letter to James Turner.
[36] Kirk, "There's a Long, Long Trail A-Winding," in *Ancestral Shadows*, 286.
[37] Ibid., 287.

And Father O'Malley says that maybe some people work out their Purgatory here on earth, and I might be one of these. He says we are spirits in the prisonhouse of the body which is like we were serving Time in the world here below and maybe God forgave me long ago and Im [sic] just waiting my time and paying for what I did and it will be alright in the end. Or maybe Im [sic] being given some second chance to set things right ... Father O'Malley even says I might not have to do the Act actually if only I just made up my mind to do it really and truly because what God counts is the intention.[38]

The intention is, indeed, all that really "counts" for God, but Sarsfield goes far beyond that in sacrificing his life to save a young mother and her children. Ray Andrew Newman agrees, adding that "God has given Frank a chance to let his goodness and his fondness of children blossom into a self-sacrificing love which allows three young girls and their mother to live and which propels his soul closer to the lasting Easter vision."[39] Like Cain, Sarsfield may yet have further to go on the "Long, Long Trail" to redemption ... but it is also possible, and perhaps more likely, that his days of tramping are done for good.

The Strait and Narrow Way

Indeed, Sarsfield's next appearance, in 1976's "Watchers at the Strait Gate," seems to confirm as much. The title alludes to Jesus' warning in the Sermon on the Mount that the path to Heaven will not be an easy one: "Because strait is the gate, and narrow is the way, which leadeth unto life, and few there be that find it."[40] Fr. Justin O'Malley strives to be one of those few, having lived an honest and virtuous life despite many frustrations. Most of these were experienced by Kirk himself, who shared O'Malley's disapproval of liturgical changes brought about by the Second Vatican Council of 1962-65. In his memoirs, Kirk decries the "widespread decay of belief in Christian dogmata" during the 1960s and 70s, as well as the "virtual secularization of Christian churches," both of which he blamed on Vatican II.[41] O'Malley, too, must contend with the forces of modernization, as represented by a "New Breed" of priests, eager for change but with little regard for the Church's two thousand years of tradition, as well as a new liturgy, which de-emphasized the fear of Hell in favor of more cheerful material.[42] For his

---

[38] Ibid., 293.
[39] Ray Andrew Newman, "Pilgrimages and Easter Destinations in the Ghostly Tales of Russell Kirk," *Modern Age* 40, no. 2 (1998): 315.
[40] Matt. 7:14.
[41] Kirk, *The Sword of Imagination*, 423.
[42] Kirk, "Watchers at the Strait Gate," in *Ancestral Shadows*, 308-09.

adherence to faith and tradition, O'Malley is regarded as a bigot, even by some of his subordinates. For instance, he had to dismiss a nun for insisting upon the right to preach from the pulpit in direct contravention of long-established prohibitions against such things.[43] O'Malley spends much of his time writing sermons and trying not to drink too much. One imagines that, had Kirk embraced the vocation of the priesthood rather than of a man of letters, he might have ended up something like O'Malley.

One night, the good priest falls asleep while working on a sermon at his desk. He wakes to find the familiar figure of Frank Sarsfield looming over him—he wants the priest to hear his confession. But there is something sinister about the man's presence and his strange request. It is the middle of the night, after all; moreover, just last month, a pair of priests had been found murdered in Detroit. O'Malley cannot help but wonder whether Sarsfield had something to do with that terrible deed. Kirk continues to ratchet up the tension during the actual confession when Sarsfield admits to his role in the bloodbath that ends "There's a Long, Long Trail A-Winding." He asks the priest to pray with him for the dead, and as they kneel together, O'Malley worries that he is about to become the man's next victim. Afterward, they begin talking ominously about post-death experiences. For an uneducated tramp, Sarsfield seems suspiciously knowledgeable about the subject:

> It's my experience, Father, that when you cross over, there's a hesitation and lingering, for a little while. Then you move on out, and that's scary, because you don't know where you're going; you've got no notion whatsoever. It's not that happy little tunnel with light at the end. Why, it's more like a darkling plain, Father. And you're all alone, or seem to be, except where those ignorant armies clash by night. On and on you go. And when you think or feel that at last you've arrived at the strait gate *which leadeth unto life*—well, then you meet the Watchers.[44]

Still, O'Malley is skeptical. What could Sarsfield possibly know about the afterlife? It is not until they return to his office, and the priest sees his own body sitting at the desk where he fell asleep, that he realizes everything Sarsfield has

---

[43] Although it continues to rage in the present, the controversy over female priests was already venerable by Kirk's time; the Church's inability to ordain women is addressed in the Catechism of the Catholic Church, 1577, and the apostolic letter *Ordinatio sacerdotalis*, issued by Pope St. John Paul II in 1994.

[44] Kirk, "Watchers at the Strait Gate," in *Ancestral Shadows*, 322. Sarsfield's reference to a "darkling plain" is probably an allusion to Matthew Arnold's famous 1867 poem, "Dover Beach." It is worth remembering that Sarsfield is depicted by Kirk as having memorized a large number of verses.

said is true. They are both dead, and Sarsfield has returned (or has been sent back) to guide O'Malley to Heaven.

As I have noted, Kirk frequently employs symbols in his fiction. Sometimes, it can be difficult to figure out exactly what those symbols are supposed to represent. In such cases, one must try not to dwell on the literal meaning of the words but focus, instead, on the larger message they are trying to convey. His characters often face a similar difficulty in making themselves understood by others. "I'm trying to put into words for you some experiences that words don't fit," Sarsfield explains to O'Malley,[45] echoing a line in the unfinished "Fragment of an Agon" by Eliot, which Kirk repeatedly quotes in *Lord of the Hollow Dark*.[46] "So when I tell you about the darkling plain," Sarsfield continues, "and about the Sleepless Ones, those Watchers, you're not supposed to take me literally, not all the way."[47] In keeping with Sarsfield's advice, the reader, too, must remember that timeless moments are metaphysical concepts about which one can attain only an imperfect understanding. Heaven, Hell, and Purgatory are states of being rather than places, even if Kirk often describes them as such for the sake of convenience or comprehensibility. One might recall his extraordinary claim in "A Cautionary Note on the Ghostly Tale": that writers of Gothic fiction should believe in their ghosts enough to be frightened by them. His stories are not intended to portray the literal truth about these matters but to capture something of their elusive, ineffable natures.

With that in mind, the stories about Sarsfield seem to symbolize the path of the ordinary sinner and penitent: one who needs to undergo purgation before entering Heaven. There is a character in Kirk's fiction who travels even further than he, metaphorically speaking, one whose wanderings take him from the deepest Hell to the highest Heaven. That character is Ralph Bain, who also appears in several stories and is one of the main characters in *Lord of the Hollow Dark*. Person describes him as an "aimless wanderer and something of a wastrel, though good-hearted …"[48] Like Sarsfield, Bain is a well-meaning vagrant who ends up sacrificing himself for the sake of others. Bain is not as innocent or naive as Sarsfield, however, nor does he show much interest in religion. In a review of *The Princess of All Lands* that is available on the Kirk Center website, Stephen Schmalhofer compares Bain to Don Quixote, "his

---

[45] Ibid.
[46] Eliot, *The Complete Poems & Plays*, 125 ("Fragment of an Agon"). The line quoted and alluded to by Kirk is "I gotta use words when I talk to you." See Chapter 8 for more on Eliot's influence on *Lord of the Hollow Dark*.
[47] Kirk, "Watchers at the Strait Gate," in *Ancestral Shadows*, 322.
[48] Person, *Critical Biography*, 120.

mind bent by shrapnel rather than sleeplessness."[49] His first appearance is in 1952's "Sorworth Place," which ends, as previously mentioned, with the character leaping to his death in order to defy a demonic being that had been haunting a beautiful widow. That demon, the widow's former husband, is clearly suffering from his timeless moment in Hell: she even speaks of him as wanting "life to drag down with him."[50] What propels Bain to save her at the cost of his own life is "an impulse beyond duty, beyond courage, beyond even the love of woman,"[51] and that moment of genuine, Christian love (*agapē*) is enough to preserve him from being tainted by his brief contact with the infernal. Both man and demon end up plunging to the depths of Sorworth Water, but only the latter must remain there for all time. Bain has earned himself a shot at redemption, and his other appearances in Kirk's fiction demonstrate how he must work out his time in Purgatory through the commission of further acts of heroism.

Although I devote the whole of Chapter 8 to *Lord of the Hollow Dark*, Bain's appearance in that novel deserves to be mentioned here since it relates directly to Kirk's beliefs about timeless moments and the afterlife. Unlike everyone else at Balgrummo Lodging, Bain is not a member of Apollinax's Gnostic cult: he quite literally crashes the gathering, somehow surviving a long plunge down the side of a cliff that borders the castle. After being roused back to consciousness, he has trouble remembering basic details about his past—a sure sign that he may be experiencing a timeless moment.[52] Later, he is given the nickname Coriolan and assigned to assist the architect, Sweeney, in his efforts to discover an entry into the Weem. Sweeney thinks there is something odd about his companion, who seems to know much more about the place than he should. He appears "substantial" and "normal looking," but there is just something odd about him.[53] Bain disappears after vowing to pass through the deepest recesses of the Weem, a path medieval pilgrims believed to have formed a "mode of purgation" through which one's mortal sins could be "washed away" or forgiven.[54] All of the characters in this book are stuck in a kind of symbolic Purgatory, represented by the Weem, through which they must advance as

---

[49] Stephen Schmalhofer, "A Dreadful Joy is Conjured," review of *The Princess of All Lands*, by Russell Kirk, *The Russell Kirk Center*, 21 October 2018, https://kirkcenter.org/reviews/a-dreadful-joy-is-conjured/.
[50] Kirk, "Sorworth Place," in *Ancestral Shadows*, 188.
[51] Ibid., 194.
[52] Kirk, *Lord of the Hollow Dark*, 75.
[53] Ibid., 112.
[54] Ibid., 239.

penance for their sins. Having already sacrificed himself to save another, Bain alone recognizes that the opportunity for him, at least, is not merely symbolic.

He seizes upon that opportunity in the novel's climax, which takes place during the long-awaited Ceremony of Innocence. Although Arcane succeeds in rescuing most of his followers, he is forced to leave Sweeney behind. Just as Apollinax is about to have the fake architect castrated, Bain intervenes. The dialogue throughout this scene helps to shed some light on his identity and reason for being there. "'You're a dead thing,' the Master [Apollinax] told Coriolan, 'and you heard my summons.' 'I was sent, not summoned,' Coriolan answered, 'and sent to block you.'" Nor does Coriolan fear to die, having already experienced a timeless moment in his plunge into Sorworth Water: "Why, I've died more than once already, I think, whatever death is, and that's my punishment, and that's my reward."[55] Before fleeing the scene, Sweeney sees Bain take a shotgun blast to the stomach at close enough range to kill any man. But when he looks for the body, he is startled to see, instead, an indistinct "shape," "shimmering, translucent, smokelike. Then it vanished altogether."[56] Bain's body will never be found, of course, because there was never a body to begin with: the whole episode was, for Bain, simply another step on his long climb up the Purgatorial mountain. "The way of purgatory is necessarily a way of pain," Person observes of this story, adding that "the possibility of purgation necessarily entails pain chosen, even embraced, for a greater good."[57] Such is the lesson learned from Bain's fate, as described in "Sorworth Place" and *Lord of the Hollow Dark*.

He makes a final appearance in 1976's "Saviourgate." Though written three years before Kirk's third novel, Bain's purgation has advanced even further in this story; he seems to be quite near to achieving the Beatific Vision, that perfect knowledge and sight of God that entails "the satisfaction of all human desires and longings …" which we shall know only in Heaven.[58] The main character in "Saviourgate," Mark Findlay, is in the same position Bain was in *Lord of the Hollow Dark*: highly disorientated and unsure of certain details from his past. One dark and stormy night, he is welcomed into the Crosskeys Hotel by Bain and the amiable Canon Hoodman, who try to convince Findlay that he is not simply lost but experiencing a timeless moment. At the Crosskeys, Bain explains,

---

[55] Ibid., 307.
[56] Ibid., 308.
[57] Person, *Critical Biography*, 126.
[58] Michael W. Dunne, "Richard FitzRalph on the Beatific Vision: *Delectatio* and *Beatitudo* in his Oxford Lectures on the Sentences (1328-29)," *Irish Theological Quarterly* 80, no. 4 (2015): 328, doi: 10.1177/0021140015598580.

Timeless Moments 99

"Time doesn't signify: there's no Time for you and me, thank God, Findley."[59] Having ignored the question in previous stories, Kirk uses the conversation between the characters to clarify how timeless moments might relate to the particular and general judgments to which every soul must be subjected (the former upon the death of one's body, the latter at the Second Coming). "Perhaps we experience the Provisional Judgment now," Canon Hoodman says, "and so remain tied, in some sense, to experiences within Time."[60] But the attempt is unsatisfactory and hardly necessary since the story works well enough on its terms as a metaphoric representation of the final stages of Purgatory. "Of all Kirk's short stories," John M. Pafford writes, "this is my favorite, the one which impressed me the most with the best combinations of spiritual depth, an imaginative and absorbing storyline, and interesting characters."[61] It is a fitting send-off for Bain, as original and unforgettable a character as Kirk ever devised.

"A Miracle, and That No More"

No discussion of timeless moments would be complete without mention of one of Kirk's shortest and most charming stories, "An Encounter by Mortstone Pond." Its epigraph is taken from the last section of Eliot's "Little Gidding," in which the references to the living and the dead and "The moment of the rose and the moment of the yew-tree" set up the poem's final vision of "the union of the timeless and the temporal,"[62] the essence of which Kirk adroitly captures in his story. But the allusion is somewhat misleading since Kirk's tale is far less obscure and metaphysical than Eliot's poem or even compared to many of Kirk's other stories. "An Encounter" offers no avenging spirits back from the dead or overbearing bureaucrats who must be taught a painful lesson in humility, but its treatment of rampant urbanization and time is unmistakably Kirk's. Its main character is a young boy grieving the sudden death of his parents. While out walking one day, he feels a presence, which grasps his hand and offers a few comforting words. Fifty years later, Gerald Price—now a major general—finds himself walking along the same path. Lonely and despondent, he feels the presence of a young boy, "intensely miserable, abandoned to despair."[63] Without even thinking, he reaches out and grabs the boy's hand, murmuring

---

[59] Kirk, "Saviourgate," in *Ancestral Shadows*, 200.
[60] Ibid., 206.
[61] John M. Pafford, *Russell Kirk*, vol. 12 of *Major Conservative and Libertarian Thinkers*, ed. John Meadowcroft (New York: Continuum, 2010), 132.
[62] Alison Jack, "'The intolerable wrestle with words and meanings': John 21, T. S. Eliot and the Sense of an Ending," *Expository Times* 117, no. 12 (September 2006): 498, doi: 10.1177/0014524606068951.
[63] Kirk, "An Encounter by Mortstone Pond," in *Ancestral Shadows*, 399.

those same words that had been spoken to him five decades ago. Had boy and man experienced together a timeless moment?

The story ends with a few brief paragraphs in which the general tries to work out what has just happened. First, he tries a rational, scientific explanation: "We are essences, the General thought, essences that flow like mercury. Each of us is a myriad of particles of energy, held temporarily in combination by purposes or forces we understand no better than did Lucretius."[64] But he soon realizes that what he has experienced far exceeds the capacity of reason or science to explain: it is "miraculous," and, as with all miracles, there is simply something "numbing" or ineffable about it. The final lines are taken from Eliot's poem, often-quoted by Kirk, and now engraved upon his tombstone in St. Michael's Cemetery, near Mecosta: "the communication / Of the dead is tongued with fire / beyond the language of the living."[65] His gloss on them is worth noting: the dead, Kirk explains, "speak with a clarity and a candor we cannot obtain from the people of our moment in time."[66] This is something that readers of his stories and novels must remember as they reflect upon his occasionally inscrutable thoughts on time and the afterlife. Though Plato, Voegelin, and Eliot provided Kirk with a solid basis for his understanding of timeless moments, they are, perhaps, in the end, something we shall understand fully only when we, too, have learned to speak the language of the dead.

---

[64] Ibid., 400.
[65] Eliot, *The Complete Poems & Plays*, 185 ("Little Gidding" I).
[66] Kirk, *Eliot and His Age*, 260.

Chapter 6

Kirk, Johnson, and the Conservative Gothic Tradition

Each of the next three chapters will focus on one of Kirk's novels. However, that focus will not be *exclusive* to them; instead, I shall devote almost equal attention to prominent conservatives who greatly influenced or inspired its composition. Thus, in Chapter 7, *A Creature of the Twilight* is contrasted with the political satires of Evelyn Waugh. Chapter 8 explores links between *Lord of the Hollow Dark* and the poems and plays of T. S. Eliot, from which Kirk borrowed many of the names for his characters. By juxtaposing Kirk and these authors, I hope to accomplish two things. First, the comparisons are intended to illuminate different aspects of his conservatism as expressed through his fiction, including his pacifist and isolationist political views and his interest in Christian mysticism. They also demonstrate the remarkable continuity of the moral imagination, which is, in Kirk's own words, "larger than the circumstances of one's time or one's private experience" and endures across vast quantities of time and space.[1] I begin with a comparative analysis of Kirk's first novel, *Old House of Fear*, and *A Journey to the Western Islands of Scotland*, a travelog by the nineteenth-century moralist and lexicographer, Samuel Johnson.

Though written by men of very different backgrounds, temperaments, and beliefs, these texts evince a similar, unmistakably conservative worldview, which can be characterized by its romanticized view of the past and a strong distrust of technological innovation and social reform. In addition, they share what can only be described as a "Gothic" sensibility, with frequent references to long-established tropes of the genre, such as haunted houses, ghosts, and other apparently unexplainable phenomena. Parts or all of both texts, finally, are set in the Hebrides, parallel chains of islands that lie off the Western coast of Scotland and are especially noted for their isolation and rugged beauty. In conceptualizing the Hebrides through a similar framework, Johnson and Kirk demonstrate the remarkable coherence of conservative thought, as revealed by the numerous passages in which the two express nearly identical opinions about related issues. In his memoirs, Kirk attempts to pass his first novel off as

---

[1] Kirk, *Eliot and His Age*, 39.

a lark, written only to alleviate his boredom.² Whatever the true nature of its inception, *Old House of Fear* deserves attention as an important entry in what I would describe as a distinctly conservative strain of Gothic fiction, which stretches back to the earliest days of both movements. In the following pages, I elucidate some of its key tenets, as revealed by Johnson and Kirk.

Walpole, Burke, and the Rise of the Gothic and Conservative Movements

The Castle of Otranto, first published in 1764 by Horace Walpole, is often cited as the first Gothic novel. I discuss Kirk's key influences in this genre in Chapter 3, but Walpole's peculiar book deserves some attention here, especially since it introduced some of the Gothic tropes favored by Kirk, including the "wild supernatural machinations" that drive the plot and its quasi-realistic, "medieval setting."³ After his son dies in a freak accident, Manfred, Prince of Otranto, decides to marry the boy's intended bride himself to ensure the preservation of the family line. Something of the novel's lurid tone can be discerned from the following passage, in which Manfred makes his intentions plain to the terrified Isabella:

> — In short, Isabella, since I cannot give you my son, I offer you myself. — Heavens! cried Isabella, waking from her delusion, what do I hear! You, my lord! You! My father in law! ... I tell you, said Manfred imperiously, [my wife] is no longer my wife; I divorce her from this hour. Too long has she cursed me by her unfruitfulness: my fate depends on having sons, — and this night I trust will give a new date to my hopes. At those words he seized the cold hand of Isabella, who was half-dead with fright and horror. She shrieked, and started from him. Manfred rose to pursue her ...⁴

Modern readers will probably find the book more ridiculous than scary, but its immediate and enduring success speaks to the impression it made on Walpole's contemporaries. An avid theater-goer, he acknowledged the strong influence of *Hamlet* on this novel; he also boasted of having invented an entirely new literary style in which the thoughts and feelings of the characters could be presented with

---

[2] Kirk, *The Sword of Imagination*, 250-51.
[3] Crystal B. Lake, "Bloody Records: Manuscripts and Politics in *The Castle of Otranto*," *Modern Philology* 110, no. 4 (May 2013): 489, doi: 10.1086/670066.
[4] Horace Walpole, *The Castle of Otranto*, ed. Nick Groom (1764; repr., Oxford University Press, 2014): 24.

more precision and feeling than ever before.⁵ The influence of Shakespeare is also evident in the book's moral conservatism: the ghosts do not appear merely to frighten the characters but to provoke them to action. In the end, Manfred is persuaded to give up his claim to Isabella and reconcile with his wife. The two withdraw from public life and spend the rest of their lives in quiet contemplation.

Aside from Shakespeare, and probably more important than he in determining the aesthetic principles that would govern *The Castle of Otranto* and the new literary genre it heralded, Walpole was also influenced by a more unlikely source: the Anglo-Irish statesman Edmund Burke, whose *A Philosophical Enquiry into the Origin of Our Ideas of the Sublime and Beautiful* was published in 1757, and remains one of the landmark texts of both the conservative and Gothic movements. The sublime was an old concept that had been reintroduced into the public consciousness in England following a 1739 translation of Longinus' *Peri Hypsos* by William Smith, which Burke redefined in a "recognizably English and, of course, Whiggish" manner:

> Burke argued that the sublime was experienced when the mind encountered and endeavored to comprehend the infinite. The key to the sublime was the imagination, which worked most powerfully when confronted with obscurity and losing itself in intimations of eternity and boundless immensity. For Burke, mistiness and murmured sounds, night and death, *Paradise Lost* and Stonehenge were mysterious, obscure, and potentially sublime, rousing the imagination to escape its own limitations. In its aesthetic extremism, Burke's *Philosophical Enquiry* became a template for the Gothic imagination.⁶

Burke's emphasis on fear and the central role of the imagination in achieving a sublime effect is apparent throughout Walpole's novel. In the opening chapter, for instance, the messenger who brings the news of Manfred's son's death is described as leaving his audience struck with "terror and amazement."⁷ These are the same emotions Burke highlights in a key section of the *Philosophical Enquiry*: he describes the former as "the ruling principle" of the sublime, which is intended to produce a powerful emotional response in the reader and is often

---

⁵ Horace Walpole, Preface to the Second Edition of *The Castle of Otranto*, in *The Castle of Otranto*, ed. Nick Groom (1764; repr., Oxford University Press, 2014): 10.
⁶ Nick Groom, introduction to *The Castle of Otranto*, by Horace Walpole (Oxford: Oxford University Press, 2014), xxii-xxiii.
⁷ Walpole, *Castle of Otranto*, 18.

found in great works of literature.[8] Although Burke's treatise on the sublime contains little hint of his social and political views, his status as one of the most important figures in modern conservatism invites speculation regarding the potential overlap between the values and objectives of the Gothic and conservative movements.

Neither Burke nor Walpole were interested in fusing the two in a more determined manner, however. That would partly be accomplished, albeit inadvertently, by a contemporary of theirs: Samuel Johnson. Before examining his achievement, it may be helpful to clarify what I mean by the term "Conservative Gothic," which I would use to describe both Kirk's fiction and Johnson's travelog. Basically, it refers to any imaginative work that employs Gothic tropes in defense of the "permanent things," the enduring norms, values, and beliefs of Western civilization.[9] This defense of the permanent things must be the *primary intention* of a Conservative Gothic text, I would argue, not merely subtext. Thus, I would not apply the label to something like *The Castle of Otranto* because its conservative inclinations function only as a "backdrop against which the plot of [the novel] unfolds."[10] In short, Walpole is more interested in scaring and entertaining his readers than he is in teaching them about virtue. But Conservative Gothic authors never lose sight of the latter responsibility. As Kirk explains in defending his own "ghostly" stories, "All important literature has some ethical end; and the tale of the preternatural—as written by George Macdonald, C. S. Lewis, Charles Williams, and other masters—can be an instrument for the recovery of moral order."[11]

Conservative Gothic authors like the ones named by Kirk tend to be sympathetic towards religion, if not deeply religious themselves, because they recognize that supernatural events and beings can only exist in a world governed by divine providence. Having an open mind about the existence of ghosts leads necessarily to questions about where they come from and who created them. Kirk makes the same point in "A Cautionary Note on the Ghostly Tale," wondering, "How is it possible to perceive a *revenant* if there cannot

---

[8] Edmund Burke, *A Philosophical Enquiry into the Origin of Our Ideas of the Sublime and Beautiful*, 5th ed. (London: J. Dodsley, 1767): 97 - 98, *Google Books*, https://www.google.com/books/edition/A Philosophical Enquiry Into the Origin/CugJAAAAQAAJ?hl=en&gbpv=0.

[9] Kirk, *Enemies of the Permanent*, 54. Note that Kirk was always careful to distinguish between norms and values, which are not the same things despite their interchangeable use in the present. See 8-9 in this same text.

[10] Annie Pécastaings, "William Marshal and the Origins of *The Castle of Otranto*," *English Studies* 100, no. 3 (2019): 298, doi: 10.1080/0013838X.2019.1574416.

[11] Kirk, "A Cautionary Note on the Ghostly Tale," in *Ancestral Shadows*, 402-03. I use this exact quote in Chapter 3, for a similar purpose.

possibly be *revenants* to perceive?"[12] This would seem to rule out Walpole's novel as a Conservative Gothic text since the author presents, at best, an ambivalent view of religion in it and subsequent works. A few years after *The Castle of Otranto*, he wrote a play, *The Mysterious Mother*, that is full of "rather standard cheap shots at priests and the Catholic Church in general" and little friendlier to organized religion "of any stamp."[13] Conservative Gothic fiction need not promote any specific creed, but many of its authors are Christians, reflecting the historical prevalence of that faith in Western culture. This is probably the most notable difference between Conservative Gothicism and other forms of that genre, especially in the present. In recent years, there has been no shortage of books, TV shows, and other media purporting to be Gothic, such as *American Gods*, *The Walking Dead*, or *The Chilling Adventures of Sabrina*. Most either ignore Christianity or openly ridicule it.

Samuel Johnson and Edmund Burke, by contrast, took their respective faiths very seriously. Neither wrote any Gothic fiction, but they were both conservative thinkers who, in different ways, influenced the subsequent development of a conservative strain in Gothic literature, as practiced by Kirk and others. Although Burke clearly influenced Walpole, it is harder to determine who was the more dominant intellectual force in his relationship with Johnson. The two disagreed on many subjects and belonged to different political parties, yet shared a basic viewpoint that is recognizably conservative, as F. P. Lock observes: "Both upheld the prescriptive rights of property, the utility of the social hierarchy, and the restriction of political rights to the educated minority."[14] Burke and Johnson were founding members of the most famous social club in England, which was known simply as "The Club," and began meeting regularly at the Turk's Head Tavern in central London in 1764.[15] Like Burke, Johnson was more than capable of offering insightful analysis of literature; his studies of Shakespeare's plays and the lives of Milton, Dryden, and other major poets continue to be held in high esteem, even by contemporary readers and scholars. James L. Battersby describes Johnson's basic approach to literary criticism thusly:

> Johnson is concerned with the moral, social, and political tendencies of works, with the larger ramifications of works as representations or

---

[12] Ibid., 403.
[13] Jeffrey N. Cox, "First Gothics: Walpole, Evans, Frank," *Papers on Language and Literature: A Journal of Scholars and Critics of Language and Literature* 46, no. 2 (Spring 2010): 127-29, MLA International Bibliography with Full Text.
[14] F. P. Lock, *Edmund Burke* (Oxford: Oxford University Press, 2006), 2:9.
[15] Leo Damrosch, *The Club: Johnson, Boswell, and the Friends Who Shaped an Age* (New Haven, CT: Yale University Press, 2019).

expressions of truth and reality and, thus, as influences on readers' conceptions of life; in short, with all those aspects of works, considered apart from their technical and formal excellence, that oblige us to consider the author in terms of the moral feelings or the view of things that he promotes, encourages, or implies.[16]

Kirk, of course, shares Johnson's concern for "the moral, social, and political tendencies of works" and their larger "ramifications."

In 1950, several years before the publication of Burke's treatise and *The Castle of Otranto*, Johnson had attacked recent works of modern fiction in an essay published in the fourth issue of his bi-weekly periodical, *The Rambler*. He seems to have had in mind such popular novels as Henry Fielding's *Tom Jones* and Tobias Smollet's *Roderick Random*,[17] picaresque works featuring realistically flawed, even reprehensible characters who, at the novel's end, manage to escape punishment or even flourish. Such narrative decisions on the part of the author, Johnson believed, represented a dramatic break with tradition, in which authors either strove to present clear examples of virtue to emulate or create scenarios that were so far-fetched that any bad behavior they contained could be easily dismissed by the reader as irrelevant to his own life. Johnson warned that, even in trying to write more "realistic" novels, authors needed to bear in mind their responsibility to the young, especially: "to teach the means of avoiding the snares which are laid by Treachery for Innocence … to give the power of counteracting fraud without the temptation to practice it; to initiate youth by mock encounters in the art of necessary defense, and to increase prudence without impairing virtue."[18] In the twentieth century, Kirk would make a similar case for the normative value of literature, which exists to "rouse and fortify the living, to renew the contract of eternal society."[19]

Like Kirk, Johnson was eager to practice what he preached, i.e., to write poems and stories that illustrated his aesthetic principles. He was not an especially prolific writer of fiction, but all of Johnson's works in that category demonstrate a keen sense of the moral imagination, which is the hallmark of all conservative literature through the ages. In 1748, he published one of his most celebrated

---

[16] James L. Battersby, "Life, Art, and the *Lives of the Poets*, in *Domestick Privacies: Samuel Johnson and the Art of Biography*, ed. David Wheeler (Lexington, KY: The University Press of Kentucky, 1987), 43.

[17] Brian Hanley, *Samuel Johnson as Book Reviewer: A Duty to Examine the Labors of the Learned* (Newark, NJ: University of Delaware Press, 2001), 270.

[18] Samuel Johnson, "The New Realistic Novel," in *The Major Works*, ed. Donald Greene (Oxford: Oxford University Press, 2008), 177.

[19] Kirk, *Enemies of the Permanent Things*, 76-77.

poems, "The Vanity of Human Wishes," an imitation of a satire by Juvenal in which he bemoans the state of modern England while urging his readers to cultivate their spiritual lives above the temporal. "Implore [God's] aid, in his decisions, rest, / Secure whate'er he gives, he gives the best."[20] Perhaps Johnson's most noteworthy creative work is *Rasselas*, a response to Voltaire's pessimistic and satirical *Candide* that was first published in 1759. His famous biographer, James Boswell, reports that Johnson wrote it in one week to help defray the costs of his mother's funeral,[21] though there is some doubt among contemporary scholars about how true that is. The story suffers from flat characterization and a plodding pace, but Chance David Pahl makes a convincing case that it essentially anticipates the *Bildungsroman* tradition of the latter half of the eighteenth century, presenting the gradual "emergence from youthful idealism to mature sobriety" of the titular character.[22] In any case, it is clearly a conservative work of fiction.

Thus, even before the modern conservative movement had formally begun (according to Kirk and others) with the 1790 publication of Burke's *Reflections on the Revolution in France*, Johnson was already exploring many of its core principles in his literary criticism and fiction. Meanwhile, *The Castle of Otranto* had proven itself a huge success, inaugurating a craze for Gothic fiction that would last for decades.[23] As with Burke's *Reflections*, which provides more of a convenient than accurate starting point for dating the rise of modern conservatism, so does *The Castle of Otranto* imperfectly signal the dawn of the Gothic era in art. In fact, traces of it were already evident in the *zeitgeist* and were addressed by the ever-prescient Johnson. In his famous dictionary, he offers definitions for "Goths," "Gothical," "Gothick," and "Gothicism," dismissing each as "uncivilized" and "barbarian."[24] Johnson's ire was directed towards a particular style of architecture that was prominent throughout the Middle Ages and widely employed in the building of cathedrals throughout Europe.[25] This architectural style evolved out of the earlier Romanesque and was described,

---

[20] Johnson, "The Vanity of Human Wishes," in *The Major Works*, 21.
[21] James Boswell, *The Life of Samuel Johnson*, ed. Christopher Hibbert (London: Penguin Books, 1979), 86.
[22] Chance David Paul, "Teleology in Samuel Johnson's 'Rasselas,'" *Renascence* 64, no. 3 (Spring 2012): 223, *Academic Search Premier*.
[23] Jan Delasara, *PopLit, PopCult and the X-Files: A Critical Exploration* (Jefferson, NC: McFarland & Company, 2000), 143.
[24] Samuel Johnson, *A Dictionary of the English Language*, 2nd revised ed. (London: William Pickering, 1828), 25, *Google Books*, https://www.google.com/books/edition/A_Dictionary_of_the_English_Language/z3kKAAAAIAAJ?hl=en&gbpv=1&bsq=Goth.
[25] David Stephenson, *Heavenly Vaults: From Romanesque to Gothic in European Architecture* (New York: Princeton Architectural Press, 2009), 155. *ProQuest Ebook Central*.

pejoratively, as "Gothic" because it supposedly originated in places (e.g., France, Germany, and Spain) outside of the main Greco-Roman sphere of influence. However much it may have been derided by Johnson and others, the movement strongly influenced the creation of Gothic fiction, to which it later gave its name. Indeed, Walpole describes its influence on himself in terms that resemble a spiritual conversion. At Strawberry Hill, the sprawling, castle-like house in London he spent much of his life designing and building, "the Gothic [had] the valence of a religion."[26]

The point is that, as with conservatism, one cannot insist too firmly upon a formal starting point of Gothicism. Walpole's novel, like Burke's *Reflections*, deserves credit for introducing many of its themes and conventions to a wider audience, but some of the former were already swirling around the literary scene in London, being vigorously debated in the salons and clubs frequented by *aesthetes* such as Johnson. Indeed, despite his hostility towards the fledgling movement, some of his works bear evidence of the genre's possible influence. Consider the moody and melancholy *Rasselas*, written (with however much haste) in the wake of his mother's death. Whatever the exact nature of his relationship with her, it was a loss that may have caused another of the periodic bouts of "religious skepticism" that plagued Johnson throughout his life.[27] Though there is nothing to rival the campy dialogue and bizarre imagery presented in *The Castle of Otranto*, the prince's brooding quest for contentment and his frequent emotional outbursts call to mind the behavior of classic Gothic heroes such as Werther or Heathcliff. Isolation enforced by a kind of natural boundary is also a frequent trope in Gothic fiction present in Johnson's story, which begins with the titular prince closely confined in the Happy Valley, a "pastoral utopia" bordered on all sides by fast-flowing rivers and impenetrable mountains.[28] Of course, one cannot truthfully describe *Rasselas* as a Gothic text or even as a Conservative Gothic one. The closest Johnson comes to the deliberate use of Gothic tropes is in the travelog he wrote following a trip to Scotland in 1773, which becomes especially noticeable in the part of it that is set in the Hebrides.

---

[26] George Haggerty, *Horace Walpole's Letters: Masculinity and Friendship in the Eighteenth Century* (Lewisburg, PA: Bucknell University Press, 2011), 39. *ProQuest Ebook Central.*
[27] Rachel Michelle Stern, "Fantasies of Choosing in *Rasselas*," *Studies in English Literature, 1500 - 1900* 55, no. 3 (Summer 2015): 533-34, *Gale Academic OneFile.*
[28] Robert Folkenflik, "Rasselas" and the Closed Field," *Huntington Library Quarterly* 57, no. 4 (Autumn 1994): 338, doi: 10.2307/3817841.

Johnson's Travelog

Boswell and Johnson each had their reasons for wanting to leave their familiar London base for the highlands of the north. Ambitious and gregarious, Boswell undoubtedly relished the chance to show off his famous friend to relatives and acquaintances back in Auchinleck, the ancestral estate he was to inherit in 1782. Johnson, for his part, had long fretted over the rapid pace of industrialization in Europe and was curious to see how that process was affecting those who lived in one of the continent's wildest and remotest parts.[29] Despite having been friends for years, the two had not actually spent much time in each other's company since Boswell's affairs frequently kept him in Edinburgh. All of that changed the day they departed for the Hebrides together: "From the time they left Edinburgh on 18 August ... until they returned on 9 November, whether alone or with others, they were seldom apart except when sleeping, or when they separated to write letters or journal entries ..."[30] Upon their return to London, Johnson immediately published his account of the trip as *A Journey to the Western Islands of Scotland*. It sold well, despite some critical remarks he made about the country, which outraged Scottish reviewers.[31] Boswell waited until after Johnson's death to issue his *Journal of a Tour to the Hebrides* in 1785. It served as a kind of trial run for the great *Life of Johnson* he had spent several decades planning, which would follow in 1791.

Johnson's dismay at the loss of traditional Scottish culture is evident from the initial pages of his travelog. Early in their journey, he and Boswell stopped at the historic university town of St. Andrews (where Kirk was later to study for his doctorate), "the most important religious center in late medieval Scotland," Bess Rhodes argues, and a frequent site of intense theological debates since the Reformation.[32] In a sudden outpouring of emotion, Johnson laments the excessive zeal of the Scottish Reformers, which led to the abandonment or destruction of so many historic buildings throughout the country, such as the town's cathedral, now fallen into ruin:

> The change of religion in Scotland, eager and vehement as it was, raised an epidemical enthusiasm, compounded of sullen scrupulousness and

---

[29] Damrosch, *The Club*, 249-50.
[30] John B. Radner, *Johnson and Boswell: A Biography of Friendship* (New Haven, CT: Yale University Press, 2012), 113.
[31] Martin Wechselblatt, "Finding Mr. Boswell: Rhetorical Authority and National Identity in Johnson's *A Journey to the Western Islands of Scotland*," ELH 60, no. 1 (1993): 120, https://www.jstor.org/stable/2873310.
[32] Bess Rhodes, *Riches and Reform: Ecclesiastical Wealth in St. Andrews c. 1520 - 1580* (Leiden, South Holland, The Netherlands: Brill, 2019), 5.

warlike ferocity, which, in a people whom idleness resigned to their own thoughts ... was long transmitted in its full strength from the old to the young, but by trade and intercourse with England, is now visibly abating, and giving way too fast to that laxity of practice and indifference of opinion in which men not sufficiently instructed to find the middle point too easily shelter themselves from rigour and constraint.[33]

Johnson was eager to leave St. Andrews, which he memorializes in bleak terms as "a university declining, a college alienated, and a church profaned and hastening to the ground."[34] In his reflections on the place, he expresses certain sentiments that correlate to some of the chief principles identified by Kirk as being shared by all genuine conservatives, including a "Recognition that change may not be salutary reform;" a "Belief in a transcendent order;" and an "Affection for the proliferating variety and mystery of human experience."[35] The emphasis on ruins and past acts of violence in this passage lends it an unmistakably Gothic tone.

As the travelers return to their carriage and draw ever closer to the Hebrides, Johnson continues to ruminate on the ravages of time and so-called progress. He complains about the effects of deforestation near Aberbrothick (modern Arbroath or Aberbrothock) and decries the "thievish" behavior of highland tribes in the mountains who, "having lost that reverence for property by which the order of civil life is preserved, soon consider all as enemies whom they do not reckon as friends, and think themselves licensed to invade whatever they are not obliged to protect."[36] At first, he thinks the mountains might have served as a natural barrier protecting those who dwelled there from the worst excesses of the changes underway in the rest of Scotland. These people had lived for many centuries, he observes, "secluded from the rest of mankind ... an unaltered and discriminated race."[37] But even the mountains, ultimately, may not suffice to preserve the unique and venerable lifestyle enjoyed by the Highlanders. "They are now losing their distinction and hastening to mingle with the general community," Johnson concludes sadly.[38] He will soon discover a sturdier barrier against the forces of modernity in the waters that surround the Hebrides.

---

[33] Samuel Johnson, *A Journey to the Western Islands of Scotland*, ed. Allan Wendt (1775; repr., Boston: Houghton Mifflin, 1965), 5.
[34] Ibid., 7.
[35] Kirk, *The Conservative Mind*, 8-9.
[36] Johnson, *A Journey to the Western Islands of Scotland*, 8, 33-34.
[37] Ibid., 35.
[38] Ibid.

In Gothic fiction, as I have noted, there is often a kind of boundary (however permeable) between the "real" world that is governed by the laws of science and reason and the realm of the Gothic, in which the forces of horror and the imagination are given free rein. "The context that depersonalizes and diffuses the forces of violence in Gothic romance may well be a specific architectural place or natural place—forest or cave—with features similar to those of the haunted castle."[39] Often enough, this border is a natural one: a river, sea, or forest. One reason, then, that Johnson's travelog often resembles a Gothic text is because of the marked increase in references to boundaries and violent weather that mark the passages set in the Hebrides. "Sky lies open on the west and north to a vast extent of ocean … Half the year is deluged with rain. From the autumnal to the vernal equinox, a dry day is hardly known, except when the showers are suspended by a tempest."[40] Sky (or Skye) is the largest and most populous of the inner Hebrides, where the travelers were accorded a more than convivial welcome due to Boswell's name and connections. And yet Johnson, who moved to London while still a young man, seems ill at ease there, unable, perhaps, to overcome a growing sense of isolation and remoteness. "In our passage from Scotland to Sky, we were wet for the first time with a shower. This was the beginning of the Highland winter, after which we were told that a succession of three dry days was not to be expected for many months."[41] The passage ends on a despairing note with unmistakably Gothic overtones: "This is not the description of a cruel climate, yet the dark months are here a time of great distress, because the summer can do little more than feed itself, and winter comes with its cold and its scarcity upon families very slenderly provided."[42]

As in previous stages of his journey, Johnson expresses disappointment at the rapid changes that have occurred in recent years and decades. "We came thither too late to see what we expected," he notes bitterly, "a people of peculiar appearance and a system of antiquated life."[43] He laments the "decay of religion" and mass emigration from the Hebrides that has left formerly thriving communities barren and bereft. Though understandable due to rather desperate living conditions, the loss of population has the unfortunate tendency of making things worse for those who choose to remain behind.[44] "Insulation and its accompanying security," Christopher Brooks claims, "is

---

[39] Eugenia C. DeLamotte, *Perils of the Night: A Feminist Study of Ninteenth-Century Gothic* (New York: Oxford University Press, 1990), 17-18.
[40] Johnson, *A Journey to the Western Islands of Scotland*, 58.
[41] Ibid., 39.
[42] Ibid.
[43] Ibid., 43.
[44] Ibid., 48, 71-72.

maintained only through a nationalistic maintenance of any country's greatest asset: its people."[45] And yet, despite great changes and challenges, more of the past manages to endure in the Hebrides than elsewhere in Scotland: "Everything in those countries has its history."[46] Johnson delights in recording the peculiar habits and attire of the locals and spends a memorable night in Raasay listening to Gaelic singing, which greatly pleases him, though he does not understand the words. As with the mountains of the highlands, the waters surrounding the Hebrides may not be perfectly inviolable, but they are still powerful barriers to change.

No Gothic text would be complete without the appearance of a ghost, vampire, or other supernatural being. Luckily for Johnson and Boswell, they did not run into any of these during their tour of the Hebrides. Johnson, however, was very keen on learning all he could about "second sight," the ability to see distant and future events.[47] He asked many of the villagers they met about it and seemed to take some of their stories as proof that it might be real. "To collect sufficient testimonies for the satisfaction of the public, or ourselves," he concludes of the matter, "would have required more time than we could bestow ... I never could advance my curiosity to conviction, but came away at last only willing to believe."[48] Johnson attempted to investigate second sight rationally and scientifically: he "explained his interest in [it] by claiming it as a national phenomenon and thus deserving of exploration."[49] Unlike Kirk, who found his interest in the supernatural easy to reconcile with his religious beliefs, Johnson could never quite bring himself to accept such things. On the existence of ghosts, Boswell reports him as saying, "All argument is against it, but all belief is for it."[50] However incongruous the passages about second sight may seem compared to his outbursts about change and reflections on Scottish customs, they contribute further to the Gothic impression made by this text. In any case, Johnson was a strong influence on Kirk, and perhaps it is not entirely coincidental that the latter chose to set at least part of his first novel in the same location as Johnson's Travelog. He was, certainly, making a more deliberate attempt to fuse conservative and Gothic themes.

---

[45] Christopher Brooks, "Johnson's Insular Mind and the Analogy of Travel: *A Journey to the Western Islands of Scotland*," *Essays in Literature* 18, no. 1 (Spring 1991): 29, *Humanities Full Text (H. W. Wilson)*.
[46] Johnson, *A Journey to the Western Islands of Scotland*, 618.
[47] Rachel Scarborough King, "Samuel Johnson and Spectral Media," *ELH* 87, no. 1 (Spring 2020): 83, doi: 10.1353/elh.2020.0002.
[48] Johnson, *A Journey to the Western Islands of Scotland*, 82.
[49] Juliet Feibel, "Highland Histories: Jacobitism and Second Sight," *Clio* 30, no. 1 (Fall 2000): 64, *Humanities Full Text (H. W. Wilson)*.
[50] Boswell, *Life of Johnson*, 239.

Old House of Fear

As mentioned previously, Kirk's interest in the occult dates to an early period of his life. He grew up surrounded by a circle of superstitious relatives in a house in which, prior to his birth, seánces had been held on a regular basis.[51] His first experience with the supernatural occurred when he was eight or nine years old: one wintry day, he spied two spectral figures standing outside of his window. But when he went outside to confront them, they had vanished without leaving any trace of their passage in the freshly fallen snow.[52] Years later, he would buy the house himself, telling visitors gleefully of the numerous ghosts supposed to haunt the place. In a letter to Eric Voegelin, he writes, "Henry James was a man with Swedenborgian forebears who didn't believe in ghosts; I am one with Swedenborgian forebears who *does* believe in ghosts; indeed, everybody who stays here in my ancestral house of Piety Hill becomes a more fervent believer than even I am."[53] Much like Samuel Johnson, he tried to find a rational basis for his belief in the supernatural. Characters in his stories often indulge in metaphysical speculation involving quasi-scientific concepts such as "waves of impulse" or "virtue." Similarly, at one point in his memoirs, Kirk speculates that the Shroud of Turin might be explained by the laws of thermodynamics.[54] There is ample proof that he speaks truthfully in declaring himself as having not an Enlightened but a "Gothic mind, medieval in its temper and structure."[55]

If needed, further confirmation could be sought from the numerous stories and novels that he wrote, almost all of which feature strong Gothic overtones. His first collection of stories, *The Surly Sullen Bell*, was published in 1962 and contains several that merely hint at the presence of the supernatural. Two—"Skyberia" and "Lost Lake"—do not even attempt as much and are rarely discussed in the context of his fictional creations.[56] His subsequent collection, *The Princess of All Lands*, shows a marked increase in supernatural phenomena, as well as a willingness by the author to have his characters acknowledge them as such without the need for any metaphysical hand-waving. It was published in 1979, well after his 1964 conversion to Catholicism. In *Watchers at the Strait Gate*,

---

[51] Felicia Kirk Flores, Facebook message to author, 18 May 2022.
[52] Kirk, *The Sword of Imagination*, 20-21.
[53] Kirk to Eric Voegelin, 19 July 1971, in *Letters*, 153.
[54] Kirk, *The Sword of Imagination*, 245. For examples of Kirk's characters discussing metaphysics, see, e.g., the stories "The Surly Sullen Bell" and "The Princess of All Lands."
[55] Ibid., 68.
[56] Person mentions "Lost Lake" in an aside, and does not discuss "Skyberia" at all. Birzer devotes more attention to both, but offers more summary than analysis. See also the discussion of "Lost Lake" in Theodore Sturgeon, "A Viewpoint, a Dewpoint," *National Review* 14, no. 6 (February 1963).

finally, one encounters tales such as "The Invasion of the Church of the Holy Ghost" or "The Peculiar Demesne of Archvicar Gerontion," in which events cannot *possibly* be explained except by resorting to the supernatural. It followed only five years after the previous collection and contains his last published fiction. Kirk's novels follow a similar track, though, compared to his first two, there is a marked increase in the number of Gothic themes and tropes in his third and last. Even so, his first is an unmistakably Gothic work. *Old House of Fear* features no ghosts but fits comfortably into the venerable tradition of Gothic romance established by authors such as Anne Radcliffe, Sir Walter Scott, and Nathaniel Hawthorne, as I discuss in Chapter 3.

The story is set in the same obscure locale as Johnson's iconic travelog: the Hebrides. One may wonder why this proudly American author would choose to set his first novel on the other side of the world, in Scotland. In fact, Kirk knew the country well and was quite taken by its shabby, genteel charm. Many of his best and oldest friends were Scottish, including the writer George Scott-Moncrieff and sculptor Hew Lorimer.[57] He bought a small house in Pittenweem, Fife, and spent some hopeful years remodeling it before growing expenses back in Mecosta forced him to sell it at a loss.[58] In addition to *Old House of Fear*, he set many of his short stories, as well as his third novel, *Lord of the Hollow Dark*, entirely in Scotland. Kirk had first visited the country many years earlier as a young graduate student pursuing his PhD at the prestigious University of St. Andrews. Whereas Johnson, in his visit to Kirk's future alma mater, lamented its already conspicuous decline, Kirk found himself confronting the exact opposite problem: over-development. Writing back to a friend from home, he complained that the beautiful, sparse countryside around the school was being ruined by the kind of "social planners" and bureaucrats lampooned in some of his best stories. "The Government appears to prefer to build hideous little bungalows and villas in the suburb below the hill, each with a silly little strip of lawn about it and a sillier name above the door."[59] Nevertheless, he felt "comfortably situated" in the town and was eager to begin exploring the surrounding countryside.

He had a special fondness for the Hebrides, which is most evident, perhaps, in his chapter on Eigg in *Beyond the Dreams of Avarice*. Though a work of non-fiction, Kirk's 1956 essay has a strong Gothic flair, and echoes many of the themes found in Johnson's travelog. It also anticipates many of the ones Kirk would explore himself in *Old House of Fear*, which makes it worthy of some

---

[57] Kirk to Henry Regnery, 1 December 1952, in *Letters*, 61. Some of the children of Scott-Moncrieff and Lorimer also become good friends with the Kirks.
[58] Kirk, *The Sword of Imagination*, 337-38.
[59] Kirk to William C. McCann, 18 October 1948, in *Letters*, 43.

attention here. Kirk begins by bemoaning the failed social policies of the English and Scottish governments, which have led to the mass exodus of most of its inhabitants. From five hundred persons in the eighteenth century, the population had declined precipitously by Kirk's day and is now even lower: a 2012 census counted only ninety-seven souls scattered across two small settlements on the northern and southern ends.[60] Kirk notes how the bleak climate and topography have contributed to the slow pace of change for the remaining inhabitants: "[Y]ou look out across the desolate beauty of this high, lonely, somnolent island to the rough sea which separates it from the deserted and broken coast of the mainland ... From the cliffs which the shearwaters nest, a half-dozen waterfalls break perpetually, converted into white torrents after a rain."[61] His description of the place after one particularly fierce summer monsoon, full of mist and screaming breakwaters, seems better suited to one of his tales of horror.[62] Kirk cannot resist mentioning Johnson's previous visit in the context of a discussion of the island's religious history.

In contrast to Johnson's dour assessment of the area's future, Kirk sees much that is worth celebrating in Eigg. Somehow, the locals have managed to resist being fully assimilated by the forces of blind progress and conforming modernity that have triumphed elsewhere in the world—at least for now. Though "so much of Hebridean culture was swept away" after the Jacobite rebellion of 1745, he writes, "storytelling and Gaelic songs lingered on until a much later date. In Eigg, a population in part illiterate and without any very elaborate means of entertainment would gather round the peat fires in the evenings and recite old tales."[63] Like Johnson, he tries to make a case for the scientific value of the island's oral tradition, thereby justifying his interest in the same. He describes the stories they tell as works of "narrative history, not works of imagination," adding that they represent "sincere attempts to preserve a record of interesting occurrences in the island."[64] The history of the place is better recorded, Kirk insists, in the memories and reminiscences of its inhabitants rather than in the daily newspapers or reports from the radio. He notes with barely concealed delight the persistent belief in fairies on Eigg,

---

[60] Rachel Creaney and Piotr Niewiadomski, "Tourism and Sustainable Development on the Isle of Eigg, Scotland," *Scottish Geographical Journal* 132, no. 3 - 4 (2016): 216, doi: 10.1080/14702541.2016.1146327. Information about the population of Eigg is from the Small Isles Community Council.
[61] Kirk, *Beyond the Dreams of Avarice*, 282-83.
[62] Ibid., 283.
[63] Ibid., 290.
[64] Ibid.

lingering at least until the last generation, and cites several sources for this claim as proof of their credibility.

Although the island does not have any traditions involving witches, Kirk found something akin to the "second sight" that so interested Johnson. "Coming events, particularly woes, cast their shadows before them, however. In Eigg, as generally in the Hebrides, the spectral funeral procession occasionally manifests itself ..."[65] He goes on to tell the story of a witness' encounter with such a procession: "Walking along the road between manse and harbor one night, he found himself suddenly prevented from going forward; although no visible obstacle intervened, his body seemed to be pressing against some substance indefinable yet impenetrable."[66] Unable to proceed any further, the man was forced to make his way through a ditch on the side of the road until he finally passed the mysterious obstacle. Kirk's discussion of Hebridean mythical beliefs ends with a final attempt to assert their objectivity: "These legends are told with an ingenuousness and occasional inconsequentiality which is strong evidence of their validity; the people of Eigg appear never to have attempted embroidering their narratives ... or remolding them into significance if they lacked meaning."[67] This passage is remarkably similar to one in Johnson's travelog, in which he writes that those who enjoy the second sight "do not boast of it as a privilege, nor are considered by others as advantageously distinguished. They have no temptation to feign, and their hearers have no motive to encourage the imposture."[68] Undoubtedly, Kirk felt the need for circumspection in his scholarly essay on Eigg. In setting his first novel in the Hebrides, on fictional Carnglass Island, and calling it a "Gothick romance," he would have freer rein to indulge his interest in the supernatural.

Nevertheless, that was not his primary intention in writing it. As I have noted, the first responsibility of Conservative Gothic authors is to their readers' moral and intellectual edification. This ethos certainly guided Kirk in all of the fiction that he wrote: his ghostly tales were, he explains, composed not merely "to impose meaningless terror upon the innocent ... What I have attempted, rather, are experiments in the moral imagination."[69] The moral imagination is no less keenly felt in his first novel, which is, at heart, a classic tale of good vs. evil. A brave man embarks upon a dangerous quest. To win the love of a beautiful woman, he must defeat a powerful rival. Even the simplest stories have much to teach us, Kirk insists. In *Enemies of the Permanent Things*, he

---

[65] Ibid., 291.
[66] Ibid.
[67] Ibid., 291-92.
[68] Johnson, *A Journey to the Western Islands of Scotland*, 82.
[69] Kirk, "A Cautionary Note on the Ghostly Tale," 402.

distinguishes between four levels of literature "by which a normative consciousness is developed": the first, suitable mainly for children, is that of fantasy, which imparts "a sense of awe—and the beginning of philosophy."[70] *Old House of Fear* was not written for children, but it inspires awe in the reader and contains hints of the larger moral and philosophical questions with which Kirk himself would grapple in his more sophisticated writings. Wonder is provoked primarily by the novel's exotic setting, which is so unfamiliar to its intended audience of American readers. One cannot help but be enchanted by the charming land of grand old houses, ancient families, and barefoot Scottish lasses that Kirk evokes.

His long-standing objection to the decline of local custom is one of the novel's major themes. It first crops up in a conversation between the protagonist, Hugh Logan, and his boss, Duncan MacAskival. Carnglass Island was once moderately prosperous, MacAskival laments. Still, it was forced to endure the same cycle of exploitative rents, clearances, and mass emigration that ruined so much of the rest of Scotland and the Hebrides. This history lesson is peppered with frequent references to usurious tax rates and failed social policies, suggesting that, like many conservatives, MacAskival blames the centralized government for most of the locals' problems. The present owner of Carnglass happens to be one of the richest women in England. But, he adds, "income tax and surtax won't let her keep much more than five thousand pounds' income, and that probably only pays the servants she has left, and for her food."[71] Left unsaid is the implication that she would be a better steward of the money than the tax accountants in Edinburgh or London. Approaching Glasgow, Logan encounters clear signs that their malfeasance is not limited to rural parts of the country, such as "rows of white-harled Scots cottages, some empty and far gone in decay" and the "ugly sprawl" of suburban housing projects.[72] Against the ruins of modernity, Kirk would shore the natural beauty and rich cultural heritage of the Hebrides, which endure despite all attempts to eradicate it by government bureaucrats.

All of this is so delicately handled by the author that it probably escaped the notice of many of the novel's early readers. Kirk does not develop the theme as fully as he does in some of his short stories. Perhaps he was trying to stick to his advice to writers of Gothic fiction. In "A Cautionary Note on the Ghostly Tale," Kirk warns against the tendency to "turn didactic moralist" in an effort to instill virtue in the reader; however much this needs to remain the focus of the author,

---

[70] Kirk, *Enemies of the Permanent Things*, 45-46.
[71] Kirk, *Old House of Fear*, 6-9.
[72] Ibid., 16.

he must not go about it in a clumsy, overbearing manner.[73] He makes a similar point in *Enemies of the Permanent Things* about writers of humane letters in general.[74] Thus, despite featuring as its main antagonist a fanatical Marxist whose philosophical and political ideology was particularly loathed by Kirk,[75] he is careful in *Old House of Fear* not to moralize. Instead, he allows the reader to reach his conclusions about the story's precepts. Only occasionally does Kirk take it upon himself to issue authoritative judgments about Jackman's moral failings. In a brief scene near the novel's end, he refers to Marxism as a "demon ideology," which has led the otherwise intelligent Jackman astray.[76] For the most part, however, he refrains from such commentary.

Just as topography and climate feature prominently in many Gothic works, including Johnson's travelog, so are they major elements in *Old House of Fear*. The novel begins, in fact, with a brief scene (only three paragraphs long) set on the coast of Carnglass Island. It is night, and the waters are restless. Five men sit in a boat, watching the shore uneasily. "So thick about them hung the fog that they could not see the great cliffs towering above them like insurmountable walls."[77] Suddenly, there is an explosion, followed by several gunshots. The men flee in understandable terror, and Kirk immediately pivots to the comfortable office of Duncan MacAskival, some three thousand miles away. The strange events that just transpired will not be explained to the reader until much later in the novel, but the opening scene is effective at establishing a sense of mystery and danger right from the start. The landscape plays an important role in accomplishing that feat, with the men's position in a small boat being tossed by choppy waters emphasizing their isolation and vulnerability. In *A Philosophical Enquiry*, Burke insists that, compared to land, the ocean is "an object of no small terror," with its vastness and inhospitable nature contributing to the sublime effect of scenes set in or near water.[78] The opening scene in Kirk's novel furnishes an excellent example of why that is so.

These paragraphs also point to the role of the waters surrounding Carnglass as a symbolic barrier between the real and Gothic worlds. The reader is given only a glimpse of the latter before being transported to MacAskival's clean, quiet office. The conversation that unfolds between him and Logan is pleasant and unhurried; even when touching upon supernatural topics, the

---

[73] Kirk, "A Cautionary Note on the Ghostly Tale," in *Ancestral Shadows*, 403.
[74] Kirk, *Enemies of the Permanent Things*, 36.
[75] Ibid., 105. Kirk describes Humanism and Marxism as being "incompossible," or diametrically opposed concepts.
[76] Kirk, *Old House of Fear*, 142.
[77] Ibid., 3.
[78] Burke, *A Philosophical Enquiry*, 97.

two treat them with the kind of skepticism expected of rational, educated persons. "There's a tale in the island that Carnglass was Eden," MacAskival reports, "man started there, and woman too, I suppose."[79] A little later, he is again careful to attribute a fantastic claim to the presumably ignorant locals who live there: "And they say there are more bogles [i.e., ghosts] stalking through the heather than there are live folk."[80] Here is a clear echo of Johnson's attempts to present himself as a mere recorder and transmitter of local superstitions despite his sympathy for them. MacAskival will not admit to believing such tales but does not want to dismiss them outright, either. As if to emphasize the significance of the change Logan will undergo in traveling from North America to the Hebrides (and perhaps reflecting the indirect influence of Radcliffe), Kirk prolongs the journey, placing a variety of obstacles in his hero's way.

Eventually, Logan does succeed in making it to Carnglass. Kirk draws the scene out for several pages, with the sense of dread and danger rising steadily throughout them. He is right to do so, for it is a key moment in the story, representing the instant Logan crosses the Gothic frontier. Once again, the waters surrounding the island represent a vague but menacing threat. As he faces land, his back to the rising sun, Logan thinks of the "perilous waters," how they could easily sweep him away from his destination—or, worse, dash him dead against the rocks.[81] Logan is genuinely frightened; only once before in his life, we learn, has he ever been so afraid, and that was when he sat in a tomb in Okinawa, hiding from Japanese soldiers. "This fearsome coast was worse than the tomb had been, for here he was utterly alone in a hostile environment."[82] Briefly, he regrets coming and longs to return to his former existence in the States, however dull and unrewarding it may have been.

At last, he reaches the shore and manages to drag the boat up to the tide line before collapsing on the sand in exhaustion. All he has really done is cross a narrow sea, yet Kirk describes the aftermath in terms of a great battle that has left the combatant mentally and physically drained.[83] Trembling with equal measures of fear and relief, he wonders what yet awaits him on the island.

After all, MacAskival had mentioned the possibility that bogles might be wandering the moors—an amusing enough thought from thousands of miles away, but quite a different matter when one is lost in those same moors in the dead of night! From his boss, Logan also hears of several quaint superstitions, which, in hindsight, he probably regrets not taking more seriously at the time.

---

[79] Kirk, *Old House of Fear*, 7.
[80] Ibid., 10.
[81] Ibid., 41.
[82] Ibid., 41-42.
[83] Ibid., 42.

It is rumored, for instance, that one of the MacAskival women had long ago been abducted by a sinister half-man, half-goat creature known as the Gabharfear or Firgower. Also, the locals believe that certain individuals are born with a spot in their foreheads that marks the presence of a "Third Eye," which grants them clairvoyant abilities.[84] This bears a striking resemblance to Johnson's "second sight," and I believe it is more likely than not that the travelog served as a source of inspiration for this idea. Even after departing for Carnglass, Logan continues to receive warnings about the "frightening legends from the past" that are said to haunt his destination.[85] In Glasgow, he learns that the late owner of the Old House of Fear, Donald MacAskival, "dwelt in dread of the wraiths of his fathers" and was rumored to "stalk the empty corridors and chambers" of the dilapidated castle.[86] Any one of these tales might have been running through his mind as he lay shaking on the shore.

The blending of myth and reality is a characteristic feature of the Gothic dating back to Walpole. As Manuel Aguirre observes, the Gothic "is fundamentally a spatial genre [which] articulates its critique of rationalist positions by pitting the familiar reality against another which is irreducible to it."[87] In Kirk's first novel, in stark contrast to his third one and many of his stories, the author remains strictly on the side of "familiar reality." Despite hints to the contrary, there is no confirmation that anything supernatural or ghostly actually happens on Carnglass. The closest he comes to suggesting otherwise is with the character of Edmund Jackman, who is repeatedly compared with, and even identified as, the mythical Firgower or goat-man. "Of course, Dr. Jackman is the Firgower," Mary MacAskival says to Logan, "he'd tell you so himself if he were candid. He has told me so. You saw the hole in his forehead: that is his third eye."[88] Jackman does have a mark on his forehead, and at one point, Logan suspects he might be trying to hypnotize him. In that same conversation, Jackman confesses to suffering from strange visions of Hell.[89] Might he be one of its denizens, let loose to wreak havoc on the living? In the end, he dies as easily as any other man. Whatever else he might be, it is safe to say that Jackman is not the Firgower.

---

[84] Ibid., 12-13.
[85] Person, *Critical Biography*, 138.
[86] Kirk, *Old House of Fear*, 26.
[87] Manuel Aguirre, "Thick Description and the Poetics of the Liminal in Gothic Tales," *Orbis Litterarum: International Review of Literary Studies* 72, no. 4 (August 2017): 299, doi: 10.1111/oli.12138.
[88] Kirk, *Old House of Fear*, 105.
[89] Ibid., 138.

Conservative Gothicism Today

Since they were founded over two hundred years ago, the conservative and Gothic movements have always enjoyed a close but uneasy association. On the one hand, many of the earliest Gothic writers, including Radcliffe, were unabashed moralists, as troubled by the "winds of change, dissolution, and chaos" they detected swirling around eighteenth-century England as Kirk would be in his own time.[90] They had no trouble directing the ghouls and terrifying events of their stories to deliberate, didactic ends. Many contemporary critics, on the other hand, regard Gothicism as a kind of off-shoot of Romanticism, itself a reaction against "the modernizing impulses of the Enlightenment that prioritized rationality, logic, production, objectivity, and control."[91] These Romantic roots of Gothicism seem an ill match for the neoclassical ones preferred by some in the modern conservative movement, an existential conflict that is evident in some of the texts by Samuel Johnson discussed earlier. Despite occasional hints to the contrary, he is no Gothic author. Likewise, many Gothic writers occasionally promoted conservative views in their works but could not accurately be described as conservative. For example, both Edgar Allan Poe and Ray Bradbury wrote ghostly stories that were greatly favored by Kirk, in which vigorous defenses of the permanent things can often be found. However much he may have admired their respective talents and imaginative powers, Kirk, as a Christian conservative, knew that neither shared his exact worldview.[92]

In the twenty-first century, Gothicism remains as popular as ever, as demonstrated by the wide array of Gothic books, shows, and movies produced every year. Many of these texts, however, are more expressive of progressive ideology than of the moral imagination, which raises interesting questions about the future of the movement as it comes to reflect an increasingly materialistic perspective. The recently-canceled *Chilling Adventures of Sabrina*, for instance, claimed to promote tolerance and diversity while featuring a cast of pagan witches who worship Satan and attend Black Masses.[93] Meanwhile, a collection from Ohio State University Press hails the 2017 Gothic horror film

---

[90] David Durant, "Ann Radcliffe and the Conservative Gothic," *Studies in English Literature, 1500 - 1900* 22, no. 3 (Summer 1982): 520, doi: 10.2307/450245.

[91] David Collinson, Owain Smolović Jones, and Keith Grint, "'No More Heroes': Critical Perspectives on Leadership Romanticism," *Organization Studies* 39, no. 11 (2018): 1628, doi: 10.1177/0170840617727784.

[92] Kirk, *Enemies of the Permanent Things*, 135. Poe regarded himself "as something of a revolutionary," Kirk observes.

[93] Jennifer Vineyard, "Real witches and pagans break down Netflix's *Chilling Adventures of Sabrina*," *Syfy.com*, 2018 November 19, https://www.syfy.com/syfywire/chilling-adventures-of-sabrina-netflix-real-witches-pagans-magic.

Get Out for calling attention to "the continuation of slavery and the deformation of the black body and mind in white, so-called progressive America."[94] What remains to be seen is what such texts have to offer in place of the Christian faith as a hermeneutic capable of providing a viable explanation for the existence of supernatural phenomena. How, without turning to failed or abandoned faiths such as paganism, can these progressive Gothic texts possibly hope to explain the existence of ghosts if they deny that of God? And if they decline to offer ghosts in the first place, how scary—how *Gothic*—can they truly be? These are questions that too few contemporary fans of the genre seem willing to ask themselves. One suspects that even fewer would be prepared, let alone brave enough, to venture an answer.

---

[94] "Jordan Peele's *Get Out*," Ohio State Press, https://ohiostatepress.org/books/titles/9780814214275.html.

Chapter 7

Kirk, Evelyn Waugh, and the Art of Political Satire

In a letter written in 1990 to Robert L. Bartley, editor of *The Wall Street Journal*, Russell Kirk expressed his opposition to the then-ongoing Gulf War in unequivocal terms: "Already President Bush and his people are putting into northern Arabia nearly as many men as President Johnson put into South Vietnam at the height of the war in Indo-China. The Catholic bishops did their duty in protesting against a war for petroleum prices." He ends with a rhetorical flourish: "Is President [H. W.] Bush emulating President Johnson? A war for Kuwait? A war for an oil-can!"[1] His disapproval of the war brought him into conflict with the conservative mainstream in America[2] but has since been echoed by many others, including political commentator Pat Buchanan and Andrew J. Bacevich, a soldier turned historian.[3] In any case, Kirk himself was nothing if not consistent in his lifelong opposition to US involvement in foreign conflicts. "Although he was a fervent patriot," Roger Kimball writes, "Kirk believed that all the wars fought by America, the Revolutionary War included, 'might have been averted.'"[4] Nor would his pacifist attitude have surprised readers of his 1966 novel, *A Creature of the Twilight: His Memorials*, "a black comedy about an African civil war" that, as chance would have it, anticipated the outbreak of such a war in Nigeria a few months after it was published.[5] Kirk knew well that life often imitates art and suspected that US involvement in the Middle East would prove no more successful than in his satire of American diplomats and volunteers bumbling about in Africa.

The decision to write a novel of political satire was an unusual one for Kirk. The seasoned author of Gothic fiction had not ventured into the genre in any of his stories written before it and would not return to it again. Perhaps he was

---

[1] Kirk to Robert L. Bartley, 12 November 1990, in *Letters*, 326-27.
[2] See, e.g., Russello, *The Postmodern Imagination of Russell Kirk*, 20.
[3] Andrew J. Bacevich, "Introduction," *The Long War: A New History of U.S. National Security Policy Since World War II*, ed. Andrew J. Bacevich (New York: Columbia University Press, 2007), ix.
[4] Roger Kimball, "Permanent Things: Russell Kirk's Centenary," *The New Criterion* 37, no. 5 (January 2019): 7.
[5] Kirk, *The Sword of Imagination*, 375.

inspired by the "satire boom" of postwar England, when "changing tastes in popular British comedy had begun to generate an unprecedented appetite for mockery and ridicule of the manners, pretensions, and pomposity of Britain's ruling elite …"6 Closer to home, American satirists such as Joseph Heller (*Catch-22*) were producing surreal works that mocked bureaucratic inefficiency and anticipated the rise of the counterculture of the 1960s. But Kirk likely drew greater inspiration from a pair of authors whose conservative sympathies lay closer to his own: the Polish-American novelist Joseph Conrad and Evelyn Waugh, perhaps the finest writer of satires in English in the past century. Between 1904 and 1911, Conrad produced a series of books (*Nostromo, The Secret Agent,* and *Under Western Eyes*) that blended serious social commentary, international political intrigue, and comedic elements. Traces of *A Creature of the Twilight* may be seen in each of them, and Kirk is outspoken in his admiration for Conrad, whom he names one of his "ten exemplary conservatives" in *The Politics of Prudence.*[7]

For whatever reason, Kirk was not as eager to praise Waugh or acknowledge his influence. This is curious because of the strong similarities between *A Creature of the Twilight* and several of Waugh's novels, especially *Scoop*, a satire of Western journalists and bureaucrats that was first published in 1938, and *Black Mischief,* which was published in 1932, and is also set in Africa, but focuses more on education and progressive reform. Indeed, in an otherwise appreciative article on the author, James Baresel criticizes *A Creature of the Twilight* for offering "a politically heavy-handed, non-comic variant on the plot line" of *Scoop*. Although Kirk's novel is more amusing than he gives it credit for being, the plot is indeed remarkably similar to that of Waugh's classic satire.[8] In this chapter, my intention is to compare these novels by Kirk and Waugh in order to illustrate some of the differences between the authors' respective approaches to writing political satire. Given the similarities between their political, social, and religious attitudes and beliefs, it is not surprising that these would overlap in certain respects. What *is* surprising is that Kirk consistently refused to acknowledge Waugh as a possible influence on this book, despite his eagerness to do so even when borrowing from the obscurest authors. I shall end with a possible explanation for why he may have been reluctant to credit Waugh in this case.

---

[6] Stuart Ward, "'No nation could be broker': the satire boom and the demise of Britain's world role," in *British culture and the end of empire*, ed. Stuart Ward (Manchester, England: Manchester University Press, 2001), 91.
[7] Kirk, *The Politics of Prudence*, 73-74.
[8] James Baresel, "Russell Kirk's fiction is unjustly ignored," *Catholic Herald*, 8 August 2019, https://catholicherald.co.uk/russell-kirks-fiction-is-unjustly-ignored/.

Redeeming the Times through Satire

Before discussing these authors' use of satire, it may be helpful to explain what it is. The ancient Romans are typically regarded as the earliest practitioners of satire, though, as with many elements of their culture, Roman satire reveals a strong Hellenic influence. Several of their best-known satirists, including Horace and Persius, claim in their works a "direct connection" between themselves and the Old Comedians of Athens.[9] Originally used to describe any text that contained a random assortment of prose and text, *satire* soon acquired its modern meaning: "use of ridicule, irony, sarcasm, etc., to expose folly or vice or to lampoon an individual."[10] Since Roman times, satire has served an important social function by promoting free speech and protecting the rights of individuals to criticize powerful members of society, though often at the risk of alienating its practitioners. Thus, over the centuries, satirists such as Geoffrey Chaucer, Voltaire, and Mark Twain have continued the practice of ridiculing the foibles of the masses and the great while experiencing varying degrees of success, ostracization—and, sometimes, both. Waugh, the premier satirist of twentieth-century England, typifies this contrast. On the one hand, his books sold well and made him wealthy and famous. On the other, his relentless mockery of friend and foe alike earned him a reputation for "snobbishness, elitism, boorishness, cruelty, misanthropy, and racism."[11]

Waugh established a name for himself with a series of early satires that feature farcical depictions of the new trends and changing mores of contemporary English society. His first novel, *Decline and Fall*, was published in 1928 and parodies several subjects, including the British education and penal systems. His second, *Vile Bodies*, aims at the "Bright Young Things," a "privileged, aristocratic coterie" of young adults whose extravagant parties and other antics were eagerly covered by the press during the interwar period, and of which Waugh, himself, was a member.[12] His later works, though less reliant on humor, still contain satirical elements. For example, in his masterpiece, *Brideshead Revisited*, Waugh employs a framing device through which he laments the rise of "Young England," as represented by the poorly-educated and desensitized

---

[9] Alan Sommerstein, "Hinc Omnis Pendet? Old Comedy and Roman Satire," *Classical World* 105, no. 1 (Fall 2011): 26, *Education Source*.
[10] *Oxford American Desk Dictionary and Thesaurus*, 2nd ed., s.v. "satire."
[11] Michael G. Brennan, *Evelyn Waugh: Fictions, Faith and Family* (London: Bloomsbury Academic, 2013), 136.
[12] Kerrie Holloway, "The Bright Young People of the late 1920s: How the Great War's Armistice influenced those too young to fight," *Journal of European Studies* 45, no. 4 (2015): 317, doi: 10.1177/0047244115599145.

soldier, Hooper.[13] Finally, in his Sword of Honour trilogy (1952-61), Waugh criticizes the Allied powers for what he regarded as their cowardly refusal to stand up to Soviet leader Josef Stalin. "For Waugh," observes Andrew J. Bacevich, "the war that Europeans date from 1939 does not qualify as good, in considerable part because Great Britain chose to wage it. Nor does he deem those who fought or endured the war particularly great. They are merely human …"[14] Guy Crouchback is the jaded hero of this story, who by its end still has sense enough to recognize that he has been offered "the chance of doing a single small act to redeem the times," and wisdom enough to act upon it.[15] This Biblical phrase ("redeem the times") is mentioned by T. S. Eliot in *Ash Wednesday*, and was often used by Kirk, as well.

Scoop is Waugh's fifth novel and fits comfortably into the satirical vein marked out by his early fiction. Its main character is the hapless William Boot, an aristocrat who writes articles on country living for the *Daily Beast* newspaper, which is based in London and favors a highly sensationalized style of reporting that is one of Waugh's primary targets. Due to a misunderstanding, Boot is sent by the paper to report on an unfolding civil war in Ishmaelia, where loyalist forces are battling a communist insurgency. Lord Copper, the owner of the *Beast*, explains the policies that should guide Boot in his reporting of the war: "What the British public wants first, last, and all the time is News. Remember that the [loyalists] are in the right and are going to win. The *Beast* stands by them four square."[16] Fidelity to truth, in other words, is not to be one of Boot's primary concerns as a reporter. Upon arriving in Ishmaelia, he discovers that it is not a main concern of anyone else there, either. His colleagues seem to spend most of their time drinking while searching for that elusive "scoop" they can be the first to report back to their impatient readers in England. Nor are they above inventing news of their own when none is forthcoming. The novel's sardonic view of journalism is aptly summarized by Boot's veteran colleague, Corker, who says, "News is what a chap who does not care much about anything wants to read."[17]

Waugh also satirizes members of the British diplomatic corps, who at the time represented one of the most powerful countries on earth—much as Kirk, thirty years later, would direct his ire towards the well-educated but thoroughly clueless members of the US State Department. Shortly after arriving in Ishmaelia, Boot meets a young Vice-Consul, Bannister, who happens to be an

---

[13] Evelyn Waugh, *Brideshead Revisited* (1944; repr., New York: Back Bay Books, 2012), 9-10.
[14] Andrew J. Bacevich, "My Guy," *Raritan* 39, no. 3 (2020): 59-60.
[15] Evelyn Waugh, *Unconditional Surrender* (1961; repr., New York: Back Bay Books, 201), 245.
[16] Evelyn Waugh, *Scoop* (1937; repr., New York: Back Bay Books, 2012), 49.
[17] Ibid., 80.

old friend of his from school. At dinner later that evening, Bannister tells him a story that is emblematic of both Waugh's understated humor and the sort of bureaucratic ineptitude he targets in the novel:

> See this place, Laku. It's marked as a town of some five thousand inhabitants, fifty miles North of Jacksonburg. Well there never had been such a place. Laku is the Ishmaelite for "I don't know." When the boundary commission were trying to get through to the Soudan in 1898 they made a camp there and asked one of their boys the name of the hill, so as to record it in their log. He said, "Laku," and they've copied it from map to map ever since.[18]

In the best satirical tradition, Waugh is an equal-opportunity offender: British, French, and Africans alike are made to look equally ridiculous. Eventually, Boot manages to score his highly successful scoop through the intervention of a mysterious secret agent, Mr. Baldwin. The war ends shortly after, and Boot is recalled to England as a hero. But the wealth and honors that are his by right devolve upon others—not that he regrets to forgo them. On the contrary, like Bilbo at the end of his long journey through Middle-Earth, Boot is happy just to have made it home to Boot Magna, the ramshackle family estate, and *Lush Places*, his weekly gardening column.

As I have noted, Kirk and Waugh shared a similar worldview, which can be described in general terms as Catholic, traditional, and conservative. Like Kirk, the evidence of Waugh's faith becomes much stronger in his later novels,[19] though Waugh was far more orthodox in practice and creed. Both expressed a preference for rural living, as well as an aversion to modern technology, which occasionally bordered on the Luddite. Kirk was one of the prominent defenders of conservative principles throughout the latter half of the twentieth century, articulating his views in countless essays and speeches. Waugh was primarily a novelist who preferred to keep his personal views to himself. However, his private correspondence reveals a similar concern for the "permanent things," the core values of Western civilization. For instance, in one of his many letters to Nancy Mitford, a lifelong friend and fellow novelist, Waugh expresses an admiration for hierarchy,[20] which accords with Kirk's defense of "artificial

---

[18] Ibid., 121-22.
[19] Laura Coffey, "Evelyn Waugh's Country House Trinity: Memory, History, and Catholicism in 'Brideshead Revisited,'" *Literature and History* 15, no. 1 (2006): 63, doi: 10.7227/lh.15.1.4.
[20] Evelyn Waugh to Nancy Mitford, 8 January 1952, in *The Letters of Evelyn Waugh*, ed. Mark Amory (New Haven, CT: Ticknor & Fields, 1980), 364. Waugh writes to his lifelong friend, "... I am afraid you are right when you say that there are no ladies & gentlemen now. It was a most important distinction basic to English health & happiness."

aristocracy" in America.[21] In a recent article, Mark Zunac describes Waugh in terms that could just as easily be applied to Kirk: "Among so many other things, Evelyn Waugh was a steadfast defender of a common, universal humanistic tradition, and devoted much of his life and work to maintaining the ever-narrowing divide between civilization and the anarchic forces that relentlessly threaten it."[22] Whereas Kirk regarded this almost hopeless task cheerfully, Waugh was prone to bouts of moodiness and despair. Perhaps his preference for satire can be regarded as a sort of coping mechanism. Unlike Waugh, Kirk is remembered fondly by almost everyone who knew him and would not have needed to turn to his fictional worlds for jovial companionship.

In their political satire, as in most of their fiction, both authors drew heavily from their own lives. *Brideshead Revisited* and *Sword of Honour* are based on Waugh's years at Oxford and in the British army, respectively; for *Scoop* and *Black Mischief*, he relied upon his experiences as a correspondent for the *Daily Mail*, on behalf of which he covered the Second Italo-Abyssinian War of 1935-36.[23] These experiences are described in detail in his letters, diary, and a work of non-fiction, *Waugh in Abyssinia*, which was published in 1936. Abyssinia, clearly, is the model for *Black Mischief*'s Kingdom of Azania, as well as *Scoop*'s oligarchic Republic of Ishmaelia, which is said to be located in "The Heart of the Dark Continent."[24] Kirk also often turned to real-life friends and experiences for material to be used in his stories and novels, as he readily admits throughout his memoirs. It seems likely that the African kingdom of Hamnegri in *A Creature of the Twilight* is based on places Kirk visited during a 1963 tour of North Africa with his friend, Thomas Molnar. For example, a description of dancing Berber tribe members offered by Mary Jo Travers in a letter to her sister closely matches Kirk's encounter with the same outside the walls of Marrakesh.[25]

Both Waugh and Kirk were conservative Christians, then, who employed political satire in their attempts to redeem the times. Whereas Waugh made frequent use of satire throughout his long career, Kirk only wrote in this style

---

[21] Kirk, *The Conservative Mind*, 220-21.
[22] Mark Zunac, "'There Was Something Gentlemanly about Your Painting': Art and Beauty's Truth in Waugh's *Brideshead Revisited*," *Renascence: Essays on Values in Literature* 7, no. 12 (Spring 2019): 96, *MLA International Bibliography with Full Text*.
[23] Ann Pasternak Slater, *Evelyn Waugh* (Tavistock, England: Northcote House Publishers, 2016), 62.
[24] Waugh, *Scoop*, 94.
[25] Kirk, *A Creature of the Twilight*, 171. Kirk's travels through Africa are described in *The Sword of Imagination*, 278-85.

once, in his "baroque romance" of a second novel.[26] The novels were written nearly thirty years apart; coincidentally, Kirk's was published the same year that Waugh died. All of this begs the question of whether Kirk was familiar with, and possibly influenced by, *Scoop*. One will not encounter the name of Waugh in many of the unpublished letters or manuscripts kept at the Kirk Center, nor is he mentioned either in Kirk's published correspondence or in his memoirs. However, Kirk *does* refer to Waugh in some of his other works, often in a highly appreciative manner. For example, in *Reclaiming a Patrimony*, a collection of lectures delivered by Kirk during the early 1980s, he uses *Helena* (Waugh's 1958 historical novel about the mother of Emperor Constantine) to illustrate a point about architecture and beauty, a dear and frequent theme of his.[27] Finally, in *Redeeming the Time*, one of Kirk's last books and a companion to the more politically-orientated *Politics of Prudence*, he includes Waugh among a select group of contemporary practitioners of the moral imagination, along with T. S. Eliot, Robert Frost, William Faulkner, and W. B. Yeats.[28] Kirk certainly read and admired Waugh, so it is possible that, whether consciously or not, he took some inspiration from him, as well. Indeed, my comparison of *Scoop* and *A Creature of the Twilight* will begin with a look at the many similarities they share.

Similarities Between *Scoop* and *A Creature of the Twilight*

One cannot help but notice, for instance, the strong resemblance between the fictional settings of these two books, which begins with their very names: Ishmaelia (*Scoop*) and Hamnegri (*A Creature of the Twilight*). The former refers to Ishmael, the first son of Abraham, patriarch of the Jews. An angel warns his mother, the handmaiden Hagar, that he will grow up to be "a wild man; his hand *will be* against every man, and every man's hand against him; and he shall dwell in the presence of all his brethren."[29] As Carol Bakhos points out, there is a long tradition in rabbinic literature of associating the descendants of Ishmael with the Arabs, which dates back to antiquity.[30] Waugh's Ishmaelites are not Muslim, but, much as Ishmael is set apart from his brother, Isaac, so are the Ishmaelites set apart from the rest of the civilized world due to their violent natures, their greed, and their ignorance, which has left them susceptible to exploitation by outside forces. These are inherited flaws, Waugh warns, dating back to the founding of

---

[26] This is how the book is described on the dust jacket of the original edition published in1966 by Fleet. In the dedication, Kirk also refers to it as a "baroque work of fancy."
[27] Russell Kirk, *Reclaiming a Patrimony: A Collection of Lectures by Russell Kirk* (Washington, D. C.: The Heritage Foundation, 1982), 90.
[28] Kirk, *Redeeming the Time*, 71.
[29] Gen. 16:12 (KJV).
[30] Carol Bakhos, *Ishmael on the Border: Rabbinic Portrayals of the First Arab* (Albany, NY: State University of New York Press, 2006), 68-69.

their tribe and divinely ordained, which no amount of Western interference can hope to improve or alleviate. In the remote highlands far from the capital city, the natives happily pursue their "traditional callings of bandit, slave or gentleman of leisure."[31] Whatever one may think of such a lifestyle, it is better not to disturb it—even and especially with the aim of improving it. Unfortunately, this is a lesson that the various foreign powers scrambling for control of Ishmaelia must learn the hard way.

Kirk also takes the name of his fictional state, Hamnegri, from an outcast figure in the Bible. Ham is a son of Noah, who survives the great flood but does something to his father later that causes his entire race of descendants to be cursed. *What* Ham has done is a question of long-standing debate; the text only relates that he "saw the nakedness of his father and told his two brethren without."[32] Whatever his indiscretion, it is Ham's son, Canaan, who ends up bearing the brunt of Noah's ire; he and his offspring are cursed to a life of servitude and disgrace. During the Middle Ages, Ham was popularly linked with Cain, the first murderer, and fratricide; more importantly, he was also regarded as the progenitor of all humans living in Africa.[33] Thus, as in Waugh's Ishmaelia, the descendants of Hamnegri are depicted as forgotten and forsaken, with a propensity for violence and disorder that runs deep in the blood. The novel opens with the country already embroiled in a bitter civil war and the deposed Sultan dead, having been disemboweled alive. Kirk's decision to name his fictional state Hamnegri is one of "dozens of plays-on-words that make the novel hilarious," according to John Willson, and that is true enough.[34] But perhaps some of the credit should go to Waugh since the name "Ishmaelia" seems like an obvious influence.

Though they were written thirty years apart, the geopolitical situation described in both novels is remarkably similar. A civil war erupts in Africa between traditionalist and progressive forces, which serves as a proxy for the larger conflict between industrialized powers. In *Scoop*, it is the English and Russians pulling the strings; the conflict in *A Creature of the Twilight* is cosmopolitan but essentially boils down to a similar divide between the democratic West and socialist East, represented by the US and China,

---

[31] Waugh, *Scoop*, 96.
[32] Gen. 9:22.
[33] Robert Kenny, "From the Curse of Ham to the Curse of Nature: The Influence of Natural Selection on the Debate on Human Unity before the Publication of 'The Descent of Man,'" *The British Journal for the History of Science* 40, no. 3 (September 2007): 370, https://www.jstor.org/stable/4500748.
[34] John Willson, "A Foreign Policy for (Probably Not Very Many) Americans," *The Russell Kirk Center*, 3 March 2009, https://kirkcenter.org/essays/a-foreign-policy/.

respectively. Ishmaelia is nominally a republic, though one in which the presidency and all three branches of government are tightly controlled by a single family, the Jacksons. The Jacksons are not native to the land but were imported to rule over it from—of all places—Alabama. They govern "with a good-humored, though somewhat despotic, inefficiency,"[35] thus resembling the dynastic sultany that, until very recently, had ruled over Hamnegri in Kirk's book. It is, in fact, with the son of the late deposed Sultan Ali that Manfred Arcane is allied. Arcane, who is really nothing more than a shrewd mercenary in this book, has no more right to rule over Hamnegri than the Jacksons do over Ishmaelia. Yet both represent the only hope for peace of these embattled states.

Waugh and Kirk use satire to effectively criticize the imposition of democracy by Western powers upon countries with incongruous attitudes, practices, and traditions. Wildly disparate groups inhabit the dangerous lands that surround the capital city of Ishmaelia: cannibals, "furious nomads," and an "inhospitable race of squireens," or small landowners; they share no common form of government, "nor tie of language, history, habit or belief," yet have been linked through the arbitrary drawing of borders and a Western desire for order, however precariously established or maintained.[36] Finding it inconvenient to hold a national election every five years, the Jacksons send out a representative to isolated parts of the country, where illiterate tribe members are induced to cast votes through the promise of food and alcohol. Arcane, similarly, proves all too willing to cynically exploit democratic ideals for his ends. Wanting to humanize his boss but without sacrificing any of his absolute authority, Arcane convinces the sultan to add "Hereditary President" to his list of illustrious titles. Early in the war, during a meeting to discuss strategy with his top leadership, Arcane speculates sarcastically about further steps that might be taken in that direction: "Construct a constitution on parchment for the United Commonwealth of Hamnegri? Bill of Rights and all? … Well, it would be no worse fraud than most constitutions today."[37] In both Ishmaelia and Hamnegri, democracy is simply another tool by which the helpless and powerless can be exploited.

The views expressed in these works reflect their authors' ambivalence on the subject. That is not to say that Waugh or Kirk were opposed to democracy; rather, they shared a concern about inherent flaws in this system of government—a concern echoed by many other conservatives throughout the centuries and aptly summarized by C. S. Lewis in a 1959 follow-up to his popular *Screwtape Letters*.

---

[35] Hena Maes-Jelinek, *Criticism of Society in the English Novel between the Wars* (1971; repr., Paris: Presses universitaires de Liège, 2013), 420
[36] Waugh, *Scoop*, 93-94.
[37] Kirk, *A Creature of the Twilight*, 38.

In "Screwtape Proposes a Toast," the titular devil explains how the meaning of *democracy* has become corrupted in modern times; strictly speaking, it should refer only to "the name of a political system, even a system of voting," and have little to do with ethics or morality.[38] However, demonic influence has led to a shift in the meaning of the word in the popular consciousness: the idea that "men should be equally treated" has been transformed into "a factual belief that all men *are* equal," resulting in a simultaneous desire to turn that belief into reality.[39] Through social pressure and, eventually, legal and political reform, *everyone* in a democracy is encouraged to conform to the mediocre standards attainable by the least promising and talented members of society. Waugh and Kirk believed these trends to be already at work in their respective homelands. In 1946, the former confided in his diary the fear that "England as a great power is done for, that the loss of possessions, the claim of the English proletariat to be a privileged race, sloth and envy, must produce increasing poverty; that this time the cutting down will start at the top until only a proletariat and a bureaucracy survive."[40] Kirk, of course, was far less despondent, arguing that "[e]ternal vigilance and incessant criticism" by conservatives could yet prevent "the perversion of a democratic society into a sea of anonymous beings, social droplets, deprived of true family, true freedom, and true purpose …"[41] In countries without a strong conservative tradition, such as in the fictional realms depicted in *Scoop* and *A Creature of the Twilight*, this leveling trend cannot be resisted so easily.

Some of the authors' sharpest satire is reserved for their blundering fellow citizens, who are oblivious to local customs and care little about the long-term well-being of the natives. The highest-ranking representative of His Majesty's Government in Ishmaelia envies Boot for what he imagines to be the higher pay and glamorous lifestyle of a professional journalist. Soon after, Bannister patiently explains to him the official line towards the civil war: though recognizing the Jacksons as "a pack of rogues," the English stand "to lose quite a lot if they start a Soviet state here." He also confesses to being a "keen supporter" of the brutal and corrupt local prison system because it saves him from having to deal with annoying suppliants and perform some of the basic responsibilities of his job.[42] The criticism of British diplomats is even stronger in *Black Mischief*: its British minister is depicted as an incompetent failure whose greatest

---

[38] C. S. Lewis, "Screwtape Proposes a Toast," in *The Screwtape Letters* (1942; repr., New York: HarperCollins, 2001), 197.
[39] Ibid. Emphasis in the original.
[40] Evelyn Waugh, *The Diaries of Evelyn Waugh*, ed. Michael Davie (Boston: Little, Brown and Company, 1976), 661.
[41] Kirk, *The Conservative Mind*, 212.
[42] Waugh, *Scoop*, 183-90.

diplomatic triumph is the "nearly successful" building of a road from the legation to the capital city.[43] In both novels, Waugh uses satire to expose both "the barrenness of civilization" and the imperialist goal of spreading it to other countries.[44] This is also a primary concern of Kirk's and may help to explain his use of this otherwise unfamiliar genre. Government officials are a frequent target of his Gothic fiction, but only in satire could he turn them into genuine objects of ridicule.

In comparison to his British counterparts, the US government's top representative in Hamnegri is a much less comical figure. "Hard-hitting" T. William Tallstall, a potential candidate for higher office, is an expert in "negotiation, compromise, and democratic ideology," according to crack journalist Jack Symmonds.[45] Tallstall has the respect of the international press corps, his colleagues at the State Department, and most of the major players in Africa. However, his grasp of the political and strategic situation on the ground is even worse than that of the British diplomats. Even though the Progressives are fanatical Marxists, he is surprised when they promptly betray him after their initial successes, confiscating the property of American citizens and sending out feelers to the Russians.[46] Still, he has sense enough to recognize in Manfred Arcane the presence of a truly great man, one with whom the US could enjoy a long and mutually beneficial relationship. Kirk nonetheless mocks Tallstall for assuming a stereotypically belligerent pose in his initial appearances. Early in the war, he recommends military action to preserve the victory of the Progressives: "I hope that it may be possible to send a United Nations force to restore democracy in Kalidu ..." he writes blithely. If not, then perhaps "unilateral American intervention" will do.[47]

It is telling that the villainous party in both books is inspired by Marxist ideology. As is evident throughout his *Sword of Honour* trilogy, Waugh recognized the danger posed by the socialists and communists of his era long before the horrors of Stalinism had made it obvious to others that, in choosing to ally with the Russians against Nazi Germany, the West had traded one existential threat for another. Kirk, for his part, agreed with the Spanish-American philosopher George Santayana that Marxism represented the "natural progression" of modern liberalism, such as that espoused by Jeremy Bentham and John Stuart Mill, and was one of the most serious threats to contemporary

---

[43] Evelyn Waugh, *Black Mischief* (1932; repr., New York: Back Bay Books, 2012), 55.
[44] Leszek S. Kolek, "*Black Mischief* as a Comic Structure," in *Evelyn Waugh: New Directions*, ed. Alain Blayac (London: Macmillan, 1992), 10.
[45] Kirk, *A Creature of the Twilight*, 61-64.
[46] Ibid., 176.
[47] Ibid., 54.

Christendom.[48] Both authors take a special delight in ridiculing the overblown speech patterns typical of would-be revolutionaries. The short-lived "Soviet State of Ishmaelia" only endures for a single night but has time enough to issue a manifesto calling for the "development of mineral resources of the workers by the workers for the workers" and the "liquidation" of the Jackson family.[49] Kirk provides the reader with numerous hilarious examples of Marxist bombast, including a passage from the venerable Soviet newspaper, *Pravda*, that refers to Tallstall as a "henchman of the American president," himself a "Wall Street hireling."[50] A radio broadcast from the Hamnegrian Radio Awala begins with a call for "Death to reactionaries, exploiters, monarchists, capitalists, colonialists, adventurists, and creatures of the twilight!"[51] With such farcical opponents and equally ridiculous allies, the novelists' critique of imperialism comes into sharp relief.

Differences Between *Scoop* and *A Creature of the Twilight*

Despite the many similarities between *Scoop* and *A Creature of the Twilight*, they also differ in several key respects. Both are satirical but rely on an entirely different kind of humor: *Scoop* is more absurdist in tone, whereas *A Creature of the Twilight* is frequently mordant. Those who knew Waugh during his adventures as a war correspondent in Abyssinia recall him as something of a practical joker,[52] and much of that spirit is evident throughout *Scoop*, undoubtedly the more successful of the two books in terms of pure comedy. Waugh's wit remains razor-sharp even in the gentle framing scenes set in England. At a dinner banquet to celebrate Boot's return from overseas, the place of honor is assumed at the last minute by his much older, far more garrulous uncle. Lord Cooper's speech about his new ("young in years") colleague will leave most readers in stitches.[53] Kirk's fun at the expense of harmlessly ignorant characters such as Tallstall or Mary Jo Travers notwithstanding, there is little situational humor in *A Creature of the Twilight*. Most of the novel's comedy comes straight from the mouth of its punning protagonist, Manfred Arcane. His highly plagiarized motivational speech on the eve of an important battle is a

---

[48] Kirk, *The Conservative Mind*, 446-47.
[49] Waugh, *Scoop*, 202. The exact quote calls for the Jacksons being "liquidated."
[50] Kirk, *A Creature of the Twilight*, 105.
[51] Ibid., 194.
[52] Michael B. Salwen, "Evelyn Waugh in Ethiopia: the novelist as war correspondent and journalism critic," *Journalism Studies* 2, no. 1 (2001): 17, doi: 10.1080/14616700120021775.
[53] Waugh, *Scoop*, 272-73.

notable highlight.⁵⁴ Though undoubtedly charismatic and beloved by most of those who knew him well, Kirk was not especially known for having a keen sense of humor. The mannered, allusive style of humor featured in his lone work of comedy is probably a good approximation of his own.

Other differences between the two novels include their respective settings and tones. Boot's travails in *Scoop* take him from rural England by plane to France and thence by sea to the shores of Africa. After an overland journey by train, he finally arrives in Ishmaelia. Through it all, he encounters a variety of ridiculous characters and must repeatedly extricate himself from the most farcical situations. As in much modern satire, Naomi Milthorpe observes, mistaken identity is a recurring theme: "From grebe to badger, and from Boot to Boot, words, objects, people, places and events are, in *Scoop*, continually mistaken for something they are not."⁵⁵ Kirk's novel is set entirely in Africa, by contrast; indeed, almost all of the main action takes place within the single country of Hamnegri. The multiple narrators and epistolary style featured in certain chapters of *A Creature of the Twilight* result in a highly variable, unpredictable tone, through which, truth be told, the author "moves skillfully" and "quite convincingly."⁵⁶ Several characters, including Arcane, have been personally affected by the Holocaust, and though their suffering provides Kirk with an opportunity to explore his interest in delayed justice and retribution, the digressions seem rather incongruous in what is supposed to be a comedy (albeit a "black" one).

Perhaps the most important difference between *Scoop* and *A Creature of the Twilight* is in their respective protagonists and the type of virtue or heroism they represent. Between Boot and Arcane, the former is much less interesting and impressive: timid and inexperienced, he is easily manipulated by others and often finds himself stuck in situations that could have easily been avoided had he been willing to stand his ground or speak up in his defense. After arriving in Ishmaelia, he begins a flirtatious dalliance with a young married German, Kätchen, who happily leaves him the moment her husband reappears on the scene—but not before milking Boot out of several pounds worth of clothing and other gifts. It is obvious where the relationship is headed the first time she hits him up for money. However, Boot remains oblivious, even as her final letter to

---

⁵⁴ Kirk, *A Creature of the Twilight*, 190-93. Arcane is praised for displaying a "burst of original eloquence," though most readers will recognize the allusions to famous speeches in history.
⁵⁵ Naomi Milthorpe, *Evelyn Waugh's Satire: Texts and Contexts* (Lanham, MA: Fairleigh Dickinson University Press, 2016), 72.
⁵⁶ Person, *Critical Biography*, 145.

him mentions an urgent need for £50, preferably in francs.[57] However, despite his flaws, the reader cannot help but admire Boot's dogged optimism and imperturbability. He has little trouble getting along with almost everyone he meets, which testifies to his understated charm. Waugh may have regarded him as a sort of alter-ego for himself, as Bill Deedes, who knew him in Abyssinia, suggests.[58]

Arcane, the self-styled "Father of Shadows," is almost the exact opposite of Boot. Suave, urbane, and sophisticated, Arcane is a seasoned military commander and a shrewd negotiator. Not only does he succeed in outwitting the Progressive forces while defying the whims of the American government, he somehow manages to engineer his private revenge on the former Nazis who had killed his lover in a concentration camp. Even his close comrades hold him in awe: "I serve Arcane because I have not any other place to go," writes one, "and because—why not say it?—I'm scared to death of him."[59] Unlike Boot, Arcane is completely at ease in the company of the opposite sex; indeed, most of the women he meets invariably find themselves attracted to him despite their very considerable differences in age. In *A Creature of the Twilight*, this applies to his relationship with both Mary Jo Travers and Melchiora, the beautiful yet deadly Sicilian who is absolutely devoted to him (and whom he marries in a subsequent work; I discuss their relationship in greater detail in Chapter 9).

Arcane is nothing like Boot, then, but there are certain intriguing parallels between him and Mr. Baldwin, the enigmatic figure in *Scoop* who plays a deciding, though shadowy, role in overthrowing the Progressives and restoring the Jacksonian government to power. Boot has several encounters with Baldwin during the journey over to Ishmaelia. It is never clear where he is going or why, and Boot is too polite to enquire about such matters, anyway. But after running into Baldwin in the dining car of his train, he is impressed by the man's meticulous style of dress and impeccable manners. "William wondered what his nationality could be and thought perhaps Turkish. Then he spoke, in a voice that was not exactly American nor Levantine nor Eurasian nor Latin nor Teuton, but a blend of them all."[60] Baldwin seems to be an expert in everything, from French wines to British hunting dogs to pre-war German poetry. Arcane, too, is a good dresser with "beautiful manners," who speaks several languages, and is

---

[57] Waugh, *Scoop*, 275.
[58] Bill Deedes, "Evelyn Waugh in Ethiopia: reflections and recollections," *Journalism Studies* 2, no. 1 (February 2001): 29, doi: 10.1080/14616700120021784.
[59] Kirk, *A Creature of the Twilight*, 67.
[60] Waugh, *Scoop*, 66.

able to discourse confidently on military, philosophical, or literary subjects.[61] His "swarthy" appearance often makes it difficult for others to identify his nationality: Travers guesses him to be, simply, "European," but he later tells her that his father was a wealthy English lord and his mother was of mixed Central European ancestry.[62] Accompanying Baldwin is a "soldierly giant" of a companion: the indefatigable Cuthbert, who is "very courageous" and "adequately armed."[63] One is reminded of Arcane's imposing bodyguard, the dreadful, mutilated Nemo Arpad.

Black Mischief features a character who resembles Arcane even more closely than Baldwin. He is Basil Seal, its "deeply attractive" protagonist: an adventurer, playboy, and short-lived Member of Parliament who bursts with "vitality and ambition."[64] The novel was first published in 1932 and is set in the fictional African kingdom of Azania, where an Oxford-educated emperor, Seth, dreams of transforming his backward state into a modern and progressive paradise. He employs Seal, a former classmate who has failed in almost every one of his previous endeavors, to help him. As Minister of Modernization, Seal comes to wield almost unchecked power over the whole of Azania, enjoying a position that resembles that of Arcane in Hamnegri. Like Arcane, he soon learns that holding on to power will require the occasional swallowing of his pride, not to mention his tongue, especially in response to the often ludicrous demands of an employer whose very word is enough to ensure one's execution.[65] For example, Seth, at one point, commissions Seal to arrange advertising for a "Birth Control Gala," meant to promote the use of prophylactics during sexual intercourse. The ignorant natives mistake Seal's poster as an advertisement for fecundity instead and begin buying tickets for the gala in droves. Seal, who knows better than to correct Seth's understanding of the reason for the gala's success, writes an article praising the locals' desire to follow the emperor's lead "in the cause of Progress and the New Age."[66] Arcane, similarly, spends much of his time composing propaganda to be dissembled through various means, including newspaper articles, radio broadcasts, and diplomatic cables. Thus,

---

[61] Kirk, *A Creature of the Twilight*, 79.
[62] Ibid., 23, 237.
[63] Waugh, *Scoop*, 64-69.
[64] Peter Wilkin, "The Temptation of Evelyn Waugh: Portrait of the Artist as Tory Anarchist," *English Studies: A Journal of English Language and Literature* 97, no. 7-8 (November 2016): 756, 2020, doi: 10.1080/0013838X.2016.1198119.
[65] Cf. Kirk, *A Creature of the Twilight*, 12, 252. Arcane had to leave Hamnegri after falling under suspicion due to rumors spread by his political opponents. He tried to warn the sultan before the outbreak of war, but was rebuffed.
[66] Waugh, *Black Mischief*, 172.

although Arcane bears similarities to Boot, Baldwin, and Seal, he is not exactly like any one of them but can best be described, perhaps, as an amalgamation of all.

Scoop and *A Creature of the Twilight* both end on a happy note for their respective heroes. Though those notes happen to be in very different keys, it is remarkable how faithful they are to one of the standard tenets of conservatism, as espoused by Kirk: that conservatives, while respecting the need for permanence and change in any society, tend to prefer the former, all other things being equal. "With Lord Falkland, they say, 'When it is not necessary to change, it is necessary not to change.'"[67] And so, despite all of the remarkable occurrences that befall Boot during his ill-advised foray into journalism, the closing pages of *Scoop* find him right back where he started: at the family home in Boot Magna, writing gentle essays on the habits of country animals to a small but devoted readership. *A Creature of the Twilight*, likewise, ends with Manfred Arcane once again firmly in control of Hamnegri, just as he was before the Civil War began. He has suffered a bullet wound and the loss of a few comrades but is otherwise none the worse for wear. The restoration of the narrative to an earlier time is one of the marked features of conservative satire, as Frank Palmeri remarks: "If the utopian vision implied by a satire looks backward towards a golden age in the past, and if it subjects to satiric parody a recently emerging, subversive position, then the satiric work defines its position as reactionary or conservative."[68] Whatever differences exist between *Scoop*, *Black Mischief*, and *A Creature of the Twilight*, no one can deny that they are all, at heart, deeply conservative works.

"That Pomposity Edmund Gosse"

But surely, these books have more in common than can be explained as mere coincidence. Given Kirk's familiarity with Waugh and his eagerness to acknowledge the work of his predecessors, it is curious that he never mentions the probable influence of *Scoop* or *Black Mischief* on his second novel. Perhaps his antipathy to one of Waugh's relatives may help to explain this uncharacteristic reticence. In 1964, Waugh published the first part of his autobiography, *A Little Learning*, which covers the early years of his life and "depicts his childhood environs as a pastoral idyll."[69] Much like Kirk, Waugh begins his memoir by attempting to trace his family tree back over several generations, making note

---

[67] Kirk, *Concise Guide to Conservatism*, 6.
[68] Frank Palmeri, *Satire in Narrative: Petronius, Swift, Gibbon, Melville, and Pynchon* (Austin, TX: University of Texas Press, 1990), 6.
[69] Muireann Leech, "'Do Not Analyse the Self': A Little Learning as Evelyn Waugh's Catholic Anti-Autobiography," *Prose Studies: History, Theory, Criticism* 37, no. 2 (August 2015): 118, doi: 10.1080/01440357.2015.1084708.

of several illustrious ancestors, including William Morgan, an important figure in actuarial science, and Lord Cockburn, a Scottish lawyer and writer. Also among the list of notable Waugh forebears is Thomas Gosse, an "itinerant portrait-painter" and writer of unpublished "allegorical epics" with titles such as *The Attempts of the Cainite Giants to reconquer Paradise*.[70] But it is Gosse's son who would prove more interesting for Kirk: Sir Edmund Gosse was a writer and critic who came to hold considerable sway over the cultural landscape of late Victorian England. Amanda L. French credits the younger Grosse as the person "most responsible for introducing the French forms, including the villanelle, into Anglophone poetry"[71]–an important development for later Symbolists and Modernists, including Ezra Pound and T. S. Eliot.

In fact, Gosse's influence was at its apex when the young Eliot arrived in England and began to establish himself as a poet. Kirk's description of those years can be found in Chapter 2 of *Eliot and His Age* and contains several unflattering references to Gosse, which are atypical of his generally charitable and genial approach, even towards subjects he dislikes. Kirk introduces him sarcastically as "England's arbiter of literary taste," noting that he was "fiercely detested" by the younger generation of poets whose fates he partially controlled.[72] A few paragraphs later, he refers to "that pomposity Sir Edmund" and quotes almost gleefully from disparaging remarks about Gosse made by Eliot, Aldous Huxley, and Waugh himself.[73] To Kirk, Gosse represented everything about the old, established order, which Eliot had to overcome in the attempt to revitalize Western civilization. It seems as if he could not forgive him for failing to recognize the brilliance of the young and still-unproven poet, who would later become his dear friend. His unwillingness to acknowledge Waugh as a possible influence on the writing of his second novel, then, might be due to his strong dislike for Waugh's distant relative, Sir Edmund Gosse.

If true, this would be most uncharacteristic of Kirk, who was known to deal fairly with even the most intransigent ideological opponents, such as the libertarians Frank S. Meyer and Frank Chodorov. "No matter the battle," writes Bradley J. Birzer, "Kirk always treated his opponents–if not always the school that opponent represented–humanely."[74] With any luck, there are unpublished letters or other materials by Kirk that will someday shed further light on the

---

[70] Evelyn Waugh, *A Little Learning: An Autobiography* (Boston: Little, Brown & Company, 1964), 12-13.
[71] Amanda L. French, "Edmund Gosse and the Stubborn Villanelle Blunder," *Victorian Poetry* 48, no. 2 (Summer 2010): 244, doi:10.1353/vp.0.0104.
[72] Kirk, *Eliot and His Age*, 12.
[73] Ibid., 13.
[74] Birzer, *American Conservative*, 325.

matter. Fortunately, Kirk was more forthcoming about the sources that influenced his next book; in fact, he named most of its characters after poems and plays of Eliot, whose exploration of "timeless moments" in *Four Quartets* also serves as a major theme. In the next chapter, I will explore characterization in Kirk's third and last novel, *Lord of the Hollow Dark*.

Chapter 8

T. S. Eliot and *Lord of the Hollow Dark*

In his memoirs, Russell Kirk is often at pains to show that he did not take the writing of fiction too seriously. He claims that he wrote his first novel, *Old House of Fear*, "mostly for his entertainment."[1] Despite its surprising success, which led to a short-lived revival of Gothic romance, he resisted calls for an immediate follow-up. "But Kirk had written the romance for his amusement," he explains, referring to himself in the third person, "and he wrote to improve rather than to entertain; years would pass before he would turn out another novel."[2] That novel is mentioned only briefly, as are the next and most, if not all, of his short stories. It is almost as if, in reflecting upon the course of his life, Kirk wished to dwell upon his fictional output as little as possible. However, some of the unpublished papers held at the Kirk Center tell a different story about Kirk's expectations for his fiction, especially regarding his last novel, *Lord of the Hollow Dark*. In advance of its 1979 publication by St. Martin's Press, he drew up several prospectuses intended to promote the book, which was known by a variety of titles, including *Essences* and *That Archaic Smile*. In one of these prospectuses, Kirk writes that he expects it to be "as readable" and to possess "more enduring significance" than *Old House of Fear*.[3] Some of the letters he wrote in the years leading up to its publication are full of hopeful references to this work-in-progress.[4]

Forty years after its initial publication, *Lord of the Hollow Dark* is still waiting to catch on with readers. Unlike *Old House of Fear*, which Kirk claimed to be his best-selling book, or his short stories, which earned him several awards and a reputation as a distinguished author of Gothic fiction, *Lord of the Hollow Dark* has never been commercially successful nor critically popular. It is a dark and thematically complicated work, as one of its few contemporary champions admits:

> *Lord of the Hollow Dark* places almost every figure to appear in a T.S. Eliot play and poem in a Scottish castle for the few days leading up to

---

[1] Kirk, *The Sword of Imagination*, 250.
[2] Ibid., 251.
[3] Russell Kirk, prospectus for "That Archaic Smile," 16 February 1977, Box 88, Russell Kirk Center for Cultural Renewal.
[4] See, e.g., Kirk to Jim Flowe, 6 May 1979, Box 50, Russell Kirk Center for Cultural Renewal.

Ash Wednesday. Also bringing in several of his own literary characters, the novel looks at the lengths to which evil will go to achieve its ends. The story itself revolves around the sacrifice of a baby for a Black Mass.[5]

Bradley J. Birzer points here to one of the novel's unique features: the fact that all of its main characters adopt pseudonyms taken from the works of T. S. Eliot. Given Eliot's enduring popularity among biographers, readers, and critics and the general interest in Kirk as one of the foremost conservative thinkers of the twentieth century, it is curious that no one has yet undertaken a formal study of the names in this book. *Lord of the Hollow Dark* may be obscure, after all, but the same cannot be said of Eliot or Kirk himself.

My purpose in this chapter is to address this oversight by exploring Kirk's motivations in assigning each character the specific pseudonym he did. If, as I have argued previously, Kirk put a great deal of thought into even the most cursory of allusions, it stands to reason that he did not choose these names lightly, especially since the cast of characters is so small. For some characters, the names have obvious significance. For instance, the fiendish cult leader, "Mr. Appollinax," is based on one of Eliot's most repellent creations. With others, Kirk's intentions are harder to discern, as is the case with the novel's protagonist, Manfred Arcane, who is dubbed after the old fool depicted in "Gerontion." Overall, I believe that the use of pseudonyms in this work represents the height of Kirk's allusive, dialogic literary style, as described in Chapter 2. By assigning each character a name based on a poem or play by Eliot, Kirk forces the reader to engage with the poet, as one cannot properly understand the novel without referring to the works cited so conspicuously therein. As much as any other work of his, *Lord of the Hollow Dark* illustrates Kirk's lifelong desire to help "refurbish what Edmund Burke called the 'wardrobe of a moral imagination,'"[6] and guide his reader to an understanding of the permanent things, however unsuited those aims might have been to satisfy popular tastes.

The Age of Eliot

For as important a writer as Kirk believed Eliot to be, the latter had a surprisingly modest output of creative works: only a few dozen poems and plays were published during his lifetime, and Eliot never dabbled in novel writing or short fiction. Even so, the impact of his verse is undeniable and

---

[5] Bradley J. Birzer, "When Russell Kirk was Really Scary," *The American Conservative*, 19 October 2018, https://www.theamericanconservative.com/articles/when-russell-kirk-was-really-scary/.
[6] Kirk, *Enemies of the Permanent Things*, 2.

endures even into the present, when poetry has ceased to be widely read or discussed. His 1922 masterpiece, *The Waste Land*, had a seismic effect on the post-war literary scene and quickly attained "a kind of eminence from which it has never been dislodged."[7] After his conversion to Christianity in 1927, Eliot's poetry became increasingly religious, as is evident in *Ash Wednesday* and *Four Quartets*; he also began to write for the stage, producing several popular and well-received dramas, including *Murder in the Cathedral*, *The Cocktail Party*, and *The Confidential Clerk*. He also exerted considerable influence as a literary and social critic, contributing essays and books on art, tradition, and culture that are still read and debated today. Eliot wrote "within a great tradition and in conformity to orthodox teaching," Kirk insists. "As philosophical poet, as dramatist, as literary critic, and as social essayist, Eliot labored for the recovery of order: the order of the soul, and the order of the commonwealth."[8] These are, of course, the primary causes on which Kirk labored so long and with so much effort.

Eliot was born in St. Louis in 1888 but moved to England shortly before the outbreak of the First World War. Kirk did not meet him until 1953, only a dozen years before Eliot's death and long after he had produced most of his great works. For most of his life, Eliot had favored an elaborate, almost archaically formal manner of dress, which prompted much twittering from friends such as Virginia Woolf and Herbert Read, as well as accusations of mendacity from later biographers eager to find (or invent) some pretense for criticizing him. "In an age more formal than our own," Tony Sharpe speculates, "Eliot seems to have stood out as more formal than most, and such formality can, of course, be a highly developed deference-mechanism, a desire to be impregnably correct."[9] Alternatively, perhaps Eliot simply preferred to dress in an old-fashioned manner. In that regard, he was not so different from Kirk, who often went sailing on the Little Muskegon River near his house in Mecosta dressed in a dinner jacket and tie. In 1963, he traveled to Africa with the writer Paul Molnar, who recalls Kirk's idiosyncratic fashion sense: "He wore, under the sun of North Africa, a suit, necktie, a felt hat, heavy shoes, and a heavy, knotty, walking stick. All the children of Tunis, and later those of mysterious Morocco, looked at us with open mouths as we passed."[10] Suppose Eliot and Kirk's manner of dress struck their contemporaries as outlandish. In that case, it may have also served

---

[7] Peter Ackroyd, *T. S. Eliot: A Life* (New York: Simon and Schuster, 1984), 128.
[8] Kirk, *Eliot and His Age*, 6.
[9] Tony Sharpe, *T. S. Eliot: A Literary Life* (New York: Palgrave Macmillan, 1991), 106. A photo of Kirk and Annette sailing down the Muskegon is included in *The Sword of Imagination*.
[10] Kirk, *The Sword of Imagination*, 278.

as a bond between them, a reflection of their mutual desire and determination to resist the ever-fickle dictates of modernity.

Although they were at very different ages and stages of their careers when they met, Kirk and Eliot had much in common and shared many mutual acquaintances. Not surprisingly, they got along well together and, in the years before Eliot's death, were able to maintain an "extensive correspondence" that ranged over a variety of topics as befitted their respective interests and learning. The relationship, as Birzer points out, was always one-sided, for though Kirk certainly influenced Eliot in his final years, "Eliot did not admire Kirk in the way that Kirk admired Eliot."[11] This may help to explain the deferential attitude Kirk often assumed in his letters to Eliot. Though he often familiarly addressed close friends, Kirk's first and last missives to Eliot begin with the formal salutation, "Dear Mr. Eliot." Throughout their correspondence, Kirk frequently and ingratiatingly refers to himself as "Your servant."[12] His final letter to Eliot, sent in June of 1963, retains the same distancing formality, though Kirk's eagerness to see Eliot at a conference in Rome later that summer belies his fondness for the dying man.[13] He was traveling with his wife, Annette, to Africa when Eliot passed away, and he did not hear about it until long after. Deprived of the chance to bid farewell to Eliot properly, Kirk would visit his gravesite in East Coker a few years later and pray for the soul of his departed friend.

Despite the brevity of their friendship and the formality of their correspondence, Kirk's friendship with Eliot affected him greatly—far more, perhaps, than his relationship with any other public figure. In his introduction to the most recent edition of *Eliot and His Age* (published by ISI Books in 2008), Benjamin Lockerd draws attention to the sheer number of scholarly and literary endeavors by Kirk that bear the direct influence of his late friend. "From at least 1953 on," he concludes, "Eliot was central to Kirk's thought."[14] After learning of his death, Kirk must have been eager to find a way to memorialize Eliot in a manner that suited his stature as one of the greatest poets in the English language, as well as the high personal esteem with which Kirk regarded him. In the 1970s, he produced two remarkable tributes to him: *Eliot and His Age* and *Lord of the Hollow Dark*, which represent, respectively, the height of his powers as a scholar and writer of fiction.

---

[11] Birzer, *American Conservative*, 218.

[12] See Kirk's letters to Eliot of 22 December 1955 and 20 May 1958, for instance, in his *Letters*, 76-78 and 83-84.

[13] Ibid., 107-08.

[14] Benjamin Lockerd, introduction to *Eliot and His Age: T. S. Eliot's Moral Imagination in the Twentieth Century*, by Russell Kirk (Wilmington, DE: ISI Books, 2008), xvi.

The breakdown of order in the soul and the commonwealth, purgation, and timeless moments—these are all ideas with which Kirk grappled repeatedly throughout his lifetime. But it is only in *Lord of the Hollow Dark*, written partly as a tribute to Eliot, that he attempted to address them all in a single text. The result is "one of Kirk's darker works of fiction and certainly his most ambitious. There is imagery of gloom, dampness, and rot throughout it. But there is also hope …"[15] The plot and tone of this novel may intimidate the unwary reader, but they are designed to match the contours of Eliot's lifelong journey from skepticism to belief, as traced by Kirk in *Eliot and His Age*. In early works, such as "The Love Song of J. Alfred Prufrock" and "Gerontion," Eliot masterfully articulates the conundrum faced by modern men and women, severed from their ancient traditions and beliefs due to the massive upheavals that afflicted Western society during the nineteenth and twentieth centuries. The religious and philosophical charlatans to which so many of them turned had nothing to offer but vacuous "spirituality" or suicidal ideology. As the characters in Kirk's novel are soon to discover, neither can avail them much in the end, for theirs is a crisis of faith, which can only be resolved by a return to faith. "Unless faith is regained … why, we end desperate as Gerontion or simian as Sweeney. We end barren."[16]

Even before his conversion, Eliot realized that the crisis of modernity had been precipitated, in large part, by the decline of Christianity in favor of the contemporary cults of Darwin, Nietzsche, and Freud. "It is clear," Denis Donoghue observes, "that Eliot's early poems are from an acutely personal context in which the predominant emotions are guilt, self-disgust, and revulsion. A religious faith that offered to make sense of guilt and suffering … would have special salience for him."[17] Thus, the representative speaker of "The Hollow Men" describes being tormented by "Eyes I dare not meet in dreams / In death's dream kingdom," unable to bring himself to believe in those things, but also knowing that his skepticism will not save him once he crosses over to "death's other kingdom."[18] The turning away from sin and despair towards hope entails a necessary process of purgation, which Eliot explores fully in *Ash Wednesday* and the "Ariel" poems of his middle period. Finally, his magisterial *Four Quartets* are devoted to a creative explication of some of the core concepts of his new-found faith, such as time, love, and ineffability. The cycle ends with

---

[15] Person, *Critical Biography*, 128.
[16] Kirk, *Eliot and His Age*, 55.
[17] Denis Donoghue, *Words Alone: The Poet T. S. Eliot* (New Haven, CT: Yale University Press, 2000), 275-76.
[18] Eliot, *The Complete Poems & Plays*, 43 ("The Hollow Men").

"a remarkable Christian affirmation, striking a note of transcendence and hope that was desperately needed in the dark days of 1942 when [it] first appeared."[19]

In *Lord of the Hollow Dark*, Kirk forces his characters to undergo the same spiritual journey in one week as Eliot, himself, had undertaken over many years. Balgrummo Lodging represents nothing more or less than a chance to save or damn themselves for all eternity. Like so many of us, the core group of pilgrims led by Arcane comes perilously close to failing the test, yet manages, in the end, to find its way home to the rose garden and the yew tree, blessed symbols of grace and redemption. Eliot evokes them repeatedly throughout *Four Quartets* and returns to them again in the closing lines of "Little Gidding": "The moment of the rose and the moment of the yew-tree / Are of equal duration."[20] Kirk's gloss on these lines clarifies his intentions in ending the novel the way he does: "For the Rose itself may be attained," he explains, "blooming eternally in the love of God."[21] Clearly, Eliot's thoughts suffuse *Lord of the Hollow Dark*, which Kirk makes no effort to disguise. Indeed, by choosing to give his characters pseudonyms taken from the poems and plays of Eliot, he presumably intended to call attention to that very fact. Now, I shall explore the significance of these pseudonyms by comparing some of the characters in this novel to their namesakes in Eliot's works.

Characterization in *Lord of the Hollow Dark*

Technically speaking, it is not Kirk who assigns the characters' pseudonyms, but Apollinax. Early in the book, Marina recalls how he had told her that "everybody at this gathering would assume some name from T. S. Eliot's poems."[22] The *assumption* here is ambiguous and could be taken to mean that everyone is free to choose their name. The matter is clarified in Chapter 6, however, when Manfred Arcane explains the strange set-up to the newly arrived Ralph Bain: "Everyone here assumes a name from T. S. Eliot's poems, and takes a role, too ... Mr. Apollinax tells us that it's all a form of spiritual therapy."[23] Arcane assumes responsibility for naming Bain but notes that he will have to seek Apollinax's approval first. All of this is important, I believe, because it helps to explain why certain characters, such as Arcane and his loyal *chatelaine*, Lady Fergusson, are given names so patently unsuitable for them (Gerontion and Madame Sesostris, respectively): the perspective is supposed to be Apollinax's,

---

[19] Barbara Newman, "Eliot's Affirmative Way: Julian of Norwich, Charles Williams, and *Little Gidding*," *Modern Philology* 108, no. 3 (February 2011): 428, doi: 10.1086/658355.
[20] Eliot, *The Complete Poems & Plays*, 197 ("Little Gidding" V).
[21] Kirk, *Eliot and His Age*, 263.
[22] Kirk, *Lord of the Hollow Dark*, 2.
[23] Ibid., 77.

rather than Kirk's. Even so, as the author, Kirk retains overall responsibility for the naming of his characters, and the choices he makes (or has Apollinax make for him) are quite revealing.

This is especially true of Arcane, the central figure in the book. He is called Gerontion, after the titular figure in one of Eliot's pre-conversion poems, whose very name, as Katrina Harrick reminds us, "evokes vague connections to old age, and is perhaps a created name or word for the *process* of aging."[24] Older people are supposed to be wise, but Gerontion is a scared and lonely old fool, "A dull head among windy spaces." Having always played it safe, he is haunted by his failure to accomplish anything of value in his life and now faces the prospect of spending his final days in a dilapidated boarding house with only a group of strangers for company. Despite his apparent belief in the afterlife, he cannot even bring himself to accept the comforts of religion, though he is wise enough to recognize that, in this era of "unnatural vices" and "impudent crimes," of destructive world wars and cannibalizing ideologies, secular belief systems (such as his preferred "History") only amount to a false God that "deceives with whispering ambitions, / [and] Guides us by vanities."[25] But such a thought can hardly prove comforting. In any case, as a nickname for Arcane, Gerontion seems far from complimentary!

On at least one superficial point of resemblance between Arcane and Gerontion, Apollinax seems to have hit the mark, however. By the time of the events described in *Lord of the Hollow Dark*, Arcane must be in his seventies, at least.[26] The pseudonym could have suggested itself due to his advanced age, then. It is important to remember, however, that Arcane is in Scotland under an assumed identity: in actuality, it is not the mysterious Minister without Portfolio last seen ruling over Hamnegri who has been given the name Gerontion, but a deceased dealer of *kalanzi*, the psychotropic drug that Apollinax uses to control his minions. The tale of how Arcane came to outwit this dealer and assume his identity is told in "The Peculiar Demesne of Archvicar Gerontion," which was first published in 1980 but is set before the events of Kirk's last novel. That story confirms that Apollinax could not have found a more fitting name for the drug-dealing archvicar in all of Eliot's works. Like Gerontion, the archvicar is old, well-traveled, and possesses a respectable level of intelligence, though it is directed towards immoral or even diabolical ends. Arcane describes him as "harmoniously perfect in his evil ... as smoothly

---

[24] Katrina Harrick, "Temporal, mnemonic, and aesthetic 'eruptions': recontextualizing Eliot and the modern literary artwork," *Yeats Eliot Review* 26, no. 2 (Summer 2009): 6, *Gale Academic OneFile*.

[25] Eliot, *The Complete Poems & Plays*, 37-39 ("Gerontion").

[26] I discuss the question of Arcane's age more in the next chapter.

foul a being as one might hope to meet."²⁷ He practices a form of black magic that calls to mind, and was probably suggested by, the poem's reference to "Madame de Tornquist, in the dark room / Shifting the candles."²⁸ Through such means, he has been able to delay the inevitability of his death but fears it just as much as the older man in Eliot's poem.

Even if not originally intended for him, the nickname "Gerontion" still describes certain aspects of Arcane's personality. Having participated in the Spanish Civil War, World War II, and the civil war in Hamnegri, Arcane has several decades' worth of combat experience and training in military tactics. The love of his life was killed during the Holocaust, and he knows how dangerous the world can be, even or especially for those who just want to be left alone. Though he has never fought in battle, Eliot's Gerontion is fully aware of its destructive potential. The "bulk" of the poem was written in the summer of 1919,²⁹ and the old man has only to look out the front windows to see the waste expanses of Europe, smashed "Beyond the circuit of the shuddering Bear / In fractured atoms."³⁰ As Jamie Wood observes, Eliot's poem "captures an immediate postwar public mood characterized by the divisions between combatants and noncombatants, the sublimation of private emotion to public memorialization, changes in international law and politics, and the acceleration of violence around the world."³¹ Arcane and Gerontion have both been shaped by the same, violent and unstable, "mood." Whereas the latter is paralyzed by it, Arcane knows that all human suffering is part of a larger plan. Nor is he dismayed by an increasingly secular and consumerist culture, which is the main stumbling block for Gerontion to turn his fear into faith. To Gerontion's house of despair might Arcane himself have gone, but for his fear of the Lord and His grace.

Such is the lesson that must be learned the hard way by Sweeney, perhaps the most interesting character in this novel after Arcane. It is something of a miracle that he does succeed in learning it while there is still time to do so. His is an example of a perfectly chosen nickname by Apollinax, although, in the closing pages, he confesses that his real name, whether by coincidence or design, also happens to be Sweeney.³² If he is not lying—and that is by no means certain, given his myriad indiscretions—it suggests, perhaps, that the character was

---

[27] Kirk, "The Peculiar Demesne of Archvicar Gerontion," in *Ancestral Shadows*, 257.
[28] Eliot, *The Complete Poems and Plays*, 37 ("Gerontion").
[29] Sharpe, *T. S. Eliot*, 61.
[30] Ibid., 39.
[31] Jamie Wood, "'Here I Am': Eliot, 'Gerontion,' and the Great War," *Biography: An Interdisciplinary Quarterly* 41, no. 1 (Winter 2018): 131, doi: 10.1353/bio.2018.0011.
[32] Kirk, *Lord of the Hollow Dark*, 334-35.

more than inspired by his namesake in Eliot's poems: he *is* that namesake, Sweeney transported directly from his final appearance in Eliot's unfinished verse drama *Sweeney Agonistes* to Kirk's mystical Gothic romance, written almost half a century later.[33] In any case, the character is mentioned in several early poems by Eliot, including "Mr. Eliot's Sunday Morning Service" and *The Waste Land*. In the former, he is depicted lounging in the bathtub while humans and animals alike perform their daily oblations, symbolizing the growing religious apathy that Eliot had already begun to see as a problematic feature of contemporary life. Kirk's Sweeney expresses a similar indifference towards the mystical aspects of his unusual position with Apollinax, as I have already noted.[34] Of course, after surviving the events of the following week, he is ready to sing a different tune.

Eliot presents a clearer impression of Sweeney in the two poems named after him that were published in his 1920 collection of work. "Sweeney Erect" signals its intentions with a bawdy pun in the title; it opens with the character shaving in a brothel while a prostitute suffers an epileptic fit on the bed. "By poem's end," remarks John Perryman, "the depictions of Sweeney shift from epic (if flawed) to bestial (if noble)."[35] Further references to Sweeney's "bestial" nature can be found in the opening stanza of "Sweeney Among the Nightingales":

> Apeneck Sweeney spreads his knees
> Letting his arms hang down to laugh,
> The zebra stripes along his jaw
> Swelling to maculate giraffe.[36]

The whole poem is suffused with a vaguely menacing air: it is "written out of fashion, but not away from it, turning a vogue into something else without leaving it behind, keeping its figures suggestively costumed, veiled in hints and names."[37] Kirk's Sweeney is also a brutish, predatory character with a checkered past and a forged diploma. He shows little interest in the beautiful, sexually

---

[33] Sharpe, T. S. Eliot, 104. *Sweeney Agonistes* was published in two parts between 1926-27 in Eliot's journal, *Criterion*, and performed for the first time in London in 1934.
[34] Kirk, *Lord of the Hollow Dark*, 17.
[35] John Perryman, "Back to the Bay Psalm Book: T. S. Eliot's Identity Crisis and 'Sweeney Erect,'" *Midwest Quarterly* 47, no. 3 (March 2006): 254, *Academic Search Premier*.
[36] Eliot, *The Complete Poems & Plays*, 56 ("Sweeney Among the Nightingales").
[37] Anne Stillman, "Sweeney Among the Marionettes," *Essays in Criticism: A Quarterly Journal of Literary Criticism* 59, no. 2 (April 2009): 125, doi: 10.1093/escrit/cgp002.

experienced Grishkin, preferring the "shrieking innocence" of the naïve single mother, Marina, instead.[38]

Sweeney's brief appearance in Part 3 of *The Wasteland* might have some bearing on this aspect of his personality:

> But at my back from time to time I hear
> The sound of horns and motors, which shall bring
> Sweeney to Mrs. Porter in the spring.[39]

These lines suggest an idyllic country rendezvous between a young man and his (married) lover. But occurring as they do in a passage that highlights the degraded nature of love in the modern era, one is tempted to see something more sinister at work in Sweeney's romantic dalliance. Eliot's note to this passage draws our attention to the myth of Actaeon, the unfortunate hunter who surprised the goddess Diana in her bath and was turned into a stag for his indiscretion.[40] Furthermore, his linking of Sweeney and Philomena in "Sweeney and the Nightingales" and his reference to the latter in a previous section of *The Waste Land* suggest that Sweeney might not be the romantic lover of Mrs. Porter after all, but her rapist. Although some critics continue to insist that "there is no reason to believe … that [Sweeney] will rape or brutalize Mrs. Porter,[41] Kirk certainly interpreted the passage in such a way, making his Sweeney guilty of repeated "offenses against women."[42] He even tries to rape Marina but is prevented from doing so at the last moment, after which, finally, he begins to demonstrate genuine repentance.

For Kirk, it is enough that Sweeney makes the effort to repent, however belated. Despite Sweeney's faults, he is among the select group of pilgrims that makes it through the events of the novel alive; it is telling, though, that his first thought upon escaping from the labyrinthian Weem is for a bit of rum.[43] Kirk seemed to believe that Eliot was headed in a similar direction with the character, especially in *Sweeney Agonistes*, a sort of jazz-infused drama that Dennell M. Downum describes as having "borrowed its structure from the comedies of

---

[38] Kirk, *Lord of the Hollow Dark*, 20.
[39] Eliot, *The Complete Poems & Plays*, 67 (*The Waste Land* 196-98).
[40] Probably the best-known version of this tale is from Ovid's *Metamorphoses*, Book III.
[41] Dennell M. Downum, "Apeneck Sweeney's penitential path," *Yeats Eliot Review* 26, no. 1 (Spring 2009): 11, *Gale Academic OneFile*.
[42] Kirk, *Lord of the Hollow Dark*, 15.
[43] Ibid., 333.

Aristophanes and its currency from the Music Hall."[44] Eliot only completed a few pages of this promising work, but several lines are quoted in *Lord of the Hollow Dark*, including "I've gotta use words when I talk to you," Sweeney's exasperated acknowledgment of the futility of trying to capture the horror and banality of modern life through words. The drama ends abruptly with symbolic cries of "Hoo ha ha" and an unanswered knocking on the door, both of which are echoed in an important dream Sweeney has early in Kirk's novel.[45] Kirk believed that part of the reason Eliot did not finish the play was that he no longer wished to write about characters in such a fallen, degenerate state.[46] Through Arcane, he is able to shepherd his own Sweeney onto the path of redemption—finishing the job started by Eliot.

The most important female character in *Lord of the Hollow Dark* is Marina, named after one of Eliot's "Ariel" poems, itself based on a scene from *Pericles*, a late romance written at least partly by Shakespeare (along with the inn-keeper George Wilkins). In the play's famous recognition scene, Pericles enjoys an unexpected reunion with his long-lost daughter, Marina, whose mother he believed to have died giving birth to her. Eliot's poem takes up from that moment, as Pericles begins to realize that the apparent resurrection of his daughter has given him a new lease on life, as well:

> This form, this face, this life
> Living to live in a world of time beyond me, let me
> Resign my life for this life, my speech for that unspoken,
> The awakened, lips parted, the hope, the new ships.[47]

As F. R. Leavis puts it in an old but influential essay on Eliot's "Later Poetry": "Thus, in the gliding from one image, evocation or suggestion to another, so that all contribute to a total effect, there is created a sense of a supreme significance, elusive, but not, like the message of death; illusory; an opening into a new and more than personal life."[48] For Kirk, the significance of "Marina" is clear and

---

[44] Rick de Villiers, "'Of the Same Species': T. S. Eliot's *Sweeney Agonistes* and Samuel Beckett's *Waiting for Godot*," *English Studies in Africa* 55, no. 2 (2012): 20, doi: 10.1080/00138398.2012.731287.
[45] Eliot, *The Complete Poems & Plays*, 125-26 (*Fragment of an Agon*).
[46] Kirk, *Eliot and His Age*, 112.
[47] Eliot, *The Complete Plays & Poems*, 110 ("Marina").
[48] F. R. Leavis, "T. S. Eliot's Later Poetry," in *T. S. Eliot: A Collection of Critical Essays*, ed. Hugh Kenner (Englewood Cliffs, NJ: Prentice-Hall, 1962), 114. This article was first published in 1942 in Leavis' own journal, *Scrutiny: A Quarterly Review*.

closely related to themes explored in *Ash Wednesday*: the poem represents the victory of life over death.[49]

At first glance, Kirk's Marina does not seem to bear much resemblance to her namesake in Eliot's poem (or, rather, in Shakespeare's play, since the poem is written entirely from the perspective of Marina's father, Pericles, and does not offer much characterization of her). We learn early on that Kirk and Eliot's Marinas cannot possibly be the same person since her real name is Deborah Fitzgerald. She is no virginal daughter lost at sea but a former nun who renounced her vows and was abandoned by her feckless lover shortly after breaking the news to him that she was pregnant with their son, Michael.[50] Her girlish manner is somewhat reminiscent of Dr. Mary Jo Travers, the star-struck PhD and Peace Corps volunteer from Kirk's second novel, *A Creature of the Twilight*. Despite having some familiarity with basic Catholic doctrine, she is easily overwhelmed by Apollinax's explanations of his complicated belief system and how she and her baby fit into his plans for Ash Wednesday.[51] What she does not realize until it is almost too late is that he intends for them to play a central role in his blasphemous Ceremony of Innocence, during which she will be married to a ghost, her son offered as a sacrifice to his *kalanzi*-crazed followers. Perhaps if she knew her Yeats as well as Kirk did, she would have been more suspicious of Apollinax's intentions. After all, he has named his ritual after a key symbol from Yeats' "The Second Coming," a poem published in 1921, in which the author decries the increasing chaos of the modern world, the decline of the Irish aristocracy, and concomitant loss of traditional values.[52] Such instability and destruction are integral to Apollinax's long-term plans, and he would gladly trade the lives of two innocent persons to bring them closer to reality.

Marina and Michael serve an important narrative function in the novel by offering the other characters a clear motivation for wanting to resist Apollinax's powerfully magnetic personality. Against his strength and scheming stand the mother and child, weak and sinful but desiring (and essentially symbolizing) the good. After all, every Gothic romance needs a heroine of some kind, and Marina, who has no friends, family, or prospects, clearly fits the standard trope of the "woman in distress," stuck or lost "in a secluded location," and in

---

[49] Kirk, *Eliot and His Age*, 114.
[50] Kirk, *Lord of the Hollow Dark*, 26-28.
[51] Ibid., 97-98.
[52] John R. Harrison, "What Rough Beast? Yeats, Nietzsche and Historical Rhetoric in 'The Second Coming,'" *Papers on Language & Literature* 31, no. 4 (1995): 368-69.

desperate need of rescue.[53] In *Lord of the Hollow Dark*, as in so many Gothic texts, even the most incorrigible of characters can earn redemption by attempting to save such women. The attempt need not prove successful, though it does, happily, for most of the would-be heroes in Kirk's novel. Ralph Bain, Sweeney, and Arcane all demonstrate their worthiness through an act of sacrifice undertaken on behalf of Marina and Michael. "I'll carry you over, Deborah Fitzgerald," Bain assures her at one point. "That's why I was sent here."[54] He is not referring only to the plank bridge across the underground river in the Weem, before which they happen to be standing.

And yet, that is the only bridge across which he can actually carry her. The other, metaphysical one, she must be willing to hazard on her own. Unlike her predecessors in Shakespeare and Eliot, Kirk's Marina is not only primarily a symbol but also a fully realized human being. Like everyone else, she suffers from Original Sin and needs herself to be saved before she can serve as a means for the redemption of others. To her credit, Marina recognizes her culpability while reading her namesake poem. Scanning the lines, she realizes how aptly they describe her failings as a former nun who renounced her vows in favor of a man who left her pregnant and penniless.[55] Her situation and the choices she faces contrast sharply with those of Shakespeare's Marina, who swears that "If fires be hot, knives sharp, or waters deep, / Untied I still my virgin knot will keep," and is somehow able to preserve her virtue even after being threatened with rape and then prostituted by a band of rowdy pirates.[56] Kirk would certainly approve of the moral lesson Shakespeare is trying to impart through her example. Still, the best that can be said of the play's Marina, perhaps, is that she is "not either a symbol of vice or virtue or a 'real' figure of female social life and discourse, but both."[57] The truth is, all of her prayers and oaths would not protect her for more than five minutes were she threatened by a drunk and determined Sweeney, let alone Apollinax and his grim band of devotees. To cope with the physical and spiritual dangers of the modern world, Kirk's Marina must be made of sterner stuff.

---

[53] Julianne Guillard, " 'You are exactly my brand of heroin(e)': Convergences and Divergences of the Gothic Literary Heroine," *Girlhood Studies* 4, no. 1 (Summer 2011): 52, doi: 10.3167/ghs.2011.040105.

[54] Kirk, *Lord of the Hollow Dark*, 291.

[55] Ibid., 26.

[56] William Shakespeare, *Pericles: Prince of Tyre*, vol. 2 of *The Complete Works of William Shakespeare*, ed. W. G. Clark and W. Aldis Wright (Garden City, NY: Nelson Doubleday, 1950), IV.ii.159-60.

[57] Bridget Escolme, "Public Eye and Private Place: Intimacy and Metatheatre in *Pericles* and *The Tempest*," *Shakespeare Bulletin: The Journal of Early Modern Drama in Performance* 36, no. 1 (2018): 124, doi: 10.1353/shb.2018.0007.

Like Marina, Eliot's Coriolan is based on a play by Shakespeare. There is no mistaking Kirk's Coriolan for the character after whom he is named, either, since he is introduced by his real name, Ralph Bain, and there are repeated references to his previous exploits in other stories. Coriolanus was a legendary Roman general who defected to the Volscians and led them in a siege of Rome in the fifth century BC; the story may have been familiar to Shakespeare from his reading of Plutarch's *Lives*, as translated into English by Sir Thomas North.[58] Eliot had begun writing poems based on the character shortly after the publication of *Ash Wednesday* in 1930 but had only finished two of the planned four-poem sequences.[59] In "Triumphal March" and "Difficulties of a Statesman," Eliot presents Shakespeare's Coriolanus as a twentieth-century man, a tragic figure whose attempts at preserving his masculine sense of "hyper-independent subjectivity" are fatally undermined by forces beyond his control and the weaknesses of his contemporaries.[60] Amidst all of the marches and the meetings, there is always the "still point of the turning world" for which Coriolan longs[61] and in which, alone, may be found "abiding wisdom and justice."[62] Kirk regarded the poem as one in which "Eliot's principles of social order [were] reflected—or perhaps best expressed."[63]

Much like his namesake (as depicted by both Shakespeare and Eliot), Bain is a natural leader with an unimpeachable sense of honor. Yet one suspects that, had he been born in a different era or a different place, perhaps he might have been recognized as a truly great man. Instead, he is adrift in feckless, post-war Britain, where opportunities to earn distinction are rare. Before his valiant death at Sorworth Place, he spends the time following his discharge from the army in a variety of profligate pursuits: "Drinks with strangers in one village, listless games of cards in the next town, inconsequential talks on buses or trains ..." Bain bears the Military Cross and a battlefield wound, which entitle him to some rest and a pension. But the forced inactivity does not sit well with him, and he feels a shameful "self-dislike" at gazing upon his reflection in the mirror.[64] Bain's discontent springs from a similar source as that of Coriolanus:

---

[58] Russell M. Hillier, " 'Valour Will Weep': The Ethics of Valor, Anger, and Pity in Shakespeare's *Coriolanus*," *Studies in Philology* 113, no. 2 (2016): 362, doi: 10.1353/sip.2016.0015.

[59] Sharpe, *T. S. Eliot*, 126.

[60] L. Monique Pittman, "Heroes, Villains, and Balkans: Intertextual Masculinities in Ralph Fiennes's *Coriolanus*," *Shakespeare Bulletin* 33, no. 2 (Summer 2015): 218, doi:10.1353/shb.2015.0022.

[61] Eliot, *The Complete Poems and Plays*, 128-30 (*Coriolan*).

[62] Kirk, *Eliot and His Age*, 164.

[63] Ibid., 165.

[64] Kirk, "Sorworth Place," in *Ancestral Shadows*, 178-81.

both suspect that "There is a world elsewhere," far from the "common cry of curs" trembling in fear and indecision before the enemies ranged against them.[65] In *Lord of the Hollow Dark*, it is Arcane, not Apollinax, who gives Bain his nickname; the wise old man does not explain his reasoning but notes one other reference to "broken Coriolanus" in *The Waste Land*.[66] Might Ralph Bain, dead and still in need of redemption, yet be revived?[67] In "Saviourgate," published in 1976 but probably set after the events of Kirk's third novel, it seems as if Bain has finally earned the peace and happiness that always eluded his namesake.

Almost all of the minor characters in *Lord of the Hollow Dark* are also given pseudonyms. These include several of Arcane's companions from Hamnegri. Lady Grizel Fergusson, his loyal and leathery *chatelaine*, is named after Madame Sosostris, a fortune teller who, in *The Waste Land*, reads the fates of various characters from a deck of Tarot cards. According to Francesca Bugliani Knox, Eliot "did not take the symbols of the Tarot at face value … he saw [it] mainly as a device to give frame and unity to the quest that follows later in the poem, anticipating its characters and elements, and hinting at their ancient and secret roots."[68] Apollinax may have chosen the name based on Lady Grizel's reputation for being wise and resourceful. However, it is worth noting that she does read from a deck of cards later in the story[69] and that Kirk used to do the same until shortly before his marriage to Annette.[70] Brasidas and his brother, Cleon, served as Arcane's bodyguards in Africa; he has brought the former with him to Scotland under the guise of Phlebas. This character is mentioned in the fourth section of *The Waste Land*, "Death by Water," in which Eliot urges the reader to "Consider Phlebas, who was once handsome and tall as you," but now is dead, a *memento mori*.[71] Perhaps Apollinax meant the nickname as a joke: in *A Creature of the Twilight*, the diminutive brothers are frequently compared to feral animals; one character describes them as "wolf-boys."[72]

Arcane's long-time companion, Melchiora, is also with him at Balgrummo Lodging, though they have wisely elected to keep their sensitive son, Guido, far

---

[65] William Shakespeare, *Coriolanus*, vol. 2 of *The Complete Works of William Shakespeare*, ed. W. G. Clark and W. Aldis Wright (Garden City, NY: Nelson Doubleday, 1950), III.iii.120-35.
[66] Eliot, *The Complete Poems & Plays*, 74 (*The Waste Land* 417).
[67] Kirk, *Lord of the Hollow Dark*, 78.
[68] Francesca Bugliani Knox, "Between Fire and Fire: T. S. Eliot's *The Waste Land*," *Heythrop Journal* 56, no. 2 (March 2015): 240, doi: 10.1111/heyj.12240.
[69] Kirk, *Lord of the Hollow Dark*, 248-56.
[70] Kirk, *The Sword of Imagination*, 267-68.
[71] Eliot, *The Complete Poems & Plays*, 71 (*The Waste Land* 321).
[72] Kirk, *A Creature of the Twilight*, 70.

away from the gathering. Melchiora, whom Arcane addresses by a wide variety of endearments, has assumed the alias of Fresca, a character referred to briefly at the end of "Gerontion." The name possesses a distinctively European air that suits the fiery, dagger-wielding Sicilian, and perhaps that is all there is to Apollinax's decision to give her that name. But Eliot's Fresca was also meant to appear in a notorious passage of *The Waste Land*, which he deleted from the manuscript at the behest of Ezra Pound. The "Fresca passage" was intended as a "pastiche" of a scene from Alexander Pope's *The Rape of the Lock*, an incongruously scatological "parody of a parody," as Patrick Deane describes it.[73] A facsimile of the manuscript with Pound's annotations was published in 1971,[74] the same year as Kirk's *Eliot and His Age*. It is unclear how soon Kirk became aware of the offending passage, but he expresses general support for Pound's work in the 1984 edition of his book, on which the most recent one is based.[75] The point is that by the time Kirk started working on *Lord of the Hollow Dark* in the 1970s, he must have known about the deleted lines from *The Waste Land*, which may have influenced his decision to name Melchiora after Fresca. The reference to her in "Gerontion" seems too cursory for such an important character.

Then again, Apollinax is the one who gave her that name; from his perspective, she is but one of several dozen "essences," a dismissive term he uses to describe the disciples and acolytes whom he plans to abandon to eternal torment in the Weem.[76] Even his most loyal and devoted follower, the seductive Grishkin, does not survive the gathering at Balgrummo Lodging. Ironically, she ends up suffering a worse fate than most, for after Marina and her child escape, Apollinax decides that the Ceremony of Innocence must end with her being crucified instead. Nor does he seem much put out by her death: "The world was full of Grishkins," he thinks to himself afterward.[77] Indeed, her disposability is suggested by the pseudonym he has given her, taken from the third of three figures mentioned in "Whispers of Immortality." In this early poem by Eliot, Grishkin's "friendly bust" is said to give "the promise of pneumatic bliss. In contrast to Daniel Webster and John Donne, who are also named in the poem, she has no interest in metaphysical questions about death

---

[73] Patrick Deane, "Rhetoric and Affect: Eliot's Classicism, Pound's Symbolism, and the Drafts of *The Waste Land*," *Journal of Modern Literature* 18, no. 1 (Winter 1992): 85, accessed 11 September 2020, *MLA International Bibliography with Full Text*.
[74] Christopher Macgowan, *Twentieth-Century American Poetry* (Malden, MA: Blackwell Publishing, 2005), 66.
[75] Kirk, *Eliot and His Age*, 63-64.
[76] Kirk, *Lord of the Hollow Dark*, 316. As mentioned above, "Essences" was one of the novel's early titles.
[77] Ibid., 318.

or the soul and cares only for her selfish pleasure. "Yet her sex appeal is without calculation," Craig Raine argues, "without consciousness. It is *unaware*, simple, shorn of complication."[78] In a former life, Grishkin had been known as Carmella di Stefano, a model and one of the jet-setting group of vapid personalities parodied by Kirk in *A Creature of the Twilight*.[79] Arcane recognizes her as such but is unable to convince her to abandon Apollinax before it is too late. She is too far gone to be saved, lost in depravity, blasphemy, and her crippling addiction to *kalanzi*.

As for her master, it is curious that he would not look harder to find a more flattering nickname for himself. "Mr. Apollinax" is another of Eliot's early poems and centers on a foreign professor who visits the United States, spreading confusion and debauchery wherever he goes. The narrator thinks him lecherous and incomprehensible: "Priapus in the shrubbery / Gaping at the lady in the swing," with a laugh that resembles "an irresponsible foetus." And yet, that laugh is "submarine and profound" enough to earn this charlatan a host of admirers, such as Mrs. Phlaccus and the otherwise respectable Channing-Cheetahs, all of whose identities are assumed by various followers of Apollinax's.[80] Kirk knew that Eliot based the character on Bertrand Russell, a Harvard professor and philosopher, with whom Eliot and his first wife briefly lived. A serial philanderer, Russell "was no ideal marriage counselor," Kirk observes dryly.[81] He believed that Russell seduced Eliot's wife, Vivienne Haigh-Wood and that Eliot retaliated by depicting Russell in an unflattering manner in this poem. In any case, the association between Apollinax and Russell lends an added layer to Kirk's motivation in making him the villain of his novel.

First, it is worth noting the close physical resemblance between the two Apollinaxes. In *Lord of the Hollow Dark*, Sweeney describes him as always looking "unfinished," with skin as smooth as a baby's. Talking with the cult leader is like "a confrontation with a clever and alarming fetus," a clear echo of the unusual description of the visitor's laughter in Eliot's poem. Though physically "infantile," he is intellectually "old, old, the old man of the sea, or perhaps of the mountain," also a rephrasing of a line from the poem.[82] But Kirk's character does more than look like Russell; he thinks and talks like him, too. Russell described himself as an agnostic but was critical of organized religion, which he blamed for many of the world's problems. He denounced the Christian attitude towards sex as "its worst feature": "an attitude so morbid and

---

[78] Craig Raine, *T. S. Eliot* (Oxford: Oxford University Press, 2006), 13.
[79] Kirk, *A Creature of the Twilight*, 133-36.
[80] Eliot, *The Complete Poems & Plays*, 31 ("Mr. Apollinax").
[81] Kirk, *Eliot and His Age*, 33.
[82] Kirk, *Lord of the Hollow Dark*, 21.

so unnatural that it can only be understood when taken in relation to the sickness of the civilized world at the time when the Roman Empire was decaying."[83] Similarly, Apollinax criticizes Eliot's "narrow" understanding of morality as "spoilt by foolish old prejudices from the childhood of the race ..."[84] He is, of course, something even worse than an atheist. From Kirk's point of view, both Russell and Apollinax are misguided prophets who represent equally dangerous rivals to the truth of the Church.

In one of his most popular and influential collections of essays, which was published in 1918 and called *Mysticism and Logic*, Russell discusses a variety of topics, ranging from the "History of Western Philosophy" to "Marriage and Morals." "The book as a whole ... is less a unity than a dialogue where logic, like mathematics, epitomizes impersonally the claims of reason, and mysticism the co-equal claims of the spiritual life."[85] Some of Russell's remarks on time sound very much like Apollinax's own words on the subject:

> Past and future must be acknowledged to be as real as the present, and a certain *emancipation from slavery to time* is essential to philosophic thought ... A truer image of the world, I think, is obtained by picturing things as entering into the stream of time from an eternal world outside, than from a view which regards time as *a devouring tyrant* of all that is.[86]

At least Russell recognizes the limitations of his approach to metaphysical issues. Apollinax arrogantly believes that he has discovered a means to achieve what is possible only through the grace of God or cooperation with the devil. In the end, he discovers that only the former is willing to keep His promises. Perhaps in assigning himself a pseudonym based on one of Eliot's most repugnant characters, he thought to achieve a sort of metafictional triumph over the long-dead poet. In fact, the name ends up suiting him more than he dared to imagine, for he dies in a manner that ensures he will join his namesake "under coral islands / Where worried bodies of drowned men drift down in the green silence."[87]

---

[83] Bertrand Russell, "Has Religion Made Useful Contributions to Civilization?" in *Russell on Religion: Selections from the Writings of Bertrand Russell*, ed. Louis Greenspan and Stefan Andersson (London: Routledge, 2003), 170.
[84] Kirk, *Lord of the Hollow Dark*, 96.
[85] Ronald Jager, *The Development of Bertrand Russell's Philosophy* (London: Routledge, 2013), 182.
[86] Bertrand Russell, "Mysticism and Logic," in *Mysticism and Logic: And Other Essays* (Totowa, NJ: Barnes and Noble Books, 1981), 23. Emphasis is mine.
[87] Eliot, *The Complete Poems & Plays*, 31 ("Mr. Apollinax").

Kirk's "Mystical Gothick Romance"

As I have noted previously, Russell Kirk was never shy about acknowledging his sources. In his dedication to *Lord of the Hollow Dark*, he claims to be inspired mainly by the novels of his forebears in the Gothic tradition, including Sir Walter Scott and Ann Radcliffe.[88] Similarly, in letters written before the novel's publication, he refers to it variously as a "Gothick romance,"[89] "mystical romance,"[90] or "mystical Scottish romance,"[91] emphasizing the debt to Scott and Radcliffe. And yet, the influence of Eliot looms large on the novel's unique blend of mysticism and horror. It ends, after all, with most of the characters dead or dying, doomed to suffer the same fate as the "hollow" men and women of Eliot's poem, whom Kirk describes as being "confined forever … in the desolation of cactus and prickly pear."[92] The novel's densely allusive style owes more to Eliot's Modernist style than to that of the Romantic authors Kirk names above. Finally, there must be a reason that he chose to name the characters after the ones in Eliot's works—not those of Scott or Radcliffe.

If Kirk was at all reticent about Eliot's influence on his last novel, it is probably because he considered it so obvious as not to be worth drawing attention to. As he writes in his memoirs, he preferred to leave his readers "to puzzle out for themselves his meanings"[93] and would have trusted them to work out the significance of Eliot's presence in the book on their own. But sales proved disappointing, and *Lord of the Hollow Dark* was soon forgotten. It has remained so ever since, even as the one-hundredth anniversary of Eliot's key works passes or draws near, and Gothicism enjoys a broader renaissance in the popular consciousness. Ironically, Kirk's decision to de-emphasize Eliot's influence may have resulted in the novel receiving less attention than it deserved. It is much better than its reception or sales would indicate and ought to be considered one of the outstanding examples of Conservative Gothic horror of the 1970s, if not the whole second half of the twentieth century. Perhaps the forthcoming celebrations of the centenaries of *Ash Wednesday* and *Four Quartets* will lead to greater interest in Kirk's final, overlooked novel.

---

[88] Russell Kirk, dedication in *Lord of the Hollow Dark* (New York: St. Martin's Press, 1979) [ii].
[89] Kirk to Kirby McCauley, 7 June 1978, in *Letters*, 207.
[90] Kirk to Folke Leander, 28 January 1978, in *Letters*, 202.
[91] Kirk to David Adam Bovenizer, 16 November 1978, in *Letters*, 210.
[92] Kirk, *Eliot and His Age*, 109.
[93] Kirk, *The Sword of Imagination*, 434.

Chapter 9

Manfred Arcane

One of the last things Russell Kirk worked on before his death was his long-awaited autobiography, *The Sword of Imagination: Memoirs of a Half-Century of Literary Conflict*. Apparently, he was still putting the finishing touches to its final chapter in the weeks before he passed away.[1] "Is Life Worth Living?" he wonders in his elegiac epilogue, answering his question a few pages later with an emphatic "yes." "This present life here below ... is an ephemeral existence, precarious, as in an arena rather than upon a stage: some men are meant to be gladiators or knights-errant, not mere strolling players. Swords drawn, they stand on a darkling plain ..."[2] Kirk knew that, in his own way, he had been one of those brave champions, fighting to defend the permanent things and restore the moral imagination in an increasingly decadent and antagonistic twentieth century. An old sword hung above the chimneypiece at Piety Hill, his ancestral home in Mecosta, and Kirk's final musings are on the possibility of being allowed to take it with him into the afterlife. "Quite conceivably imagination of the right sort may be so redemptive hereafter as here. Forward!"[3] May he ever brandish that sword!

Nevertheless, one suspects that he would have liked to do more than emulate those gladiators and knights-errant of the past ... that he (or a part of him) longed to play a more vigorous role in shaping the dramatic events that unfolded throughout his lifetime. During World War II, he served in the Army but never left the United States. A letter written in 1943, in which he complains of British and American inaction, suggests something of the frustration he must have felt, sitting on the sidelines while important battles were being fought across Europe, Asia, and Africa.[4] Decades later, in *The Roots of American Order*, Kirk describes the two "types of humanity [who] were the wonder of medieval Europe: the great saint and the great knight. In later ages, their descendants would be the scholar and the gentleman."[5] Having declined to accept any permanent academic appointment throughout his lifetime, Kirk may have viewed himself as more of a gentleman than a scholar, a descendant—along with

---

[1] Person, *Critical Biography*, 17. Kirk died of natural causes on 29 April 1994.
[2] Kirk, *The Sword of Imagination*, 475-76.
[3] Ibid., 476.
[4] Kirk to Margaret, Jane, and Frank Pierce Jr., 31 October 1943, in *Letters*, 34.
[5] Kirk, *The Roots of American Order*, 200.

T. S. Eliot, Samuel Johnson, and Edmund Burke, none of whom were primarily "scholars"—of the warmongering John of Brienne, king, emperor, and scourge of the Saracens.

As Kirk acknowledges in his memoirs, his battles were figurative; his opponents were the enemies of the permanent things, against whom he clashed in the "arena" of public life, armed only with his trusty typewriter. There is another sense in which his battles were figurative, however, which he seems to have overlooked in his own reflections about the past. As I have argued throughout this book, Kirk's moral imagination was never more potent and fully realized than in his fiction, despite his relatively modest output in that genre. Surely, it is in his fictional worlds, and especially in the male and female heroes who populate them, that Kirk was best able to live up to the calling of the formidable John of Brienne. Of all his memorable protagonists, none better represents him as a knight and gentleman than Manfred Arcane, Kirk's alter ego and the hero of several stories and novels. Arcane was formally introduced in Kirk's second novel, *A Creature of the Twilight*, as "Minister without Portfolio" in the fictional African kingdom of Hamnegri; eventually, he proves victorious in the civil war that is being fought there between progressive and reactionary forces. In Kirk's third and last novel, *Lord of the Hollow Dark*, a much older Arcane returns as part of a group of pilgrims struggling to resist the diabolic schemes of a homicidal cult leader. He also appears in two stories set between those books. Traces of the character are evident, however, in at least one of the earliest pieces of fiction Kirk wrote during the 1950s. Thus, it is fair to say that Arcane, in some form or another, was present throughout almost the whole of his literary career. By exploring the development of this character through the years, much light can be shed, perhaps, on the author's evolving conception of himself. In this final chapter, I try to answer the question: What can the "Father of Shadows" teach us about the "Wizard of Mecosta"?

The Knight of the Devious Ways

Kirk offers biographical information about Arcane only in a piecemeal fashion, resulting in a fragmentary life story that must be pierced together through careful cross-checking of the available sources. Some of the confusion seems deliberate on Kirk's part. One of his favorite tricks is to have other characters relate information about Arcane that basically amounts to hearsay, and which is, subsequently, neither confirmed nor denied by others (let alone by Arcane himself). Early in *A Creature of the Twilight*, for instance, the American envoy, T. William Tallstall, confesses to a colleague his doubts about Arcane's sinister past. "He may have been an officer of Nazi S. S., though this cannot be confirmed as yet."⁶ A businessman, Thomas Whiston, reveals similarly lurid details about Arcane in "The Peculiar Demesne of Archvicar Gerontion": "They say he knows where the bodies are buried …" ⁷ Even his basic nationality is a matter of speculation: "According to some sources," journalist Jack Symonds reports, "Arcane is partly of Turkish or Egyptian extraction."⁸ The reader's initial impression of Arcane, therefore, is likely to be unfavorable. After all, he is rumored to be not only a Nazi but a member of the dreaded S. S., a paramilitary branch of the Party that was responsible for some of the most atrocious human rights violations committed during the Second World War. As it turns out, Arcane was, himself, a victim of the Holocaust whose own beloved perished in the concentration camps. Nor is he of shadowy, Middle Eastern heritage: his father was English, and his mother was Central European. However, it is some time before the reader is made aware of these facts.

The task of assembling a complete biography of the character is further complicated by the eagerness with which Arcane and his associates prove willing to confirm his reputation as a source of mystery, rumor, and disinformation. "I have been artful in disguises and pseudonyms," he proudly admits.⁹ In *Lord of the Hollow Dark*, Arcane arrives at Balgrummo Lodging under the alias of Archvicar Gerontion, a drug dealer in Hamnegri who is supposed to play a major role in the ceremony planned by Apollinax. Aside from his loyal retinue, none of the other characters know his true identity, though the skeptical Sweeney does find something incongruent between the Gerontion he knew in Hamnegri and Arcane.¹⁰ A conversation between Marina and Madame Sosostris / Lady Grizelda, meanwhile, only adds to the confusion over Arcane's background. "Why," the latter says, "the Archvicar's orders are quite valid: Mr. Apollinax inquired into that. The Archvicar had himself ordained by the Bishop of Utrecht, ever so long ago, to make sure of it."¹¹ It is difficult, if not impossible, to determine whether Grizelda is speaking here of Arcane or the real Gerontion. Not for nothing does "The Peculiar Demesne" end with one bewildered character wondering which of the two managed to escape from Gerontion's lair. When dealing with Arcane, the reader, too, often faces a difficult task in separating fact from fiction.

However, there are at least two occasions on which Arcane is willing to drop all pretense and provide information about himself in a relatively straightforward

---

⁶ Kirk, *A Creature of the Twilight*, 55.
⁷ Kirk, "The Peculiar Demesne of Archvicar Gerontion," in *Ancestral Shadows*, 252.
⁸ Kirk, *A Creature of the Twilight*, 98.
⁹ Kirk, "The Peculiar Demesne of Archvicar Gerontion," in *Ancestral Shadows*, 259.
¹⁰ Kirk, *Lord of the Hollow Dark*, 14.
¹¹ Ibid., 9.

manner. The first occurs near the end of *A Creature of the Twilight*, in a private account of his life written for the young and impressionable Mary Jo Travers. Nonetheless, it is telling that, rather than employ the standard conventions of autobiography, he chooses to present the story of his life to her in mythopoeic terms. Thus, he refers to himself not as Manfred Arcane but as Tancred, "Knight of the Devious Ways," the illegitimate son of a "grand baron in the land of Albion."[12] After spending the first part of his life in Vienna, Arcane is sent to school in England, where he is taunted for his "swarthy" appearance and "exotic" ways.[13] Upon the death of his father, he receives a sizable inheritance and spends most of his early manhood traveling throughout Europe, Africa, and Asia as a sort of mercenary-for-hire, gaining valuable experience in military strategy, which would serve him well later. Eventually, he settles in Spain, fighting on the side of the Republicans in the civil war there. Then he moves to Italy, where he falls in love with a certain "delicious" countess.[14] This is shortly before the outbreak of the Second World War, which would provide Arcane with exactly the sort of desperate chance to prove his heroism that was sorely lacking during Kirk's time at Dugway Proving Ground in the deserts of Utah. Considering how things turned out for Arcane, perhaps he was fortunate in that.

Disaster strikes one day when, while attempting to smuggle Jews out of Italy, the countess falls into the hands of the Nazis, who send her to a concentration camp. Arcane devises a daring, if highly improbable, plan to rescue her, which involves assuming the guise of a Macedonian S. S. colonel and convincing the inhabitants of a small town next to the camp to join him in attempting to liberate it. There is something of John of Brienne in Arcane's grim determination to see the mission through despite impossible odds: "He made resolve to act, however frantically, as men of old had done, venturing all upon one audacious deed of violence, as liking death better than defeat."[15] Remarkably, he almost succeeds in pulling the whole thing off, but the countess dies before he can reach her. Broken-hearted, Arcane retreats with his ragged band of followers to Spain. Though he has failed in his primary mission, he has met a few of the colorful desperadoes who would later join him in Hamnegri, including the future commander of his Interracial Peace Volunteers, Colonel Fuentes, and the fearsome, mutilated judge, Arpad Nemo. At the end of this lengthy tale, Arcane confesses to having fallen in love with the much younger Travers, who is clearly smitten with him. However, with the fate of a nation at stake and out of loyalty to his deceased lover, he decides against pursuing the matter any further. Given

---

[12] Kirk, *A Creature of the Twilight*, 237.
[13] Ibid., 238.
[14] Ibid., 240-41.
[15] Ibid., 244.

his fondness for Travers, it is likely that the account he offers here is factually correct. One imagines that the whole scene partly derives from, and seeks to replicate, Kirk's fondness for story-telling. His daughter, Cecilia, recalls him regaling her and her sisters with many an impromptu bedtime tale. "He related these stories as installments beside the fireplace ... developing the characters and plots as he spoke."[16] Arcane (at this stage of his life) has no children of his own but seems to have inherited his creator's narrative gifts.

He tells another version of his life story in "The Last God's Dream," published over a decade after *A Creature of the Twilight* in 1979. His audience here is a pair of American tourists whom he has never met before. However, despite having felt the need to frame his past in mythical terms with Travers, a woman he knew well and loved, Arcane is willing to speak freely with these two strangers, reflecting, perhaps, his supreme confidence in himself after having led his followers to victory in the Hamnegrian civil war. The story is set a few years after the events related in *A Creature of the Twilight*, and Arcane offers several details about himself that make it possible to pin down some of the uncertainty regarding his age and background. His mother, we learn, was from the "mountains south of Spalato," in modern-day Croatia: a "gypsy" dancer.[17] Arcane's father was not a British peer but an officer, though still very wealthy. His mistress really had been a countess who perished during the Holocaust. Before the attempted rescue, he had served as a double agent for Italy, Germany, and Spain. Late in the story, there is a reference to one of the tourists winning "a personality contest" in 1978, a year before the story was published. Given Arcane's earlier reference to visiting the town for the first time in 1913 as an "adventurous and willful boy," it is possible to deduce that he is now about 70 years old.[18]

Kirk, himself, was in his early 60s when he published "The Last God's Dream." Most of Kirk's biographers, taking the author at his word, present his decision to convert to Christianity in 1964 as a natural extension of his earlier and lifelong interest in Stoicism. "The Stoicism of [my] military years was not effaced," Kirk explains in his autobiography, "but it was transmuted very gradually. Stoic insights had blended with Christian revelation in the early years of the Church ... so it came to pass in [my] meditations also."[19] However imperfectly, his conversion offers a convenient point at which the early and late

---

[16] Cecilia A. Kirk, "'The Box of Delights': A Literary Patrimony," in *The Unbought Grace of Life: Essays in Honor of Russell Kirk*, ed. James E. Person (Peru, IL: Sherwood Sugden & Company,1994), 62.
[17] Kirk, "The Last God's Dream," in *Ancestral Shadows*, 219.
[18] Ibid., 222.
[19] Kirk, *The Sword of Imagination*, 231.

stages of his life and career may be divided. After all, in addition to assuming a new faith, Kirk was also married in 1964. He and his new bride settled down in Mecosta and soon began to raise a family. In August of 1965 came that memorable evening with Martin D'Arcy, S. J., in which the Kirks were assured by the Jesuit priest that they would be married forever, even after death. He was active on the national political scene during these years, campaigning and writing speeches for Barry Goldwater.[20] Finally, in 1966, *A Creature of the Twilight* was published, giving birth to Kirk's greatest literary creation, Manfred Arcane. I believe that, in this first memorable appearance, the character mostly reflects the life his creator had led before the transformative events of 1964. In his future appearances, there would be more in him of the married, contented Kirk.

Introducing Manfred Arcane

In fact, traces of Arcane are evident in stories written much earlier than Kirk's second novel, suggesting an even longer gestation period than the author may have realized. In 1951, he published one of his earliest stories, "Uncle Isaiah," which features a titular character who bears a strong resemblance to Arcane. Like the future "Father of Shadows," Isaiah is a sinister figure about whom even his family members prefer to speak only in whispers. He has not been seen in many years after he was declared insane and sent to a mental asylum. He later escaped and had the insanity plea overturned by his lawyers. Despite his past, Daniel Kinnaird knows his uncle to be a decent man, one who, even at his best, remains "a force to be feared."[21] He manages to get in touch with Isaiah, who agrees to help his nephew deal with the extortionist threatening his livelihood. In the end, everyone gets what they deserve, especially the gangster whose days of robbing his neighbors are brought to a permanent end.

Uncle Isaiah plays the familiar, retributive role that is seen in so many of Kirk's stories, including several featuring Arcane. However, Isaiah resembles him in other, more direct ways. For instance, they seem to share a similar taste in clothes and are known to be perfect gentlemen, especially in the company of ladies. "His manners were exquisite with everyone," Daniel's wife, Alma, recalls, "and he dressed beautifully." A closer physical description is offered in the story's final pages: "It was a self-assured old man, small but squarely built, dressed with care; he played with a good walking stick; his head was bare, and in the flicker of the candle [the gangster] Costa could see that he had thick white hair, a fresh pink skin, and great eyebrows that made his eyes circles of shadow."[22] After meeting Arcane for the first time, Mary Jo Travers is similarly impressed with

---

[20] Ibid., 261-342.
[21] Birzer, *American Conservative*, 303.
[22] Kirk, "Uncle Isaiah," in *Ancestral Shadows*, 37, 47-48.

his magisterial bearing: "He's quite dark, but his hair and short beard are snow-white, and his English is simply beautiful." A few pages later, she adds that he is "a brisk bearded man, in a kind of white tunic, carrying only a heavy dark stick in his hand."[23] Both Isaiah and Arcane are elderly and short, with stark white hair, yet still imposing; both like to carry walking sticks. After getting to know Arcane a little better, Travers confirms that he also has "beautiful manners."[24] Thus, there is much to suggest that if Kirk envisioned Arcane as his own alter ego, the character was given a sort of trial run in one of his earliest stories.

Indeed, the two characters even have an identical way of talking, which highly resembles Kirk's own erudite and allusive manner of speech. Here are Isaiah's words of greeting to a nephew he has not seen in nine years: "In me, Daniel, decades of celibacy and sobriety are rewarded. I'm as hearty as I was when we last met. But if you will pardon my recurrent eccentricity, we will keep this door shut."[25] He peppers his conversation with snatches of folk songs, verses from the Bible, and quotes from the Stoic philosopher Marcus Aurelius. His insults are no less learned: "I look upon you, sir," he tells the hapless gangster, Costa, "as an interesting phenomenon of social disintegration, a representative specimen of these depraved days."[26] Mark C. Henrie describes the characteristic features of Kirk's prose in terms that would apply just as easily to the speaking styles of both Isaiah and Arcane: "the meandering sentences, the unattributed references to Bunyan, the promiscuous use of aphorisms and epigrams, the sheer, untroubled confidence of the historical and theoretical assertions."[27] The similar word choice between these characters extends even to interjections. When asked why he refuses to come home with Kinnaird, Isaiah replies, "[W]hy, candidly—I fear Alma wouldn't survive the shock without some preparation, eh?" Arcane, too, favors his *why*s and *eh*s.

"Uncle Isaiah" was published in *The London Mystery Magazine* in 1951, two years before *The Conservative Mind* would make Kirk a household name and 15 years before *A Creature of the Twilight* heralded the arrival of Arcane. Kirk had spent the years immediately preceding the writing of this story enrolled in graduate school at St. Andrews, traveling much throughout Scotland and Europe. He had already published several articles in which hints of his mature writing style may be discerned. In his memoirs, he draws attention to one such

---

[23] Kirk, *A Creature of the Twilight*, 17-23.
[24] Ibid., 79.
[25] Kirk, "Uncle Isaiah," in *Ancestral Shadows*, 44.
[26] Ibid., 48.
[27] Mark C. Henrie, "Russell Kirk and the Conservative Heart," *The Imaginative Conservative*, 16 November 2011, https://theimaginativeconservative.org/2011/11/russell-kirk-and-conservative-heart.html.

essay, written in 1944, when he was still serving in the Army, and published in 1945 in *The South Atlantic Quarterly*.

> It might not be surprising to hear the headmaster of a military preparatory school expounding a doctrine which exalts above his victim the legionary who slew Archimedes; but to listen to this cry of "sound, sound the clarion, fill the fife" coming from the ivory tower is another matter. It is an opinion which differs only in degree from an important article in faith in the credo of those states now contesting with us the mastery of the earth, whose intellectual principles we profess to despise.[28]

One imagines that Uncle Isaiah might respond in much the same manner had he ever been prompted for a declamation on the state of modern education in the 1940s. Even in this brief passage, there are traces of some of the hallmarks of Kirk's later style: elaborate sentence structures, literary allusions to classical and literary authors, and an impressive vocabulary.

Kirk did not yet have Isaiah's shock of white hair, but the similarities between him and his fictional creation do not end there. Isaiah's regard for the opposite sex is surely patterned after the author's reputation as something of a perfect gentleman. During his early travels throughout Europe, Kirk recalls in his memoirs, he was often accompanied by young, pretty women. Their relations were entirely "chaste," he hastens to assure the reader, and Kirk remained life-long friends with most of them.[29] After reviewing letters written during that time, Birzer concludes that Kirk's embrace of chastity was perhaps more reluctant than he lets on here;[30] still, there is no denying that he was known for having graceful manners and wrote often enough of his ideal gentleman as being "well-educated, well-read, and virtuous."[31] The walking sticks carried by Uncle Isaiah and Arcane were probably inspired by the author's preference for them; he carried such devices on his early tours of Scotland, and they remained a constant feature of his adult life.[32] Finally, despite being a poor graduate student, Kirk was always careful to make sure that he did not look like one. While still in high school, he had inherited several pairs of expensive suits from his well-dressed uncle, Glenn

---

[28] Kirk, *The Sword of Imagination*, 78. The article is titled, "A Conscript on Education."
[29] Ibid., 83-84.
[30] Birzer, *American Conservative*, 91-92.
[31] Ben Reinhard, "Russell Kirk's Literary Gentlemen," *The Imaginative Conservative*, 8 April 2020, https://theimaginativeconservative.org/2020/04/russell-kirk-literary-gentlemen-ben-reinhard.html.
[32] Kirk, *The Sword of Imagination*, 95. His penchant for walking sticks can be seen, for instance, on the cover of the 2002 paperback edition of his memoirs.

"Potter" Jewell, which served him well for many years.[33] In a letter written late in 1951, he claims to be the only American wearing a cape in St. Andrews.[34] It is not at all difficult to believe.

Uncle Isaiah, then, deserves to be considered as a kind of forerunner of Manfred Arcane, with both characters representing the alter egos of Kirk himself. Both have many of the same speech patterns, sartorial preferences, and mannerisms of their creator. Of course, Kirk's life underwent several changes in the 15 years that separate the two characters; I have already noted that he was both married and converted to Christianity in 1964, two years before *A Creature of the Twilight* was published. Undoubtedly, however, the biggest event of the preceding decade was the 1953 publication of *The Conservative Mind*, which turned Kirk into a major figure in the conservative movement almost overnight. "*The Conservative Mind*," Person observes, "went on to become one of the most widely discussed works of political theory written in the twentieth century."[35] In a pair of letters written to T. S. Eliot towards the end of the year, Kirk reported robust sales and favorable reviews in dozens of influential journals and magazines.[36] He was immediately deluged with requests to speak, write, and lecture around the world, which continued unabated for the rest of his life. Uncle Isaiah, envisioned and written when Kirk was just a poor student, had been content to intervene in the minor affairs of his own family, his only adversary a two-bit gangster who hardly seems worth the trouble of divine retribution. Nevertheless, the author had much grander ambitions for Manfred Arcane, which suited his own as a successful man of letters.

Arcane is not after world domination, but his geopolitical and personal goals are only somewhat less audacious. Throughout *A Creature of the Twilight*, he refers to himself variously by the names of Dionysius, Dis, and Ares. The pseudonyms—all taken from the names of Greco-Roman deities—are meant to suggest the expansive scope of his myriad talents, which range from mastery of social etiquette to knowledge of military tactics. In any case, Arcane spends much of the novel playing Ares, god of war, as he successfully guides the forces of Hamnegri to victory not only against the Marxist usurpers who had deposed the late monarch but also in defiance of global powers such as the US and Soviet Russia, who would turn the civil war in Hamnegri into yet another proxy battle in their endless struggle for world domination. Arcane is in the

---

[33] Ibid., 43.
[34] Kirk to Fay Jewell, 22 December 1951, in *Letters*, 50.
[35] Person, *Critical Biography*, 11.
[36] Kirk to T. S. Eliot, 10 September 1953 and 21 October 1953, in *Letters*, 63-66. Of course, the fact that Kirk (a recent graduate) was able to write to, and expect a reply from, the greatest living poet in English is further confirmation of his improved status.

background for most of the war, directing his men like pieces on a chessboard, but does assume personal command during the climactic Battle of the Krokul Fords, at the end of which he is shot in the back by a traitor.[37] It is as Ares, perhaps, that Arcane is most unlike his predecessor, Uncle Isaiah, and Kirk himself. After all, his struggles and eventual triumph on the battlefield could not be further removed from the safety and tedium of Kirk's actual tour of duty. One cannot help but wonder how much of the character's political and military acumen was inspired by Kirk's frustrating experiences with the Barry Goldwater campaign of 1964. After finding himself excluded from the candidate's inner circle, his influence abruptly neutralized. Kirk may have intended for Arcane to be the forceful and dominant leader to whom the same thing could never happen.[38]

There is undoubtedly more in Arcane of both his predecessor and creator under the guise of Dionysius, god of wine and symbol of "inspired artistic genius" since the time of Horace.[39] Like them, he gets along well with women and always impresses them with his manners. Unlike Isaiah and Kirk, however, Arcane proves instantly attractive to almost every woman he meets and is strongly desired by both of the main female characters in *A Creature of the Twilight*: his Sicilian companion, Melchiora, and the American aid worker, Mary Jo Travers. Both are much younger than he, though Melchiora has a child of her own and is more mature than Travers, about whom Arcane muses condescendingly, "The delicious child has no mind."[40] Without jealousy, Kirk's widow, Annette, admits that Melchiora and Travers were both patterned after female friends of hers and denies that there is much of herself in either.[41] One is tempted to conclude that Kirk intended for Arcane to enjoy opportunities that had been denied to him throughout his long life as a bachelor. At the same time, he adored Annette, as is clear from a letter he wrote her shortly before they were married: "I am rather frightened at the prospect, I confess: I feel as a mortal man must have felt who won the favors of one of the Olympian goddesses. For you really have been my goddess, Annette girl, ever since I first saw you at the Wellington Hotel."[42] Perhaps Arcane is better understood, then,

---

[37] Kirk, *A Creature of the Twilight*, 277-90.
[38] For more on Kirk's experiences during the Goldwater campaign, Chapter 7 in Birzer, *American Conservative*, 245-282, and Chapters 10 and 11 of Kirk's memoirs, 249-298.
[39] John F. Moffitt, *Inspiration: Bacchus and the Cultural History of a Creation Myth* (Leiden, The Netherlands: Brill, 2005), 64. Bacchus is the Roman name for the Greek god known as Dionysius.
[40] Kirk, *A Creature of the Twilight*, 111.
[41] Annette Kirk, interview by author, Mecosta, MI, 15 April 2021, https://creativecommons.org/licenses/by-nc-sa/4.0/.
[42] Kirk to Annette Y. Courtemanche, 20 March 1964, in *Letters*, 109.

as an attempt to create a persona worthy of such luck as Kirk himself enjoyed: a god capable of wooing a goddess.

As Dis, finally, Arcane seems to embody some of the darker aspects of both Uncle Isaiah and Kirk, though surpassing both. In classical mythology, Dis (Roman *Pluto*) is the god of the underworld, whose appeal to the Gothically-inclined Kirk should be obvious enough. Even as a young man, he had taken the existence of ghosts quite seriously, a belief supported by whatever authoritative and empirical means were at hand: namely, family lore and his infrequent encounters with them. Later, sounding very much like Arcane, he would tell his new bride, "The darkness belongs to us."[43] Though he strenuously avoids including ghosts and other supernatural elements in his first two novels (perhaps in the hope of securing them a wider audience), he is less ambivalent about their use in his early stories, several of which feature hauntings, vengeful spirits, etc. "Uncle Isaiah" attempts to strike a middle ground, suggesting that there is something uncanny about the titular character but declining to confirm the reader's suspicions about who or what he really is. Isaiah certainly sounds as if he had escaped—or been set loose from—Purgatory. "[Y]et you will understand that I am here on sufferance; my tenure is precarious; and my present arrangements require that our intercourse take place wholly *per vox* …"[44] The story ends with Isaiah cornering the gangster who had been threatening his nephew; the reader is left to imagine the well-deserved fate that awaits the man. Uncle Isaiah would not be out of place, one suspects, among the crew of misfits that comprise Arcane's entourage in Haggat, his base in Hamnegri.

The young Kirk fully believed in the possibility of an afterlife; Isaiah might have proven its existence; only Arcane could get away with calling himself its ruler: Dis, the Father of Shadows. Having traveled to a concentration camp in a failed attempt to rescue the love of his life, he has every reason to think that he has been to Hell and back. In a recorded message to Travers, he refers to himself as "such a one as Orestes, and as doomed to slay and to be slain."[45] His enduring grief over those events may be another reason he chooses to frame his life story to her as a kind of fable, with himself in the role of the "Knight of the Devious Ways." Though calling himself Dis, Arcane also resembles, in part, one of the underworld's most famous mythical visitors: Orpheus. In most versions of his oft-retold tale, Orpheus descends into Hell to rescue his wife, Eurydice, after Dis / Pluto abducts her. He succeeds in winning her back with a song but is warned not

---

[43] Kirk, *The Sword of Imagination*, 22. He describes ghostly encounters at Mecosta in the preceding pages.
[44] Kirk, "Uncle Isaiah," in *Ancestral Shadows*, 44.
[45] Kirk, *A Creature of the Twilight*, 229.

to look at her until after they have returned to the world of the living. He cannot prevent himself from doing so, of course, and ends up losing her again, this time forever. "The myth of Orpheus and Eurydice has been retold time and again since Ovid's *Metamorphoses*," notes Efrossini Spentzou.[46] It is retold once again, or at least alluded to, in *A Creature of the Twilight*.

Nevertheless, towards the end of the novel, with his victory assured, Arcane once again assumes the familiar role of Dis. Unlike Orpheus, who has no choice but to slink back to the world of the living without his prize, Arcane spends the years after his descent into Hell planning his revenge on those who took his beloved away from him. He manages to lure the former Nazis who ran the camp in which she perished to the roof of his mansion in Hamnegri, where he confronts them with one of their other victims: the ruined judge Arpad Nemo, now playing Rhadamanthus to Arcane's Dis. As with Uncle Isaiah's moment of triumph, Kirk leaves the details of Nemo's revenge to the reader's imagination.[47] Afterward, Arcane is finally free to retire the Dis persona. He and Melchiora are married, and there is every reason to believe they will be as happy together as Kirk had found married life with his new, beautiful bride. By the time he resumes writing stories about Arcane over a decade later, both he and his alter ego will have changed considerably.

The Father of Shadows in Old Age

Kirk turned 48 in 1966, the year in which *A Creature of the Twilight* was published. Arcane would not appear again in his work until 1979, when Kirk was 61. That was a kind of *annus mirabilis* for his fiction, with the publication of his second collection of stories, *The Princess of All Lands*, and his last novel, *Lord of the Hollow Dark*. Arcane features conspicuously in several of the former's new tales and is the main character in the latter. Kirk would produce one more collection of stories, 1984's *Watchers at the Strait Gate*, but only about half of the stories in it were new. He was clearly losing interest in the writing of fiction. In a letter to Ray Bradbury written in 1980, he mentions longing to "rest on [his] laurels, so far as fiction is concerned" after finishing one last "longish uncanny tale."[48] How much Kirk's life had changed in the intervening years is evident from a letter sent in 1976 to Brigid Boardman, a long-time family friend. In it, he discusses the forthcoming publication of *The Princess of All Lands*, as well

---

[46] Efrossini Spentzou, "Orpheus, Byblis, Myrrha: Towards a Matrixial Ethics of Encounter in Ovid's Metamorphoses," *International Journal of the Classical Tradition* 26, no. 4 (December 2019): 419, doi:10.1007/s12138-019-00512-8. Three especially influential versions of the Orpheus myth are told by Vergil, Ovid, and Boethius.

[47] Kirk, *A Creature of the Twilight*, 313.

[48] Kirk to Ray Bradbury, September 1980, in *Letters*, 232.

as a planned trip to California to confer with then-Governor Ronald Reagan about the possibility of filming his great historical treatise on *The Roots of American Order*. Finally, he sends Boardman the love of his much-enlarged family, consisting of his wife, Annette, and his four daughters, Monica, Cecilia, Felicia, and the "ever-cheerful" Andrea, then only one-year-old.[49]

Though he had spent his first forty years as a bachelor, Kirk took to life as a family man with gusto. His happiness with Annette is evident in the evolving relationship between Arcane and Melchiora over the years. I have already noted how Annette Kirk believes her husband to have modeled this character after two of her friends, but something of herself must have been added to the mix, also. In *A Creature of the Twilight*, Arcane already has many nicknames for his future wife, most of which are identical to those employed by Kirk for Annette. For instance, both husbands favor the unusual endearment, "Persephone." In Greek mythology, Persephone was a young virgin abducted by Dis / Pluto, who was then forced to become his bride and rule as queen of the underworld. Kirk may have found the name fitting because, in the early days of their courtship, he feared that Annette might look upon the prospect of being married to him with some degree of horror.[50] "Persephone" also suggests something of Annette's regal nature; in his memoirs, Kirk describes being struck occasionally by her "hauteur."[51] In *Lord of the Hollow Dark*, Arcane and Melchiora are still happily wedded and as fond of each other as ever. He has taken to addressing her by two other nicknames: "Hypatia," after the celebrated Greek mathematician and philosopher, and "Pomegranate," which is a fruit that has often been closely associated with Persephone.[52] Kirk also used both for Annette.

There is further evidence to suggest that Melchiora was at least partly patterned after Kirk's wife. For example, they seem to resemble each other physically. Early in *Lord of the Hollow Dark*, Kirk offers the following description of Melchiora: "Then [Marina] saw a darkly lovely young woman, wild-looking, down her back a splendid mane of black hair, her face at once passionate and controlled …"[53] In "The Peculiar Demesne of Archvicar Gerontion," first published in 1980, Melchiora is described thusly: "sibylline and haughty, her

---

[49] Kirk to Brigid M. Boardman, 5 December 1976, in *Letters*, 197-98.
[50] Kirk to Annette Y. Courtemanche, 20 March 1964, in *Letters*, 108.
[51] Kirk, *The Sword of Imagination*, 290.
[52] Ovid, *The Metamorphoses*, trans. A. D. Melville (Oxford: Oxford University Press, 2008), 109-16. After Persephone's abduction, her mother, Demeter, begged Zeus to free her, but it was discovered that Persephone had already eaten some pomegranate seeds, and could thus not fully return to the world of the living. As a compromise, she was allowed to leave Hell for part of the year.
[53] Kirk, *Lord of the Hollow Dark*, 36.

mass of black hair piled high upon her head, her black eyes gleaming in the lamplight."[54] Here is how Kirk recalls Annette at their first meeting: "Hers was an exquisite beauty, a unique one, difficult to describe. One was hard put to say from what race she came ... That splendid and somewhat haughty face (relieved by sweetness and innocence of expression) was crowned by long, long black hair, admirably groomed."[55] The age gap between Arcane and Melchiora is identical to the one that existed between Kirk and Annette. Melchiora is more mature than either Mary Jo Travers, Didi, or Marina (the main female characters in *A Creature of the Twilight*, "The Last God's Dream," and *Lord of the Hollow Dark*, respectively), and is probably in her mid to late twenties by the time of her first appearance in Kirk's second novel. Shortly before marrying Annette, Kirk had fretted that, at 44, he was already twice her age and, therefore, too old for her. He even modestly wondered what she could see in him.[56] Arcane's relationship with Melchiora offered him a chance to explore this question through his fiction.

Like Annette, Melchiora is a devout Catholic. Kirk's wife had been born in the faith and insisted that their children be raised in it, as well. The couple's embrace of Christian charity began quite literally at home, as they welcomed countless refugees and immigrants to Piety Hill over the years. "Unwilling to say no to almost anyone," Lee Edwards writes, "Russell and Annette were in danger of being eaten out of house and land. It became necessary to sell property, but the Kirks sought consolation and confirmation of their faith in the motto above the entrance to their home: 'God helping, work prospers.'"[57] One of their long-time though sporadic guests, Clinton Wallace, was a homeless vagabond who had been in and out of jail most of his life and probably suffered from a mild form of mental illness. "Unschooled and unmachined, Clinton was unemployable by anyone except the Kirks"—and so the Kirks, inspired by Annettte's Christian values, continued to feed and clothe him until he died six years later.[58] Perhaps their generosity towards others helps to explain why Kirk always depicts Arcane as being surrounded by a crew of misfits: whether in Haggat or Scotland, he seems to attract to himself those with nowhere else to go and few viable skills to offer anyone, like the mutilated Arpad Nemo or the failed architect, Sweeney. Melchiora also lives by his sufferance, along with her son, Guido. She is revealed to be Catholic early in *A Creature of the Twilight*

---

[54] Kirk, "The Peculiar Demesne of Archvicar Gerontion," in *Ancestral Shadows*, 252.
[55] Kirk, *The Sword of Imagination*, 261.
[56] Ibid., 289.
[57] Lee Edwards, "The Marriage That Shaped American Conservatism," *Intercollegiate Studies Institute*, 20 August 2019, https://isi.org/intercollegiate-review/marriage-shaped-american-conservatism/.
[58] Kirk, *The Sword of Imagination*, 353.

when she crosses herself while talking to Arcane.[59] Just as Annette's faith influenced Kirk's treatment of others, so too did Melchiora's affect her future husband.

Certainly, both women had a moderating effect on the religious views of their respective spouses, who were baptized in middle age but never proved to be especially devout. According to Person, Kirk stopped attending church regularly during the mid-1970s.[60] He continued to identify as Catholic but did not feel the need to observe all of the associated rituals. He was also dismayed by many of the liturgical changes enacted after Vatican II, as reflected not only in his memoirs but in his fiction, as well.[61] As for Arcane, there is little evidence of him being a Christian in *A Creature of the Twilight*, even though Kirk wrote the book after his conversion. Instead, he manifests the same admiration for the pagan culture of classical Greece and Rome that prompted Kirk to write "lovingly if purely symbolically of myth, gods, demigods, and heroes."[62] Once again, Arcane's characterization in this novel seems to reflect more the life Kirk had led before the memorable events of 1964. In later appearances, he would admit to being a "papist" and generally expresses views that are more consistent with Christianity. Perhaps as a way of atoning for the occasional lapse in reverence in both himself and his alter ego, Kirk makes sure that the last scene featuring Arcane shows him in a devout light: before leaving the room at the end of "The Peculiar Demesne of Archvicar Gerontion," he genuflects before a crucifix hanging on the wall.[63]

At least one major difference between Melchiora and Annette is worth noting. Kirk's courtship of the young "Conservative beauty" was a protracted affair, lasting several years. Again, he was troubled by doubts about their compatibility. She, as an attractive woman with many suitors, must have also been reluctant to commit herself to a man so much older, however much she may have admired him as a thinker and writer. In any case, Kirk was very much the submissive, pursuing partner in their relationship. His description of their courtship confirms that she was more than a little haughty towards him: she very much had him wrapped around her finger, and they both knew it. Birzer calls Annette completely "untamable": "a force of nature" who could "readily tame those around her"—including her husband![64] And yet, in the relationship

---

[59] Kirk, *A Creature of the Twilight*, 44.
[60] Person, *Critical Biography*, 13.
[61] Kirk, *The Sword of Imagination*, 423-24. His dislike of Vatican II is particularly evident in "Watchers at the Strait Gate" and *Lord of the Hollow Dark*.
[62] Birzer, *American Conservative*, 376.
[63] Kirk, "The Peculiar Demesne of Archvicar Gerontion," in *Ancestral Shadows*, 275.
[64] Birzer, *American Conservative*, 383.

between Arcane and Melchiora, the roles are reversed, with Arcane being the dominant one and Melchiora completely submissive. This is especially noticeable in *A Creature of the Twilight* but also true in the final story Kirk wrote that features the pair, "The Peculiar Demesne of Archvicar Gerontion." After hearing him speak about his encounter with Gerontion, she responds in a melodramatic fashion: "'Only you, Manfred, could have had will strong enough to come back from that place,' Melchiora told her husband. She murmured what I took for Sicilian endearments. Her fine eyes were wet, though she must have heard the fearful story many times before. Her hands trembled badly."[65] Making Melchiora so passive contributes to her husband's mystique as a powerful and attractive man. Still, Annette in real life was far from docile. She remains a "force of nature," even into her 80s—as anyone who has visited Piety Hill in recent years can attest.

Of course, it is quite easy to view Kirk's mythologizing of his friends and family in an unflattering light, to make the mistake of assuming that, because most of his characters were based on people he knew, he was willing to exploit his relationships for the sake of his fiction. Indeed, that is the claim made by Adrina Tran in a prize-winning essay from 2016, published in *The Michigan Historical Review*. She focuses on Kirk's relationship with Clinton Wallace, the "hobo in residence" at Piety Hill for some years starting in the mid-1960s, whom Kirk portrays in several stories as the good-hearted wandering tramp Frank Sarsfield.[66] Tran objects to Kirk's depiction of Wallace in "There's a Long, Long Trail A-Winding." Due to the author's fictional treatment of his friend, she argues, "the memory of Clinton Wallace would be absorbed into the mythology of Frank Sarsfield," who does not erase his namesake but "consigns him to the hazy space between fact and fiction."[67] Perhaps something similar might be said about the portrayals of Annette Kirk mentioned above, except that her refusal to remarry in the years after his death and her hard work in preserving and transmitting to others her husband's legacy suggests the folly of believing that Kirk was capable of using his friends and loved ones in so cynical a manner. In Wallace's case, it is doubtful that any "memory" of the man would exist at all had he not been immortalized in Kirk's stories and in the frequent columns he wrote about him. It is also important to remember that Sarsfield is *not* Wallace but is only based on him; in equating the two, Tran seems to make the very mistake she accuses Kirk of committing.

---

[65] Kirk, "The Peculiar Demesne of Archvicar Gerontion," in *Ancestral Shadows*, 273-74.
[66] Kirk, *The Sword of Imagination*, 350.
[67] Adrina Tran, "An Experiment in the Moral Imagination: Russell Kirk, Clinton Wallace, and Conservative Hobohemia," *The Michigan Historical Review* 42, no. 1 (Spring 2016): 30-31.

In any case, there is clearly much textual evidence to support the idea that Kirk regarded Arcane as his alter ego. Long before writing *A Creature of the Twilight*, he had experimented with creating characters that reflected certain aspects of himself: his style, manners, appearance, and inimitable way of speaking. This is most evident in the titular figure from "Uncle Isaiah," though his fiction certainly furnishes other examples of mannered, articulate heroes (and villains). In his first appearance, Arcane seems to reflect more the earlier, carefree lifestyle his author had led until the fateful year in which he married Annette and converted to Christianity. Even early reviewers, such as Thomas Quinn, found it easy to pinpoint Kirk's intentions with this strange, though undoubtedly arresting, character: "Manfred is a jolly schemer, a manly lover, a noble character and, alas, quite out of place anywhere but in this quasi-Medieval African land. There are hints of a spiritual autobiography here."[68] Through the years, as Kirk settled into a happy marriage, his love for his wife deepened, and he sought to give his hero a spiritual and marital happiness to match his own. The elderly Arcane who returns in his final stories and *Lord of the Hollow Dark* is a slower, more reflective man, much changed from the reckless and dashing figure who had so confounded US and Soviet authorities as the de-facto ruler of a tiny African kingdom. Then again, Kirk, too, had changed.

Russell Amos Kirk: Wizard and Prophet

One thing that never changed, of course, was his abiding love of literature. Certain authors were always favorites of his, including J. R. R. Tolkien. His daughter, Cecilia, recalls him reading from *The Hobbit* and *The Lord of the Rings* to her and her sisters.[69] In *Enemies of the Permanent Things*, Kirk praises Tolkien as a powerful defender of traditional values. "The tremendous popularity of his fable ... suggests that the moral imagination of our rising generation, starved though it has been by dominant Logicalism and flabby Sociability in our education system, still may be waked."[70] Kirk was surely familiar with "Leaf by Niggle," an allegorical story published by Tolkien in 1945. Its hero is an unassuming painter who knows that he must someday embark upon a long journey he dreads to undertake. In the meantime, he becomes obsessed with one of his creations, a painting of a tree crowned with leaves and, in the background, a glimpse of forest and mountains fading off in the distance. "Niggle lost interest in his other pictures, or else he took them and tacked them

---

[68] Thomas Quinn, "Summer Reading: You Need Help, Charlie Brown" (review of *A Creature of the Twilight*), *Reporter*, August 1964, Russell Kirk Center for Cultural Renewal.
[69] Cecilia Kirk, "The Box of Delights," in *The Unbought Grace of Life*, 61.
[70] Kirk, *Enemies of the Permanent Things*, 131.

on to the edges of his great picture."⁷¹ Eventually, but long before the painting is done, he is forced to depart. He visits many different places and eventually reaches one that is very similar to his painting; in fact, he realizes it *is* his painting, or at least, it is the real place he had been attempting to capture through his art. The story has been interpreted on many different levels but works quite well as an allegorical depiction of Tolkien's intentions as an author.⁷² Like Niggle, he spent much of his life toiling away in the obscure labor related to his vast legendarium, which remained unfinished at the time of his death. He could only trust that others would find meaning and value in that work, not knowing how many millions of souls it would eventually touch and continue to inspire!

Perhaps Kirk wrote fiction for a similar reason, though on a much more modest scale, obviously. It is true that he did not spend his whole life writing about Arcane or his world and tended to disparage his creative efforts. However, he did produce stories and novels throughout much of his adulthood and clearly put many of his hopes and desires into the character. Indeed, in a 1990 letter to Gloria Whelan, a fellow Michigan writer, Kirk explains that he would have continued writing stories had there existed a market for his Gothic fiction and refers to himself as "the last master of the uncanny tale" following the death of Robert Aickman nearly a decade prior.⁷³ Whatever frustrations he may have felt during the lonely years of his bachelorhood or after the failure of the Goldwater campaign, Kirk never lost sight of what he really wanted to do with his life, which was to redeem the times by guiding others to an understanding and appreciation of the permanent things. He sought to do this not through force or pure ("defecated") reason, which is the way of the ideologue, but through something far more powerful than either: the moral imagination. Ultimately, he hoped to prove, like Arcane, a wizard and prophet capable of leading misguided pilgrims through the wasteland of the contemporary world. At the end of *Lord of the Hollow Dark*, Arcane comforts his followers thusly: "What matters about time, I think, is not duration, but intensity—that is, how we spend it. If we spend it well, we are promised, then we shall transcend time."⁷⁴ With such words did Kirk seek to assure his wife that they would always be together in Heaven … with such words did he seek to assure all readers of his fiction, however few or many they might be, that they, too, could hope to enjoy the same eternal happiness as Kirk believed to be waiting for him after death.

---

[71] J. R. R. Tolkien, "Leaf by Niggle," in *The Tolkien Reader* (New York: Ballantine Books, 1966), 101.
[72] Marie Nelson, "J. R. R. Tolkien's 'Leaf by Niggle': An Allegory in Transformation," *Mythlore* 28, no. ¾ (2010): 11.
[73] Kirk to Gloria Whelan, 18 November 1990, in *Letters*, 328.
[74] Kirk, *Lord of the Hollow Dark*, 335.

Bibliography

Abrams, M. H. "On the Transformation of English Studies: 1930-1995." *Daedalus* 126, no. 1 (Winter 1997): 105-31. *JSTOR*, https://www.jstor.org/stable/20027411.

Ackroyd, Peter. *T. S. Eliot: A Life*. New York: Simon and Schuster, 1984.

Aguirre, Manuel. "Thick Description and the Poetics of the Liminal in Gothic Tales." *Orbis Litterarum: International Review of Literary Studies* 72, no. 4 (August 2017): 294-17. doi: 10.1111/oli.12138.

Allitt, Patrick. Review of *Russell Kirk: American Conservative*, by Bradley J. Birzer. *Catholic Historical Review* 103, no. 1 (2017): 163-64. *Academic Search Premier*.

Anderson, Elizabeth. "Burnt and Blossoming: Material Mysticism in *Trilogy* and *Four Quartets*." *Christianity and Literature* 62, no. 1 (Autumn 2012): 121-42. doi: 10.1177/014833311206200107.

Andrews, Corey E. "Venders, Purchasers, Admirers: Burnsian 'Men of Action' from the Nineteenth to the Twenty-First Century." *Scottish Literary Review* 2, no. 1 (2010): 97-115. *Academic Search Premier*.

Bacevich, Andrew J. *The Long War: A New History of U.S. National Security Policy Since World War* II. New York: Columbia University Press, 2007.

———. "My Guy." *Raritan* 39, no. 3 (2020): 59-70.

Bakhos, Carol. *Ishmael on the Border: Rabbinic Portrayals of the First Arab*. Albany, NY: State University of New York Press, 2006.

Barasel, James. "Russell Kirk's fiction is unjustly ignored." *The Catholic Herald*, 8 August 2019. https://catholicherald.co.uk/russell-kirks-fiction-is-unjustly-ignored/.

Barry, Peter. *Beginning Theory: An Introduction to Literary and Cultural Theory*. Manchester, England: Manchester University Press, 2009.

Battersby, James L. "Life, Art, and the *Lives of the Poets*. In *Domestick Privacies: Samuel Johnson and the Art of Biography*, edited by David Wheeler, 26-56. Lexington, KY: The University Press of Kentucky, 1987.

Beauchamp, Scott. "Horror and Eternity." *Modern Age* 60, no. 3 (2018): 49-56.

———. "Russell Kirk's Ghostly Tales: Horror and Eternity." *The Imaginative Conservative*, 25 October 2018. Accessed 24 September 2020. https://theimaginativeconservative.org/2018/10/horror-eternity-russell-kirk-ghost-scott-beauchamp.html.

Berkowitz, Peter. "The Liberalism of Edmund Burke." *Policy Review*, no. 176 (December 2012 / January 2013): 51-68. *Academic Search Premier*.

Binney, Matthew W. "Edmund Burke's Sublime Cosmopolitan Aesthetic." *Studies in English Literature, 1500-1900* 53, no. 3 (2013): 643-66. *Gale Academic OneFile*.

Birzer, Bradley J. *Russell Kirk: American Conservative*. Lexington, KY: University Press of Kentucky, 2015.

———. "The Permanence of Humanism." *Modern Age* 59, no. 2 (2017): 53-63.

———. "When Russell Kirk Was Really Scary." *The American Conservative*, 19 October 2018. https://www.theamericanconservative.com/articles/when-russell-kirk-was-really-scary/.

Boswell, James. *The Life of Samuel Johnson*. Edited by Christopher Hibbert. London: Penguin Books, 1979.

Bowers, Katherine. "Ghost Writers: Radcliffiana and the Russian Gothic Wave." *Victorian Popular Fictions* 3, no. 2 (2021): 153-79. doi: 10.46911/TVCT9530.

Bradizza, Luigi. Review of *Imaginative Conservative: The Letters of Russell Kirk*. *Independent Review* 23, no. 4 (2019): 636-39. *Academic Search Premier*.

Brattston, David W. T. "Avarice and Greed." *Catholic Insight* 15, no. 3 (2007): 39-40.

Brennan, Michael G. *Evelyn Waugh: Fictions, Faith and Family*. London: Bloomsbury Academic, 2013.

Bristol, Michael. "Macbeth the Philosopher: Rethinking Context." *New Literary History* 42, no. 4 (2011): 641-662. *JSTOR*, https://www.jstor.org/stable/41328990.

Brooks, Christopher. "Johnson's Insular Mind and the Analogy of Travel: *A Journey to the Western Islands of Scotland*." *Essays in Literature* 18, no. 1 (Spring 1991): 21-36. *Humanities Full Text (H. W. Wilson)*.

Buckley, William F. "Russell Kirk, R. I. P." *National Review* 46, no. 10 (30 May 1994): 19-20.

Burke, Edmund. *A Philosophical Enquiry into the Origin of Our Ideas of the Sublime and Beautiful*. 5th ed. London: J. Dodsley, 1767. *Google Books*, https://www.google.com/books/edition/A_Philosophical_Enquiry_Into_the_Origin/CUgJAAAAQAAJ?hl=en&gbpv=0.

———. *Reflections on the Revolution in France*. Edited by L. G. Mitchell. 1790. Reprint, Oxford: Oxford University Press, 2009.

Castle, Gregory. *The Literary Theory Handbook*. Hoboken, New Jersey: Wiley-Blackwell, 2013.

Catechism of the Catholic Church. 2nd ed. New York: Doubleday, 1994.

Chow, Andrew R. "Historians Decode the Religious Symbolism and Queer Iconography of Lil Nas X's 'Montero' Video." *Time*. 30 March 2021. https://time.com/5951024/lil-nas-x-montero-video-symbolism-explained/.

Clery, E. J. "The Genesis of 'Gothic' Fiction." In *The Cambridge Companion to Gothic Fiction*, edited by Jerrold E. Hogle, 21-40. Cambridge: Cambridge University Press, 2002.

Coffey, Laura. "Evelyn Waugh's Country House Trinity: Memory, History, and Catholicism in 'Brideshead Revisited.'" *Literature and History* 15, no. 1 (2006): 59-73. doi: 10.7227/lh.15.1.4.

Collinson, David, Owain Smolović Jones, and Keith Grint. "'No More Heroes': Critical Perspectives on Leadership Romanticism." *Organization Studies* 39, no. 11 (2018): 1625-647. doi: 10.1177/0170840617727784.

Continetti, Matthew. "The Forgotten Father of American Conservatism." *The Atlantic*, 19 October 2020. https://www.theatlantic.com/ideas/archive/2018/10/russell-kirk-father-american-conservatism/573433/.

Cooper, Barry. *Eric Voegelin and the Foundations of Modern Political Science*. Columbia, MO: University of Missouri Press, 1999.

Cordner, Colin. "The diagnosis of scientism: Eric Voegelin and Michael Polanyi on science and philosophy." *Appraisal* 9, no. 3 (March 2013): 1-12. *Gale Academic OneFile*.

Cox, Jeffrey N. "First Gothics: Walpole, Evans, Frank." *Papers on Language and Literature: A Journal of Scholars and Critics of Language and Literature* 46, no. 2 (Spring 2010): 113-35. *MLA International Bibliography with Full Text*.

Creaney, Rachel and Piotr Niewiadomski. "Tourism and Sustainable Development on the Isle of Eigg, Scotland." *Scottish Geographical Journal* 132, no. 3 - 4 (2016): 210-33. doi: 10.1080/14702541.2016.1146327.

Dalby, Richard. "Obituary: Russell Kirk." *The Independent*, 30 June 1994.

Damrosch, Leo. *The Club: Johnson, Boswell, and the Friends Who Shaped an Age*. New Haven, CT: Yale University Press, 2019.

Deane, Patrick. "Rhetoric and Affect: Eliot's Classicism, Pound's Symbolism, and the Drafts of *The Waste Land*." *Journal of Modern Literature* 18, no. 1 (Winter 1992): 77-93. *MLA International Bibliography with Full Text*.

Deedes, Bill. "Evelyn Waugh in Ethiopia: reflections and recollections." *Journalism Studies* 2, no. 1 (February 2001): 27-29. doi: 10.1080/14616700120 021784.

DeLamotte, Eugenia C. *Perils of the Night: A Feminist Study of Ninteenth-Century Gothic*. New York: Oxford University Press, 1990.

Delasara, Jan. *PopLit, PopCult and the X-Files: A Critical Exploration*. Jefferson, NC: McFarland, & Company, 2000.

Ding, Katherine. "'Searching After the Splendid Nothing': Gothic Epistemology and the Rise of Fictionality." *ELH* 80, no. 2 (2013): 543-73. *JSTOR*, https://www.jstor.org/stable/24475517.

Donoghue, Denis. *Words Alone: The Poet T. S. Eliot*. New Haven, CT: Yale University Press, 2000.

Dougal, Josephine. "Popular Scottish Song Traditions at Home (and Away)." *Folklore* 122, no. 3 (2011): 283-307. *JSTOR*, https://www.jstor.org/stable/4130 6603.

Downum, Dennell M. "Apeneck Sweeney's penitential path." *Yeats Eliot Review* 26, no. 1 (Spring 2009): 2-16. *Gale Academic OneFile*.

Duncan, Ian. "Primitive Inventions: Rob Roy, Nation, and World System." *Eighteenth Century Fiction* 15, no. 1 (2002): 81-102. doi: 10.1353/ecf.2002.006 1.

Dunderberg, Ismo. *Beyond Gnosticism: Myth, Lifestyle, and Society in the School of Valentinus*. New York: Columbia University Press, 2008.

Dunne, Michael W. "Richard FitzRalph on the Beatific Vision: *Delectatio* and *Beatitudo* in his Oxford Lectures on the Sentences (1328-29). *Irish Theological Quarterly* 80, no. 4 (2015): 327-43. doi: 10.1177/0021140015598580.

Durant, David. "Ann Radcliffe and the Conservative Gothic." *Studies in English Literature, 1500 - 1900* 22, no. 3 (Summer 1982): 519-30. doi: 10.2307/450245.

Edwards, Lee. *Educating for Liberty: The First Half-Century of the Intercollegiate Studies Institute*. Washington, D.C.: Regnery Publishing, 2003.

———. "The Marriage That Shaped American Conservatism." *Intercollegiate Studies Institute*, 20 August 2019. https://isi.org/intercollegiate-review/marri age-shaped-american-conservatism/.

Edwards, Mickey. *Reclaiming Conservatism: How a Great American Political Movement Got Lost — and How It Can Find Its Way Back.* Oxford: Oxford University Press, 2008.

Eliot, T. S. *The Complete Poems & Plays.* 1969. Reprint, London: Faber and Faber, 2004.

———. *The Idea of a Christian Society.* 1939. Reprint, New York: Houghton Mifflin Harcourt, 2014.

———. "Tradition and the Individual Talent." In *Selected Essays: 1917-1932*, 3-11. New York: Harcourt, Brace and Company, 2014.

Escolme, Bridget. "Public Eye and Private Place: Intimacy and Metatheatre in *Pericles* and *The Tempest*." *Shakespeare Bulletin: The Journal of Early Modern Drama in Performance* 36, no. 1 (2018): 111-30. doi: 10.1353/shb.2018.0007.

Feibel, Juliet. "Highland Histories: Jacobitism and Second Sight." *Clio* 30, no. 1 (Fall 2000): 51-77. *Humanities Full Text (H. W. Wilson).*

Flores, Felicia Kirk. Facebook message to author. 18 May 2022.

Folkenflik, Robert. "'Rasselas' and the Closed Field." *Huntington Library Quarterly* 57, no. 4 (Autumn 1994): 337-52. doi: 10.2307/3817841.

Francisconi, Michael Joseph. "Political Sociology and Anthropology in Education: A Manifesto for Subversive Education." *New Proposals: Journal of Marxism and Interdisciplinary Inquiry* 1, no. 2 (2008): 5-8. https://doaj.org/article/dcc7425711754626939ba553364d3622.

French, Amanda L. "Edmund Gosse and the Stubborn Villanelle Blunder." *Victorian Poetry* 48, no. 2 (Summer 2010): 243-66. doi:10.1353/vp.0.0104.

Gable, Harvey L. "Inappeasable Longings: Hawthorne, Romance, and the Disintegration of Coverdale's Self in the *Blithedale Romance*." *New England Quarterly* 67, no. 2 (1994): 257-78. doi: 10.2307/366081.

Garside, Peter. "Popular Fiction and National Tale: Hidden Origins of Scott's Waverley." *Nineteenth-Century Literature* 46, no. 1 (1991): 30-53. doi: 10.2307/3044962.

Gefin, Laszlo K. "False Exists: The Literary Allusion in Modern Fiction." *Papers on Language & Literature* 20, no. 4 (1984): 431-52. *Academic Search Premier.*

Goldsworth, Adrian. *How Rome Fell: Death of a Superpower.* New Haven, CT: Yale University Press, 2009.

Gorday, Peter. "'He Recited in a Low Voice the Splendid Hymns of the Roman Church': Sir Walter Scott and Catholic Romanticism in the Thought of Henri Bremond." *Logos: A Journal of Catholic Thought & Culture* 25, no. 4 (2022): 74-99. Doi: 10.1353/log.2022.0030.

Groom, Nick. Introduction to *The Castle of Otranto*, by Horace Walpole, ix-xxxviii. Oxford: Oxford University Press, 2014.

Guillard, Julianne. "'You are exactly my brand of heroin(e)': Convergences and Divergences of the Gothic Literary Heroine." *Girlhood Studies* 4, no. 1 (Summer 2011): 49-66. doi: 10.3167/ghs.2011.040105.

Guroian, Vigen. Introduction to *Ancestral Shadows: An Anthology of Ghostly Tales*, by Russell Kirk, vii-xvii. Grand Rapids, MI: Eerdmans, 2004.

Haber, Tom B. "The Chapter-Tags in the Waverley Novels." *PMLA* 45, no. 4 (1930): 1142-149. Accessed 9 May 2019. *JSTOR*, doi: 10.2307/457832.

Hadley, Sean. "Russell Kirk and Reenchanting the Political Imagination." *Voegelin View*, 16 September 2023. https://voegelinview.com/reenchanting-the-political-imagination-russell-kirk/.

Haggerty, George. *Horace Walpole's Letters: Masculinity and Friendship in the Eighteenth Century.* Lewisburg, PA: Bucknell University Press, 2011. *ProQuest Ebook Central.*

Hall, Lauren. "Rights and the Heart: Emotions and Rights Claims in the Political Theory of Edmund Burke." *The Review of Politics* 73, no. 4 (Fall 2011): 609-31. https://www.jstor.org/stable/41345995.

Hanley, Brian. *Samuel Johnson as Book Reviewer: A Duty to Examine the Labors of the Learned.* Newark, NJ: University of Delaware Press, 2001.

Harrick, Katrina. "Temporal, mnemonic, and aesthetic 'eruptions': recontextualizing Eliot and the modern literary artwork." *Yeats Eliot Review* 26, no. 2 (Summer 2009): 3-15. *Gale Academic OneFile.*

Harrison, John R. "What Rough Beast? Yeats, Nietzsche and Historical Rhetoric in 'The Second Coming.'" *Papers on Language & Literature* 31, no. 4 (1995): 362-88.

Hartwell, David G. Introduction to "There's a Long, Long Trail a-Winding," in *The Dark Descent*, 59. Edited by David G. Hartwell. New York: Tor, 1987.

Hawthorne, Nathaniel. "Chiefly About War Matters." *The Atlantic Monthly*, July 1862. https://www.theatlantic.com/magazine/archive/1862/07/chiefly-about-war-matters/306159/.

———. *Hawthorne: Tales and Sketches.* The Library of America, 1996.

———. Preface to *The House of Seven Gables.* In *The Best of Hawthorne*, edited by Mark Van Doren, 399-401. New York: The Ronald Press Company, 1951.

———. *The House of the Seven Gables.* Signet Classics, 1961.

———. *The Scarlet Letter.* New York: Penguin Books, 2003.

Henrie, Mark C. "Conservative Minds Revisited." *Modern Age* 45, no. 4 (2003): 291-365. *OmniFile Full Text Mega (H. W. Wilson).*

———. "Russell Kirk and the Conservative Heart." *The Imaginative Conservative*, 16 November 2011. https://theimaginativeconservative.org/2011/11/russell-kirk-and-conservative-heart.html.

Herodotus. *The Histories.* Translated by Robin Waterfield. Oxford: Oxford University Press, 2008.

Herron, Don. "Russell Kirk: Ghost Master of Mecosta." In *Rediscovering Modern Horror Fiction I*, edited by Darrell Schweitzer, 21-47. Berkeley Heights, NJ: Wildside Press, 1999.

Hillier, Russell M. "'Valour Will Weep': The Ethics of Valor, Anger, and Pity in Shakespeare's *Coriolanus.*" *Studies in Philology* 113, no. 2 (2016): 358-96. doi: 10.1353/sip.2016.0015.

Holloway, Kerrie. "The Bright Young People of the late 1920s: How the Great War's Armistice influenced those too young to fight." *Journal of European Studies* 45, no. 4 (2015): 316-30. doi: 10.1177/0047244115599145.

Honan, William H. "Russell Kirk is Dead at 75, Seminal Conservative Author." *The New York Times*, 30 April 1994. Section 1, 13.

The Imaginative Conservative. "About Us." Accessed 23 May 2023. https://theimaginativeconservative.org/about-us.

Inglis, David, and Roland Robertson. "From Republican Virtue to Global Imaginary: Changing Visions of the Historian Polybius," *History of the Human Sciences* 19, no. 1 (2006): 1-18. doi: 10.1177/0952695106062144.

Irwin, William. "What Is an Allusion?" *Journal of Aesthetics & Art Criticism* 59, no. 3 (2001): 287-297. *Academic Search Premier.*

Jack, Alison. "'The intolerable wrestle with words and meanings': John 21, T. S. Eliot and the Sense of an Ending." *Expository Times* 117, no. 12 (September 2006): 496-501. doi: 10.1177/0014524606068951.

Jager, Ronald. *The Development of Bertrand Russell's Philosophy.* London: Routledge, 2013.

Johnson, Samuel. *A Dictionary of the English Language*, 2nd revised ed. (London: William Pickering, 1828), 25, *Google Books*, https://www.google.com/books/edition/A_Dictionary_of_the_English_Language/z3kKAAAAIAAJ?hl=en&gbpv=1&bsq=allusion.

———. *A Journey to the Western Islands of Scotland.* Edited by Allan Wendt. 1775. Reprint, Boston: Houghton Mifflin, 1965.

———. *The Major Works.* Edited by Donald Greene. Oxford: Oxford University Press, 2008.

"Jordan Peele's Get Out." Ohio State Press. Accessed 27 May 2023. https://ohiostatepress.org/books/titles/9780814214275.html.

Kay, Tristan. "Redefining the 'matera amorosa': Dante's *Vita nova* and Guittone's (anti-)courtly 'canzoniere.'" *Italianist* 29, no. 3 (2009): 369-99. doi: 10.1179/026143409X12584559181732.

Kenny, Robert. "From the Curse of Ham to the Curse of Nature: The Influence of Natural Selection on the Debate on Human Unity before the Publication of 'The Descent of Man.'" *The British Journal for the History of Science* 40, no. 3 (September 2007): 367-88. https://www.jstor.org/stable/4500748.

Kevin, William. "Dialect of the Tribe: Modes of Communication and the Epiphanic Role of Nonhuman Imagery in T. S. Eliot's *Four Quartets.*" *Harvard Theological Review* 108, no. 1 (Jan. 2015): 98-112. http://dx.doi.org/10.1017/S001781601500005X.

Kimball, Roger. "Permanent Things: Russell Kirk's Centenary." *The New Criterion* 37, no. 5 (January 2019): 4-7.

King, Rachel Scarborough. "Samuel Johnson and Spectral Media." *ELH* 87, no. 1 (Spring 2020): 65-90. doi: 10.1353/elh.2020.0002.

Kirk, Annette. Interview by author. Mecosta, MI, 15 April 2021. https://creativecommons.org/licenses/by-nc-sa/4.0/.

Kirk, Cecilia A. "'The Box of Delights': A Literary Patrimony," in *The Unbought Grace of Life: Essays in Honor of Russell Kirk.* Edited by James E. Person, 59-66. Peru, IL: Sherwood Sugden & Company, 1994.

Kirk, Russell. *America's British Culture.* London: Routledge, 1993.

———. *Ancestral Shadows: An Anthology of Ghostly Tales*, edited by Vigen Guroian. Grand Rapids, MI: Eerdmans Publishing Company, 2004.

———. *Beyond the Dreams of Avarice: Essays of a Social Critic.* 1956. Reprint, Peru, IL: Sherwood Sugden & Company, 1991.

———. "Bishop Has Perfect Faith in the Séance." *Progress-Index*, 13 October 1967, 6. Quoted in Bradley J. Birzer, *Russell Kirk: American Conservative*. Lexington, KY: University Press of Kentucky, 2015.

———. "A Cautionary Note on the Ghostly Tale." *The Russell Kirk Center*, 19 March 2007. https://kirkcenter.org/kirk/a-cautionary-note-on-the-ghostly-tale/.

———. *Concise Guide to Conservatism*. 1957. Reprint, Washington, DC: Regnery, 2019.

———. *The Conservative Mind: From Burke to Eliot*. 1953. Reprint, New York: Regnery, 2016.

———. *A Creature of the Twilight: His Memorials*. New York: Fleet Publishing Corp., 1966.

———. *Eliot and His Age: T. S. Eliot's Moral Imagination in the Twentieth Century*. 1971. Reprint, Wilmington, DE: ISI Books, 2008.

———. *Enemies of the Permanent Things: Observations of Abnormity in Literature and Politics*. 1984. Reprint. Peru, IL: Sherwood Sugden & Company, 1988.

———. *The Essential Russell Kirk*. Edited by George A. Panichas. Wilmington, DE: ISI Books, 2007.

———. *Imaginative Conservative: The Letters of Russell Kirk*. Edited by James E. Person. Lexington, KY: University of Kentucky Press, 2018.

———. *Lord of the Hollow Dark*. New York: St. Martin's Press, 1979.

———. "Lost Lake." *Southwest Review* 42 (1957): 318-24.

———. *Old House of Fear*. 1961. Reprint, Grand Rapids, MI: Eerdmans Publishing, 2007.

———. *The Politics of Prudence*. Bryn Mar, PA: Intercollegiate Studies Institute, 1994.

———. Prologue to *The Princess of All Lands*, vii - viii. Sauk City, WI: Arkham House Publishers, 1979.

———. *Reclaiming a Patrimony: A Collection of Lectures by Russell Kirk*. Washington, D. C.: The Heritage Foundation, 1982.

———. *Redeeming the Time*. Wilmington, DE: ISI Books, 1996.

———. *The Roots of American Order*. 1974. Reprint, Wilmington, DE: ISI Books, 2014.

———. *The Surly Sullen Bell*. New York: Fleet Publishing Corp., 1962.

———. *The Sword of Imagination: Memoirs of a Half-Century of Literary Conflict*. 1995. Reprint, Grand Rapids, MI: Eerdmans, 2002.

Kirk, Russell. ed. Introduction to *The Portable Conservative Reader*, xi-xl. New York: Penguin Books, 1982.

Kitto, H. D. F. "The Greek Chorus." *Educational Theatre Journal* 8, no. 1 (March 1956): 1-8. *JSTOR*, doi: 10.2307/3203909.

Knox, Francesca Buliani. "Between Fire and Fire: T. S. Eliot's *The Waste Land*." *Heythrop Journal* 56, no. 2 (March 2015): 235-48. doi: 10.1111/heyj.12240.

Kolek, Leszek S. "*Black Mischief* as a Comic Structure." In *Evelyn Waugh: New Directions*, ed. Alain Blayac, 1-21. London: Macmillan, 1992.

Ladenson, Elisabeth. *Dirt for Art's Sake: Books on Trial from* Madame Bovary *to* Lolita. Ithaca, NY: Cornell University Press, 2007.

Lake, Crystal B. "Bloody Records: Manuscripts and Politics in *The Castle of Otranto*." *Modern Philology* 110, no. 4 (May 2013): 489-512. doi: 10.1086/670066.

Leavis, F. R. "T. S. Eliot's Later Poetry." In *T. S. Eliot: A Collection of Critical Essays*, ed. Hugh Kenner, 110-24. Englewood Cliffs, NJ: Prentice-Hall, 1962.

Leech, Muireann. "'Do Not Analyse the Self': A Little Learning as Evelyn Waugh's Catholic Anti-Autobiography." *Prose Studies: History, Theory, Criticism* 37, no. 2 (August 2015): 112-27. doi: 10.1080/01440357.2015.1084708.

Leitch, Vincent B. *Literary Criticism in the 21st Century: Theory Renaissance*. London: Bloomsbury Academic, 2014.

Lewis, C. S. *The Screwtape Letters*. 1942. Reprint, New York: HarperCollins, 2001.

Lewis, Jane. "'No Color of Language': Radcliffe's Aesthetic Unbound." *Eighteenth-Century Studies* 39, no. 3 (2006): 377-90. *JSTOR*, https://www.jstor.org/stable/30053478.

Li Tonglu. "New Humanism." *Modern Language Quarterly* 69, no. 1 (March 2008): 61-79. Accessed 28 October 2020. doi: 10.1215/00267929-2007-025.

Lock, F. P. *Edmund Burke*. Vol. 2. Oxford: Oxford University Press, 2006.

Lockerd, Benjamin. Introduction to *Eliot and His Age: T. S. Eliot's Moral Imagination in the Twentieth Century*, by Russell Kirk, xiii-xxxi. Wilmington, DE: ISI Books, 2008.

Machacek, Gregory. "Allusion." *PMLA* 122, no. 2 (2007): 522-36.

Macgowan, Christopher. *Twentieth-Century American Poetry*. Malden, MA: Blackwell Publishing, 2005.

Macrae, Lucy. "'A vast o' bits o' stories:' Shortreed, Laidlaw, and Scott's *Minstrelsy of the Scottish Borders*." *Scottish Literary Review* 7, no . 2 (2015): 95-117. *Academic Search Complete*.

Maes-Jelinek, Hena. *Criticism of Society in the English Novel between the Wars*. 1971. Reprint, Paris: Presses universitaires de Liège, 2013.

McDonald, W. Wesley. *Russell Kirk and the Age of Ideology*. Columbia, MO: University of Missouri Press, 2004.

McMahon, Robert. "Eric Voegelin's Paradoxes of Consciousness and Participation." *The Review of Politics* 61, no. 1 (1999): 117-39. https://www.jstor.org/stable/1408650.

Meregaglia, Alex. "An Introduction to the Short Stories of Russell Kirk: 'Not Written for Children.'" *The Imaginative Conservative*. 15 March 2011. https://theimaginativeconservative.org/2011/03/introduction-short-stories-russell-kirk-not-for-children.html.

Miles, Robert. *Ann Radcliffe: The Great Enchantress*. Manchester: Manchester University Press, 1995.

Miller, Adam. "Ann Radcliffe's Scientific Romance." *Eighteenth Century Fiction* 28, no. 3 (2016): 527-45. doi: 10.3138/ecf.28.3.527.

Milthorpe, Naomi. *Evelyn Waugh's Satire: Texts and Contexts*. Lanham, MA: Fairleigh Dickinson University Press, 2016.

Moffitt, John F. *Inspiration: Bacchus and the Cultural History of a Creation Myth*. Leiden, The Netherlands: Brill, 2005.

Nash, George H. *The Conservative Intellectual Movement in America Since 1945.* Wilmington, DE: Intercollegiate Studies Institute, 1998.

Nelson, Marie. "J. R. R. Tolkien's 'Leaf by Niggle': An Allegory in Transformation." *Mythlore* 28, no. ¾ (2010): 5-19.

Newman, Barbara. "Eliot's Affirmative Way: Julian of Norwich, Charles Williams, and *Little Gidding.*" *Modern Philology* 108, no. 3 (February 2011): 427-61. doi: 10.1086/658355.

Newman, Ray Andrew. "Avoiding Hell in Russell Kirk's Uncanny Tales." *St. Croix Review*, 2004. http://www.stcroixreview.com/archives_nopass/200412/Newman.htm.

———. "Deliver Us from Evil: An Introduction to Russell Kirk's Supernatural Fiction." Order No. EP74662, University of Nebraska at Omaha, 1998. In *Proquest Dissertations & Theses Global.* https://search-proquest-com.ezproxy.fhsu.edu/docview/1706289457?accountid=27424.

———. "Pilgrimages and Easter Destinations in the Ghostly Tales of Russell Kirk." *Modern Age* 40, no. 2 (1998): 314-18.

———. "Spirit world." *National Review* 55, no. 25 (2003): 39-40.

Nisbet, Robert. *The Quest for Community.* 1953. Reprint, Wilmington, DE: ISI Books, 2010.

Norton, Richard. *Mistress of Udolpho: The Life of Ann Radcliffe.* London: Leicester University Press, 1999.

"Nothing to Fear." *The New Criterion* 38, no. 2 (2019): 3.

Obert, Julia C. "Yes Scotland?: The Political Ecologies of the Borders in Walter Scott's Minstrelsy of the Scottish Border and Lay of the Last Minstrel, and in Contemporary Scottish Poetry." *Scottish Literary Review* 11, no. 2 (2019): 81-99. *Project MUSE*, https://muse.jhu.edu/article/741712.

Ovid. *The Metamorphoses.* Translated by A. D. Melville. Oxford: Oxford University Press, 2008.

Pafford, John M. *Russell Kirk.* New York: Bloomsbury, 2013.

———. *Russell Kirk.* Vol. 12 of *Major Conservative and Libertarian Thinkers.* Edited by John Meadowcroft. New York: Continuum, 2010.

Palmeri, Frank. *Satire in Narrative: Petronius, Swift, Gibbon, Melville, and Pynchon.* Austin, TX: University of Texas Press, 1990.

Panero, James. "The ghosts of Russell Kirk." *The New Criterion* 37, no. 5 (January 2019): 27-30.

———. "The Haunting of Russell Kirk." *The Spectator*, 29 November 2019. Accessed 24 September 2020. https://spectator.us/haunting-russell-kirk/.

———. "Introduction" to *Old House of Fear*, by Russell Kirk, vii-xiv. New York: Criterion Books, 2019.

Panichas, George A. Preface to *The Essential Russell Kirk*, by Russell Kirk, xi-xxvi. Wilmington, DE: ISI Books, 2007.

Paul, Chance David. "Teleology in Samuel Johnson's *Rasselas.*" *Renascence* 64, no. 3 (Spring 2012): 221-32. *Academic Search Premier.*

Pécastaings, Annie. "William Marshal and the Origins of *The Castle of Otranto.*" *English Studies* 100, no. 3 (2019): 291-300. doi: 10.1080/0013838X.2019.1574416.

Perryman, John. "Back to the *Bay Psalm Book*: T. S. Eliot's Identity Crisis and 'Sweeney Erect.'" *Midwest Quarterly* 47, no. 3 (March 2006): 244-61. *Academic Search Premier*.

Person, James. *Russell Kirk: A Critical Biography of a Conservative Mind*. 1999. Reprint, Lanham, MA: Rowman & Littlefield, 2016.

Pittman, L. Monique. "Heroes, Villains, and Balkans: Intertextual Masculinities in Ralph Fiennes's *Coriolanus*." *Shakespeare Bulletin* 33, no. 2 (Summer 2015): 215-44. doi: 10.1353/shb.2015.0022.

Plato. *Symposium*. Translated by Alexander Nehamas and Paul Woodruff. In *A Plato Reader: Eight Essential Dialogues*, edited by C. D. C. Reeve, 153-208. Indianapolis: Hackett Publishing Company, 2012.

Radcliffe, Anne. *Romance of the Forest*. Philadelphia: J. B. Lippincott & Co., 1865.

Radner, John B. *Johnson and Boswell: A Biography of Friendship*. New Haven, CT: Yale University Press, 2012.

Raine, Craig. *T. S. Eliot*. Oxford: Oxford University Press, 2006.

Reinhard, Ben. "The Haunting of America: Russell Kirk's Ghostly Fiction." *The Imaginative Conservative*. 16 March 2020. https://theimaginativeconservative.org/2020/03/haunting-americas-russell-kirk-ghostly-fiction-ben-reinhard.html.

———. "Russell Kirk's Literary Gentlemen." *The Imaginative Conservative*. 8 April 2020. https://theimaginativeconservative.org/2020/04/russell-kirk-literary-gentlemen-ben-reinhard.html.

Rhodes, Bess. *Riches and Reform: Ecclesiastical Wealth in St. Andrews c. 1520 - 1580*. Leiden, South Holland, The Netherlands: Brill, 2019.

Rodden, John. "A Young Scholar's Encounter with Russell Kirk." *Modern Age* 49, no. 3 (2007): 290-98.

Rousseau, Jean-Jacques. *The Social Contract*. Translated by Christopher Betts. Oxford: Oxford University Press, 1994.

Russell, Bertrand. "Has Religion Made Useful Contributions to Civilization?" In *Russell on Religion: Selections from the Writings of Bertrand Russell*, ed. Louis Greenspan and Stefan Andersson, 169-85. London: Routledge, 2003.

The Russell Kirk Center for Cultural Renewal. "About Us." Accessed 5 May 2023. https://kirkcenter.org/about-us/.

Russello, Gerald. *The Postmodern Imagination of Russell Kirk*. Columbia, MO: University of Missouri Press, 2007.

Salwen, Michael B. "Evelyn Waugh in Ethiopia: the novelist as war correspondent and journalism critic." *Journalism Studies* 2, no. 1 (2001): 1-25. doi: 10.1080/14616700120021775.

"Satire," in *Oxford American Desk Dictionary and Thesaurus*, 2nd ed. (New York: Berkley Books, 2001), 741.

Schmalhofer, Stephen. "A Dreadful Joy is Conjured." Review of *The Princess of All Lands*, by Russell Kirk. *The Russell Kirk Center*, 21 October 2018. https://kirkcenter.org/reviews/a-dreadful-joy-is-conjured/.

Schmidt, Michael. *The Novel: A Biography*. Cambridge, MA: Harvard University Press, 2014.

Schmitz, Matthew. "The Haunting of Russell Kirk." *First Things*. December 2023. https://www.firstthings.com/article/2023/12/the-haunting-of-russell-kirk.
Scott, Walter. *The Antiquary*. Edited by Nicola Watson. London: Oxford University Press, 2009.
———. *The Bride of Lammermoor*. Edinburgh: A. L. Burt Company, 1857.
———. *The Lives of the Novelists*. London: Oxford University Press, 1906.
———. *The Talisman, My Aunt Margaret's Mirror, The Tapestried Chamber*. New York: Funk and Wagnalls Company, 1900.
———. *Waverley, Or 'Tis Sixty Years Since*. London: J. M. Dent & Co., 1906.
"Secret Life of Russell Kirk." Review of *Old House of Fear*, by Russell Kirk. *Time*, 7 July 1961.
Shakespeare, William. *Coriolanus*. Vol. 2 of *The Complete Works of William Shakespeare*. Edited by W. G. Clark and W. Aldis Wright. Garden City, NY: Nelson Doubleday, 1950.
———. *Pericles: Prince of Tyre*. Vol. 2 of *The Complete Works of William Shakespeare*. Edited by W. G. Clark and W. Aldis Wright. Garden City, NY: Nelson Doubleday, 1950.
———. *The Riverside Shakespeare*. Edited by G. Blakemore Evans, 1856. Houghton Mifflin: Boston, 1997.
Sharpe, Tony. *T. S. Eliot: A Literary Life*. New York: Palgrave Macmillan, 1991.
Sharples, Robert W. *Peripatetic Philosophy 200 BC to 200 AC: An Introduction and Collection of Sources in Translation*. Cambridge: Cambridge University Press, 2010.
Sherman, Nancy. "Of Manners and Morals." *British Journal of Educational Standards* 53, no. 3 (2005): 272-89. *JSTOR*, https://www.jstor.org/stable/3699243.
Slater, Ann Pasternak. *Evelyn Waugh*. Tavistock, England: Northcote House Publishers, 2016.
Sommerstein, Alan. "Hinc Omnis Pendet? Old Comedy and Roman Satire." *Classical World* 105, no. 1 (Fall 2011): 265-38. Accessed 1 October 2020. *Education Source*.
Soud, David. "'The Greedy Dialectic of Time and Eternity': Karl Barth, T. S. Eliot, and *Four Quartets*." *ELH: English Literary History* 81, no. 4 (Winter 2014): 1363-91.
Spentzou, Efrossini. "Orpheus, Byblis, Myrrha: Towards a Matrixial Ethics of Encounter in Ovid's Metamorphoses." *International Journal of the Classical Tradition* 26, no. 4 (December 2019): 417-32. doi:10.1007/s12138-019-005128.
Steinfels, Peter. *The Neoconservatives: The Men Who Are Changing America's Politics*. New York: Simon and Schuster, 1979.
Stephenson, David. *Heavenly Vaults: From Romanesque to Gothic in European Architecture*. New York: Princeton Architectural Press, 2009. *ProQuest Ebook Central*.
Stern, Rachel Michelle. "Fantasies of Choosing in *Rasselas*." *Studies in English Literature, 1500 - 1900* 55, no. 3 (Summer 2015): 523-36. *Gale Academic OneFile*.

Stillman, Anne. "Sweeney Among the Marionettes." *Essays in Criticism: A Quarterly Journal of Literary Criticism* 59, no. 2 (April 2009): 116-41. doi: 10.1093/escrit/cgp002.

Stouck, David, and Janet Giltrow. "'A confused and doubtful sound of voices': Ironic contingencies in the language of Hawthorne's Romances." *Modern Language Review* 92, no. 3 (1997): 559-72. doi: 10.2307/3733384.

Strong, Tracy B. "Hawthorne, the Politics of Sin, and Puritanism." *Telos* 178 (2017): 121-42. doi: 10.3817/0317178121.

Sutherland, Kathryn. Introduction to *Redgauntlet*, by Walter Scott, vii-xxiii. Oxford: Oxford University Press, 2011.

Thomassen, Bjørn. "Reason and Religion in Rawls: Voegelin's Challenge." *Philosophia* 40, no. 2 (2012): 237-52. https://www.dx.doi.org/10.1007/s11406-011-9351-4.

Tolkien, J. R. R. *The Tolkien Reader*. New York: Ballantine Books, 1966.

Tran, Adrina. "An Experiment in the Moral Imagination: Russell Kirk, Clinton Wallace, and Conservative Hobohemia." *The Michigan Historical Review* 42, no. 1 (Spring 2016): 1-34.

Villiers, Rick de. "'Of the Same Species': T. S. Eliot's *Sweeney Agonistes* and Samuel Beckett's *Waiting for Godot*." *English Studies in Africa* 55, no. 2 (2012): 18-28. doi: 10.1080/00138398.2012.731287.

Vineyard, Jennifer. "Real witches and pagans break down Netflix's *Chilling Adventures of Sabrina*." *Syfy.com*, 2018 November 19. https://www.syfy.com/syfywire/chilling-adventures-of-sabrina-netflix-real-witches-pagans-magic.

Voegelin, Eric. *The New Science of Politics*. Chicago: Chicago University Press, 1952. Quoted in Russell Kirk, *The Essential Russell Kirk*, ed. George A. Panichas. Wilmington, DE: ISI Books, 2007.

———. "Notes on T. S. Eliot's *Four Quartets*," in *The Drama of Humanity and Other Miscellaneous Papers 1939-1985*. Edited by Gilbert Weiss and William Petropulous. Columbia, MO: University of Missouri Press, 2004. Quoted in Stephen J. Costello, *Philosophy and the Flow of Presence: desire, Drama, and the Divine Ground in Being*. Newcastle upon Tyne, England: Cambridge Scholars Publishing, 2013.

Walpole, Horace. *The Castle of Otranto*. Edited by Nick Groom. 1764. Reprint, Oxford University Press, 2014.

Wallace, Tara Ghoshal. "Historical *Redgauntlet*: Jacobite Delusions and Hanoverian Fantasies." *Romanticism* 21, no. 2 (2015): 145-59. doi: 10.3366/rom.2015.0225.

Walsh, Catherine Henry. "The Sublime in the Historical Novel: Scott and Gil y Carrasco." *Comparative Literature* 42, no. 1 (1990): 29-48. doi: 10.2307/1770311.

Ward, Stuart. "'No nation could be broker': the satire boom and the demise of Britain's world role." In *British culture and the end of empire*, ed. Stuart Ward, 91-110. Manchester, England: Manchester University Press, 2001.

Waugh, Evelyn. *Black Mischief*. 1932. Reprint, New York: Back Bay Books, 2012.

———. *Brideshead Revisited*. 1944. Reprint, New York: Back Bay Books, 2012.

———. *The Diaries of Evelyn Waugh*. Edited by Michael Davie. Boston: Little, Brown and Company, 1976.

———. *The Letters of Evelyn Waugh*. Edited by Mark Amory. New Haven, CT: Ticknor & Fields, 1980.
———. *A Little Learning: An Autobiography*. Boston: Little, Brown & Company, 1964.
———. *Scoop*. 1937. Reprint, New York: Back Bay Books, 2012.
Wechselblatt, Martin. "Finding Mr. Boswell: Rhetorical Authority and National Identity in Johnson's *A Journey to the Western Islands of Scotland*." *ELH* 60, no. 1 (1993): 117-48. https://www.jstor.org/stable/2873310.
Welsh, Alexander. "Contrast of Styles in the Waverley Novels." *NOVEL: A Forum on Fiction* 6, no. 3 (1973): 218-28. *JSTOR*, https://www.jstor.org/stable/1344834.
Weier, Gary M. "Perspectivism and Form in Drama: A Burkean Analysis of *Julius Caesar*." *Communication Quarterly* 44, no. 2 (1996): 246-59. doi: 10.1080/01463379609370013.
Whitney, Gleaves. "Russell Kirk: The Wizard of Mecosta," *Michigan History* 102, no. 4 (August 2018): 29-34.
———. "The Swords of Imagination: Russell Kirk's Battle with Modernity." *Modern Age* 43, no. 4 (2001): 311-20.
Wilson, James Matthew. "Conservative Critics of the Bourgeoisie." *Modern Age* 55, no. 3 (2013): 14-26. *Academic Search Premier*.
Willson, John. "A Foreign Policy for (Probably Not Very Many) Americans." *The Russell Kirk Center*, 3 March 2009. https://kirkcenter.org/essays/a-foreignpolicy/.
Wineapple, Brenda. *Hawthorne: A Life*. New York: Random House, 2004.
Wood, Jamie. "'Here I Am': Eliot, 'Gerontion,' and the Great War." *Biography: An Interdisciplinary Quarterly* 41, no. 1 (2018): 116-142. EBSCO*host*, doi: 10.1353/bio.2018.0011.
Woods, Robert M. "The Other Side of the Keyhole: Russell Kirk's Ghost Stories." *The Imaginative Conservative*, 13 February 2012. https://theimaginativeconservative.org/2012/02/other-side-of-keyhole-russell-kirks.html.

Index

A

Arnold, Matthew, xv, 95

B

Babbitt, Irving, xii, xiv, xv, 26
Benson, Robert Hugh, 45
Bible, The, 23, 30, 31, 32, 41, 56, 67, 130, 167
Blackwood, Algernon, 45
Boswell, James, 105, 107, 109, 111, 112, 180, 181, 188, 191
Bradbury, Ray, 26, 44, 121, 172
British. *See* England
Buckley, William F., xi, 1, 6, 7, 180
bureaucracy. *See* government
Burke, Edmund, xii, 2, 4, 8, 10, 23, 24, 25, 26, 34, 43, 51, 53, 66, 80, 82, 102, 103, 104, 105, 106, 107, 108, 118, 142, 162, 179, 180, 183, 185, 186
  A Philosophical Enquiry into the Origin of Our Ideas of the Sublime and Beautiful, 24, 103, 104, 118, 180
  Reflections on the Revolution in France, xi, 5, 24, 25, 107, 108, 180
Burns, Robert, 30, 33, 37, 54, 57

C

Carroll, Lewis, 34
Catholicism, xiii, 3, 7, 36, 45, 46, 47, 50, 52, 53, 54, 59, 62, 67, 69, 72, 85, 86, 89, 90, 92, 93, 94, 105, 113, 123, 124, 127, 138, 152, 158, 165, 174, 175, 179, 180, 182, 186
Chodorov, Frank, 139
Christianity, 7, 11, 12, 20, 26, 27, 46, 47, 60, 67, 73, 75, 76, 87, 88, 90, 91, 94, 97, 101, 105, 121, 122, 128, 143, 146, 157, 165, 169, 174, 175, 177, 179, 182
Cicero, 2, 29, 31, 36, 85
Coleridge, Samuel Taylor, 45
communist. *See* Marxism
Conrad, Joseph, xix, 124
conservatism, xi, xii, xviii, 2, 3, 5, 6, 7, 27, 28, 36, 42, 53, 65, 67, 77, 101, 103, 104, 107, 108, 110, 117, 132, 138

D

D'Arcy, Martin, xvii, 11, 86, 89, 166
Dante, 6, 19, 20, 23, 26, 29, 35, 36, 38, 41, 184
Defoe, Daniel, 45
democracy, 1, 9, 13, 62, 130, 131, 132, 133
Dickens, Charles, 45

E

education, xii, 3, 37, 67, 68, 69, 124, 125, 168, 177
Eliot, T. S., xi, xii, xiii, xv, xvii, xix, xx, 6, 7, 8, 9, 10, 20, 23, 24, 25, 26, 27, 30, 32, 35, 36, 37, 38, 39, 41, 48, 67, 75, 78, 83, 86, 87, 88, 89, 96, 99, 100, 101, 126, 129, 139, 140, 141, 142, 143, 144, 145,

146, 147, 148, 149, 150, 151, 152, 153, 154, 155,156, 157, 158, 159, 162, 169, 179, 181, 182, 183, 184, 185, 186, 187, 188, 189, 190, 191
Four Quartets, xviii, 87, 88, 89, 140, 143, 145, 146, 159, 179, 184, 189, 190
The Waste Land, 32, 143, 149, 150, 155, 156, 181, 185
England, xv, xvii, xviii, 3, 8, 9, 12, 23, 24, 28, 29, 30, 31, 43, 46, 48, 55, 56, 57, 58, 59, 61, 62, 66, 67, 78, 88, 103, 104, 105, 107, 108, 110, 115, 117, 121, 124, 125, 126, 127, 128, 130, 131, 132, 134, 135, 137, 139, 143, 144, 151, 154, 163, 164, 167, 169,179, 181, 182, 184, 186, 187, 189, 190

F

Ford, Ford Maddox, 47
freedom, xvii, 3, 13, 26, 46, 132
Freud, Sigmund, 46, 47, 145

G

ghosts, xvi, 1, 12, 14, 15, 39, 41, 42, 43, 44, 45, 46, 47, 49, 50, 52, 54, 62, 72, 74, 76, 82, 90, 91, 96, 101, 103, 104, 112, 113, 114, 119, 122, 171, 179, 187
Goldwater, Barry, 8, 166, 170, 178
Gosse, Edmund, 139, 182
Gothic fiction, xi, xvi, xviii, 17, 19, 24, 39, 42, 43, 44, 45, 46, 47, 48, 49, 50, 51, 52, 53, 54, 55, 56, 57, 58, 59, 61, 62, 69, 72, 75, 84, 92, 96, 101, 102, 103, 104, 105, 107, 108, 110, 111, 112, 113, 114, 116, 117, 118, 119, 120, 121, 122, 123, 133, 141, 149, 152, 153, 159, 171, 178, 179, 180, 181, 182, 189

government, xvii, 4, 12, 13, 19, 31, 62, 66, 71, 77, 78, 82, 83, 115, 117, 131, 133, 136

H

Hardy, Thomas, 26
Hawthorne, Nathaniel, xvii, 43, 44, 45, 58, 59, 60, 61, 62, 69, 74, 114, 182, 183, 190, 191
  "Roger Malvin's Burial", 60
  "The Birth-Mark", 59
  "Earth's Holocaust", 60
  "Young Goodman Brown", xvii, 60
  The Blithedale Romance, 58, 60
  The House of Seven Gables, 58, 61, 62, 183
  The House of the Seven Gables, xvii
  The Scarlet Letter, xvii, 58, 59, 183
Heaven, xvii, xviii, 11, 12, 16, 35, 87, 89, 92, 93, 94, 96, 98, 178
Hell, 12, 35, 38, 70, 71, 72, 74, 81, 85, 87, 89, 90, 91, 92, 93, 94, 96, 97, 120, 171, 172, 173, 187
Hitler, Adolf, 73
Hobbes, Thomas, 66
Hoffmann, E. T. A., 47
Homer, 25, 27, 29, 30
Huxley, Aldous, 139

I

ideology, xiv, 5, 6, 18, 30, 33, 36, 69, 71, 72, 73, 75, 76, 79, 118, 121, 133, 139, 145, 147, 178, 186
Irving, Washington, 43

J

James, M. R., xvi, 43, 45, 46, 56

Johnson, Lyndon B., xvii, 8, 123
Johnson, Samuel, xv, xviii, 27, 28, 46, 67, 101, 102, 104, 105, 106, 107, 108, 109, 110, 111, 112, 113, 114, 115, 116, 118, 119, 120, 121, 162, 179, 180, 181, 183, 184, 187, 191

K

Keats, John, 34
Kipling, Rudyard, 30, 34, 57
Kirk, Annette, xii, xvii, 7, 10, 11, 15, 50, 89, 143, 144, 155, 170, 173, 174, 175, 176, 177, 184
Kirk, Russell
  "A Cautionary Note on the Ghostly Tale", xvi, 44, 46, 48, 59, 61, 96, 104, 116, 117, 118, 185
  "An Encounter by Mortstone Pond", 16, 99
  "Balgrummo's Hell", 19, 70, 91, 93
  "Behind the Stumps", xvii, 13, 14, 50, 61, 71, 77
  "Ex Tenebris", xvii, 53, 61, 71, 77, 90
  "Fate's Purse", xx, 61
  "Lex Talionis", xvii, xx, 71, 79, 92, 93
  "Lost Lake", 14, 55, 113
  "Saviourgate", 15, 53, 65, 93, 98, 155
  "Skyberia", 14, 113
  "Sorworth Place", 13, 52, 97, 98, 154
  "The Last God's Dream", xx, 54, 165, 174
  "The Peculiar Demesne of Archvicar Gerontion", xx, 16, 114, 147, 163, 173, 175, 176
  "The Princess of All Lands", 15, 55, 73, 74, 80, 113
  "The Reflex-Man in Whinnymuir Close", 56, 57, 74
  "The Surly Sullen Bell", 28, 50, 53, 61, 72, 78, 113
  "There's a Long, Long Trail A-Winding", 80, 93, 95, 176
  "Uncle Isaiah", 13, 70, 79, 83, 167, 171
  A Creature of the Twilight, xix, xx, 15, 16, 18, 20, 23, 30, 31, 33, 37, 38, 39, 40, 101, 123, 124, 128, 129, 130, 132, 134, 135, 136, 138, 152, 155, 157, 162, 164, 165, 166, 167, 169, 170, 172, 173, 174, 175, 176, 177, 185
  America's British Culture, 33, 184
  Beyond the Dreams of Avarice, 68, 114, 115, 184
  Enemies of the Parmenent Things, xiv, 26, 27, 29, 51, 65, 106, 116, 117, 118, 121, 142, 177, 185
  Lord of the Hollow Dark, xviii, xix, xx, 16, 17, 19, 20, 23, 30, 31, 32, 35, 37, 38, 41, 43, 50, 65, 75, 96, 97, 98, 101, 114, 140, 141, 142, 144, 145, 146, 147, 150, 151, 153, 155, 156, 157, 159, 162, 163, 172, 173, 174, 177, 178, 185
  Old House of Fear, xvi, xvii, xviii, xx, 12, 16, 17, 18, 30, 31, 33, 34, 37, 39, 40, 43, 50, 57, 73, 74, 76, 101, 102, 114, 117, 118, 120, 141, 185, 187, 189
pacifism, 101, 123

Politics of Prudence, xix, 124, 129, 185
Randolph of Roanoke, 3
religious views, 7, 12, 15, 21, 31, 45, 47, 67, 73, 175
Stoicism, 4, 11, 165
The Conservative Mind, xi, xiv, xvi, 1, 4, 5, 12, 27, 51, 59, 60, 67, 77, 167, 169, 185
The Roots of American Order, xvii, 9, 31, 62, 161, 173, 185
The Sword of Imagination, xiii, xvi, 2, 6, 8, 10, 11, 12, 43, 50, 65, 83, 86, 89, 94, 101, 113, 128, 129, 141, 159, 161, 162, 167, 168, 170, 173, 175

L

Lawrence, D. H., 26
Le Fanu, Sheridan, 46, 56
Lewis, C. S., 15, 45, 46, 104, 131, 186
liberalism, 5, 12, 26, 27, 32, 87, 133, 179

M

Macdonald, George, 45, 46
Marxism, 17, 18, 40, 50, 73, 74, 76, 118, 133, 134, 169, 182
Maupassant, Guy de, 45, 47
Meyer, Frank S., 139
Mickiewicz, Adam, 30
Milton, John, 19, 30, 33, 39, 105
moral imagination, xi, xiv, xv, xx, 2, 8, 23, 25, 26, 27, 28, 34, 42, 45, 46, 53, 54, 66, 72, 82, 101, 106, 116, 121, 129, 142, 161, 162, 177, 178, 190
More, Paul Elmore, 26

N

Nisbet, Robert, 67, 68, 187
Nixon, Richard, 85, 89

O

O'Connor, Flannery, 26, 44
order, xii, xvi, xvii, xx, 7, 8, 13, 18, 25, 26, 32, 37, 41, 42, 46, 59, 60, 62, 65, 66, 67, 68, 69, 71, 73, 74, 75, 76, 77, 78, 79, 80, 82, 83, 87, 97, 104, 110, 130, 131, 139, 143, 145, 154
Orwell, George, 46, 47
Ovid, 32, 172, 187, 189

P

permanent things, xi, xiv, 2, 6, 7, 8, 23, 27, 29, 42, 65, 68, 69, 71, 85, 104, 121, 127, 142, 161, 162, 178
Plato, xii, 26, 29, 34, 65, 86, 87, 88, 100, 188
Plutarch, 32, 154
Polybius, 31, 184
Pound, Ezra, 139, 156
progressivism, 2, 5, 18, 19, 60, 62, 66, 67, 68, 72, 115, 122, 124, 130, 133, 136, 137, 162
Purgatory, xviii, 12, 38, 82, 85, 90, 92, 93, 94, 96, 97, 98, 99, 145, 171

R

Radcliffe, Ann, xvi, 16, 17, 43, 44, 48, 49, 50, 51, 53, 57, 58, 61, 114, 119, 121, 159, 181, 186, 187, 188
Rousseau, Jean-Jacques, 26, 66, 188
Russell, Bertrand, 157, 158, 188

S

Santayana, George, 133
satire, xiii, xix, 18, 31, 38, 101, 107, 123, 124, 125, 126, 127, 128, 131, 132, 133, 134, 135, 138, 186, 187, 188, 189, 190
Scotland, xviii, xix, 3, 4, 6, 13, 17, 20, 33, 37, 38, 39, 42, 43, 51, 53, 54, 55, 56, 57, 58, 70, 73, 75, 89, 90, 101, 108, 109, 110, 111, 112, 114, 115, 116, 117, 139, 141, 147, 155, 159, 167, 168, 174, 179, 180, 181, 184, 186, 187, 191
Scott, Walter, xvi, 11, 16, 17, 19, 33, 39, 43, 44, 45, 48, 50, 51, 52, 53, 54, 55, 56, 57, 58, 61, 62, 114, 159, 182, 186, 187, 189, 190
Shakespeare, William, 11, 28, 29, 30, 32, 38, 39, 40, 41, 103, 105, 151, 152, 153, 154, 182, 183, 188, 189
Stalin, Josef, 73, 126
supernatural, xiii, xvi, xvii, xviii, 12, 13, 14, 15, 17, 38, 41, 42, 43, 44, 45, 46, 47, 48, 49, 50, 58, 61, 72, 74, 82, 102, 104, 112, 113, 114, 116, 118, 120, 122, 171, 187

T

Tennyson, Alfred, 30, 33, 34, 39
timeless moments, xviii, 16, 20, 75, 83, 85, 86, 89, 92, 93, 96, 97, 98, 99, 100, 140, 145
Tolkien, J. R. R., 6, 177, 178, 187, 190
tradition, xii, xiv, xv, xviii, 4, 5, 8, 25, 32, 36, 37, 42, 43, 46, 47, 53, 54, 55, 56, 58, 61, 62, 65, 72, 78, 82, 94, 95, 106, 107, 109, 114, 115, 116, 127, 128, 129, 130, 131, 132, 143, 145, 152, 159, 177

V

Vergil, 6, 19, 29, 30, 32, 172
virtue, 9, 37, 38, 66, 67, 68, 69, 74, 82, 104, 106, 113, 117, 135, 153
Voegelin, Eric, 61, 65, 86, 87, 88, 100, 113, 180, 181, 183, 186, 190

W

Wallace, Clinton, 15, 57, 174, 176, 190
Walpole, Horace, 17, 43, 45, 48, 53, 102, 103, 104, 105, 108, 120, 181, 182, 183, 190
Waugh, Evelyn, 123, 124, 125, 126, 127, 128, 129, 130, 131, 132, 133, 134, 135, 136, 138, 139, 180, 181, 185, 186, 188, 189, 190, 191
  Black Mischief, xix, 124, 128, 132, 133, 137, 138, 185, 190
  Brideshead Revisited, 125, 126, 127, 128, 180, 190
  Decline and Fall, 125
  Scoop, xix, 124, 126, 128, 129, 130, 131, 132, 134, 135, 136, 137, 138, 191
  Vile Bodies, 125
Wharton, Edith, 45
Williams, Charles, xvi, 43, 46, 104, 187
Wordsworth, William, 34

Y

Yeats, W. B., 12, 34, 37, 45, 129, 147, 150, 152, 181, 183

www.ingramcontent.com/pod-product-compliance
Lightning Source LLC
Chambersburg PA
CBHW072235290426
44111CB00012B/2101